ACADEMIE DU VIN
WINE COURSE

To Alan
all my love
Barbara

ACADEMIE DU VIN
WINE COURSE

ACADEMIE DU VIN
WINE COURSE

The complete course in wine appreciation, tasting and study
of the Paris Académie du Vin

STEVEN SPURRIER
& MICHEL DOVAZ

Introduction by Michael Broadbent

CENTURY PUBLISHING
LONDON
in association with
Christie's Wine Publications

First published in Great Britain in 1983
by Century Publishing Co. Ltd.,
76, Old Compton Street, London W1V 5PA
in association with
Christie's Wine Publications

British Library Cataloguing in Publication Data

Spurrier, Steven
  Académie du Vin master wine course.
  1. Wine tasting
  I. Title   II. Dovaz, Michel
  III. Académie du Vin
  641.2'2   TP548.5.A5

ISBN 0 7126 0163 5

**Designed and produced by
Quintet Publishing Limited, London**

Editorial Director
Clare Howell

Editor
John Gilbert

Art Editor
Christopher White

Designer
Martin Atcherley

Cartographer
John Mitchell

Phototypesetting by
Ashwell Print Services Ltd., Norwich

Black-and-white and colour illustration
origination by
East Anglian Engraving Limited, Norwich

Printed and bound in Italy by L.E.G.O., Vicenza

Special Contributors

Muriel de Potex
Special Studies

Ian Jamieson
Germany

Fenella Pearson
Italy

Geoffrey Roberts
California, Australia & New Zealand

Note: Measurement Conversion

Measurements of volume and area
in the sections on European wines
have been expressed in hectolitres
(hl) and hectares (ha):

1 hectolitre = 26.4 U.S. gallons
1 hectare   = 2.471 acres

CONTENTS

The Académie du Vin

The purpose of the Académie du Vin is to teach people about wine. The method is a Wine Course, or series of classes in which are blended factual information and practical tasting experience.

While a certain amount of theoretical knowledge is necessary to appreciate different wines (and the more knowledge he possesses, the more a taster will look for in a given wine), nothing is more important than direct experience of what individual wines actually taste like and why. Wines are as different and as varied as people themselves. Wines should, by their heritage or *appellation*, follow a certain style and behave in certain ways. Given the same grape variety and the same soil, all things being equal, wines should be identical every year. But all things are not equal, from the climatic conditions to the man who makes the grapes into wine. The differences are infinite, yet there are reasons for all of these differences and these are the answers to why the wine tastes exactly the way it does. Our approach at the Académie du Vin is to present the facts and allow the wines to illustrate these facts through comparative tastings linked by a common theme.

Since the creation of the Académie du Vin in Paris in 1972, we have concentrated almost exclusively on French wines. The courses at the Académie du Vin in New York and at the Christie's Wine Course (held in association with the Académie du Vin) in London deal with wines from other countries, but draw strongly from our experience of teaching about French wine. Although this book does give pre-eminence to French wines, other major wine-producing regions are covered in both the theoretical and the tasting courses. But the courses printed here are not intended to be a survey of the wines of the world: the Académie du Vin *Wine Course* sets out deliberately to bring the reader to a greater and subtler understanding of all wines.

The Académie du Vin courses are entirely tuition-supported, so we are very grateful to all our students, past and present. The many wine producers, *négociants*, *sommeliers* and even government officials who have helped and encouraged us are too numerous to mention and have our continuing thanks. Of the 'staff' at the Académie in Paris, Michel Dovaz has co-authored and Muriel de Potex has contributed to this book, and I would particularly like to mention and thank Jon Winroth, who founded L'Académie du Vin with me, Patricia Gastaud-Gallagher, my co-director, who describes herself quite correctly as 'the architect of policy', and Isabelle Bachelard, who enacts this policy with tireless dedication.

Steven Spurrier

Introduction

If you are a beginner, this will set you on the right track; if you are already a keen wine drinker the book will open the doors to a deeper understanding. It is a practical and relevant book.

The background is really quite extraordinary. As one might imagine, it would take a rather special sort of person – particularly if a foreigner – to set up shop, literally, in the heart of Paris and proceed to tell the French how to appreciate their own wine. Not only that, but for a very English Englishman then to introduce premium California wines in direct competition in blind tastings was, surely, to add insult to injury. It says much for old-world tolerance and civility for Steven Spurrier to have been accommodated in the role of devil's advocate; it says much of Steven that his approach has quietly triumphed.

But the influence has been two-way. It is perfectly apparent to anyone reading this book that the author, as I do, regards France as the seedbed of wine culture. He has clearly been greatly influenced by the now considerable number of years he has lived and worked in France, and this shows. The French in turn should be grateful to one who has done so much to further the appreciation of the extraordinary range of wines produced in that large, surprisingly varied country. Not that the book is exclusively devoted to French wine, far from it. I personally think that the unusual combination of British impartiality and a French approach makes the author, and us in turn, see other wines from other areas in a truer perspective. This is the main relevance of the book.

The practical aspect is easier to explain. The whole approach is based on the experience of running wine courses, first of all introduced, then honed and polished in Paris at his Académie du Vin (like most Englishmen I am charmed by a French 'accent': somehow the phrase 'Académie du Vin' has a lighter and more evocative touch than 'Wine Academy', which sounds pompous, or 'Wine School', which is just boring). Having practised and made perfect, the move to New York was natural; and, it seems, the grafting of the Académie du Vin to Christie's Wine Course is as effective as that of a noble vine variety to a sympathetic root stock. In short, the book is soundly based on practical and successful wine teaching.

In fact, the best way to learn is to teach. As lecturers, both Steven and I have benefited immeasurably over the years from the experience we have gained explaining wine, putting it over, above all exploring the whys and wherefores of taste. Like all communicators, we are the first to admit that teaching is a two-way affair. One learns from the listeners' reactions and from the questions asked. Steven has gone several steps further as an educator for he first formalized his lectures into courses, and has now translated his speech into the printed word.

With this book in hand we can *all* benefit from a step-by-step logical approach knowing that it is a formalized, yet highly readable, version of intensely practical sessions. It represents the single-handed achievement of a remarkable, yet diffident, educator.

I enjoyed it and learned a lot. I am sure all fellow enthusiasts, no matter how new or how proficient, will do so too.

Michael Broadbent,
Christie's, Summer, 1983.

THE ACADEMIE DU VIN COURSES

1
FOUNDATION COURSE

2
INTERMEDIATE COURSE

3
ADVANCED COURSE

4
SPECIAL STUDIES

1
FOUNDATION COURSE

As an introduction to the main subject areas of the Foundation Course (tasting, vine cultivation, vinification, and the purchase, transport and storage of wine), it may be helpful to say something about identifying wine.

Even before protective legislation had been introduced, it was generally recognized that different wines needed to be clearly defined in the interests of authenticity. This was basically in order to protect the producer, who would otherwise be vulnerable to inferior imitations which might eventually damage both the prestige of his wine and his business.

It was soon evident that the best way to assure and protect the authenticity of various wines was to adopt a system based on the place of origin. French wine producers, in any event, were in the habit of forming regional federations, since they had to deal with similar problems of cultivation on similar types of soil, using identical grape varieties. As a consequence, their wines were bound to have much in common.

Nowadays, the area which forms the basis of wine identification may be very large or tiny. It is obvious that a wine from a small, well-defined region is more likely to maintain a consistently high quality. By the same token, wines from a vast area will not be given individual identification. These are simply brand wines, the familiar *vins de table*. To label such wines as the produce, say, of the European Economic Community or the United States, would provide a vague, unhelpful indication of origin; and even to describe a wine as coming from France, California, Italy or Spain, is fairly meaningless. These would still be wines of very imprecise identification, way down the scale.

Tasting/Aims

There are two distinct types of wine-tasting, which can broadly be termed 'technical' and 'hedonistic'. They differ both in method and purpose.

Technical tasting is for the professionals and its principal aim is to assess the wine from a commercial viewpoint. It has to determine, firstly, whether the wine has any faults, and secondly whether it conforms to the characteristics of its *appellation* and satisfies certain requirements of quality. Technical tasting must endeavour to be as objective as possible. The taster, in fact, is required to answer a series of questions set out on a tasting card. The pleasurable experience afforded by a given wine is not a prime consideration in this context. As a rule, wines are tasted at a uniform temperature of 15°C; ideally this may often be too cold or too warm, but it does provide an additional criterion by which the wines can be compared, and it is, in fact, a suitable temperature for critical tasting.

Hedonistic tasting is quite a different matter, for the emphasis here is on the actual pleasure afforded by drinking the wine. The taster must experience the wine as fully and subtly as possible in the best possible conditions. Thus it is a question of intelligent drinking – leading, it is to be hoped, to intelligent buying. To know that it is a good investment is to enhance the pleasure of drinking the wine.

Our experience at the Académie du Vin has shown us, however, that the two types of tasting do overlap. Neither should be pursued to the exclusion of the other. The most rewarding experience for the drinker comes from combining the strict technique and the pleasurable art of tasting.

Acquiring the technical expertise for tasting is really a matter of mastering a series of operations which, after a time, virtually become automatic. Once this happens, the taster can quickly go on to appreciate bouquet, aromatic strength, length of taste in the mouth, and so on. A more 'cultural' experience of wine takes much longer to acquire and does need a lengthy apprenticeship. It requires, for instance, a knowledge of *appellations* and their characteristics, and an ability to recognize the influence of the vintage. At an even more subtle level, it may be possible to distinguish the individual qualities of a particular wine maker and the vital importance of grape variety, soil, climate and vinification techniques.

Opposite Perfect conditions for a professional tasting at the Académie du Vin in Paris.

Below Hedonistic tasting: members of the wine cooperative of Vaux-en-Beaujolais (the original of Gabriel Chevallier's 'Clochemerle') sample the previous year's vintage, while waiting for the start of the vendange.

Tasting/Conditions

The only adjunct to the taster's own skill and experience is the wine glass – though not, as we shall see, just any glass. The other important conditions relate to the taster himself and the setting for the actual tasting. Firstly, the taster must be in good physical shape; a cold or influenza makes tasting impossible. The palate must be fresh, and have had no recent contact with spicy dishes, chocolate, mint, strong drink or cigarettes. The best time for tasting is about 10 or 11 a.m.

The setting is also very important. Ideally, the room should be quiet, well lit and well aired, to banish any lingering smells; needless to say, no odour of perfume, tobacco or cooking should be allowed to seep in. The room should have light walls and a table with a white cloth. The temperature should be 20–22°C and humidity 60–70%. These conditions are about standard for any dining room in which fine wines are to be drunk.

Such preparations, however, are pointless, if the glasses themselves are unsuitable. Various types of glass have been studied by specialist bodies; the form of glass generally recognized to be the best has now been internationally adopted and conforms to standards laid down by the International Standards Organization (ISO).

The standard glass is clear and relatively thin. It has the exceptional quality of being suitable for tasting all kinds of drinks: champagne, sparkling wines, all reds and whites, ports and other fortified wines, and *eaux-de-vie* made from wine, fruit and grain. The tulip form of this perfect and universally applicable glass both retains the bouquet within the glass and also enables the processes of oxidation and oxygenation to take place through contact with the surrounding air. The foot and stem make it possible for tasters to hold it without warming the liquid; it is also an easy form to handle during the various actions which precede the tasting proper.

The ISO Wine Glass

Total height 155mm ± 5
Bowl height 100mm ± 2
Base and stem height 55mm ± 3
Diameter of top 46mm ± 2
Diameter of bowl at its widest 65mm ± 2
Thickness of stem 9mm ± 1
Diameter of base 65mm ± 5
Total capacity 215ml ± 10
Tasting quantity 50ml

Tasting/The Eye 1

The glass must first be placed on a white surface and filled up to one-third of its volume. The eye is then the first organ used in the tasting of wine. Even though it is nowadays rare to find wines possessing faults which can be seen by the eye alone, all tastings must begin visually by the inspection of the disc, the robe and, finally, the 'legs'.

The disc

The disc is the upper surface of the wine in the glass. It should be examined from above and then from the side. The surface of the disc should be bright and free from all dust or other solid matter. If the disc is matt, this is almost certainly a sign that all is not well with the wine, which is probably suffering from a microbic ailment. Lateral examination of the disc may reveal flocculation and deposits. The presence of any floating matter in the wine, so-called 'fliers', is clearly unacceptable, for it is a sure sign that the wine has been vinified badly and will therefore not age. The best that can be said about such a wine is that it is 'dubious'.

The collection of deposits at the bottom of the glass is not serious. These are generally made up of insoluble crystals, or precipitates of potassium bitartrates (cream of tartar), a sign that the wine has been subjected to a cold shock after bottling and the wine maker has not precipitated the bitartrates.

The results of these first visual examinations are described in very simple terms. Good wines are **limpid, bright** or **brilliant**: the others are **troubled, dubious, opaque, hazy, milky, flocculent, dim, murky,** etc.

The robe

The robe is the colour of the wine; it is assessed for its hue and the intensity of the hue. These two factors change together as the wine ages and are often pointers to its condition and quality. The robe also helps to assess the vintage of a wine, whether white, rosé or red and, in the case of the latter, to recommend how long it should be kept. The hue of white wines may range from light yellow to bronze, and once again colour can be used to evaluate age.

Colour is such an important factor in the wines of Bordeaux, that one well-known *négociant* made it his major criterion when buying. He painted the courtyard wall opposite his office white, and whenever he had to judge a wine he filled the glass and flung its contents at the wall. He always bought the wine which stained the wall (which needed regular repainting) most deeply. This procedure was not as eccentric as might at first appear. In comparing the vintages of 1960 and 1961 or 1969 and 1970, it would certainly have led him to choose the better ones (1961 and 1970). Indeed, colour is so important that certain grape varieties are planted solely for the purpose of colouring the wine. Such varieties, called *teinturiers*, produce special grapes containing a dark juice. The best known of these is the Alicante Bouschet, and more than 60,000 hectares of this variety are planted in France. An older procedure is to add the juice of elderberries. Such practices do not apply to fine wines.

Left The robe and disc seen to best advantage in a standard ISO tasting glass.

Appearance and Colour

White wines are often described in the following terms:
colourless, yellow, yellow linked to the words *pale, straw, lemon, green, golden, dark* and *gold*; furthermore there is *white gold*, with additional nuances expressed by *pale gold, green gold, red gold* and *bronze gold*; and older wines may be termed *topaz, burnt topaz, maderized, amber, brown, caramel, mahogany* or *black*.

Rosé wines are often termed *grey, light red, 'partridge eye', rose* or *violet*; and older rosés may be described as *rosé yellow, rosé orange, russet, salmon pink* or even as *having the colour of onion skin*.

Red wines are often described as *light, violaceous, dark, garnet, ruby, vermilion, purple* or *black*; and older reds are termed *bisque, orange, tile-red* or *maroon*.

Tasting/The Eye 2

Opposite *The taster inclines his glass, then allows the wine to run back down the sides, leaving the 'legs' to trickle down more slowly.*

The vocabulary used to describe the visual appearance of wines is essentially one of analogy. Flowers, fruits, woods, precious stones – all these are regularly used to evoke the colour of wine; but, although in theory the range of this vocabulary and system of analogies is limitless, a restricted number of terms have become almost standard by reason of frequent use.

Such terms are mainly intended to evoke the nuance and shade of a wine, which can of course be of a greater or lesser intensity. The robe of the wine can therefore be further qualified by such words as **deep, consistent, ample, dense, rich, heavy** or, in contrast, **light, weak, poor.** The description of a wine's hue is almost always accompanied by an opinion on the ageing of the wine, and the vocabulary may thus be extended by such terms as **fresh, sound, clear, true,** or **faded, over-aged, past its best, worn out, oxidized, maderized.**

Although the hue of a wine can nowadays be measured scientifically with a spectrometer, the taster's eye still remains the surest method of relating colour to quality by the comparative method. Professional tasters are offered four wine samples of varying degrees of colour intensity, positioned in front of a light source. They will arrive at their opinion of a particular wine by comparing it with the other samples offered for inspection.

The 'legs'

The 'legs' are the subject of the third type of visual examination.

Below *The effect of 'legs' or 'tears' on the side of a glass.*

The taster inclines his glass or makes a circular movement with it, so that the wine rises and then runs back down the sides of the glass. As this happens, the wine will form 'legs' or 'tears' which trickle down more slowly. This is the result of two processes. The first is due to the differences in surface tension between water and alcohol, which creates a capillary effect; the second is related to the viscosity of the wine, the 'legs' or 'tears' being formed by glycerols and residual sugar together with the alcohol. There has been much inconclusive discussion about the relationship between the quality of a wine's taste and the degree to which it forms 'legs'. Suffice it to say that the presence of the 'legs' is no guarantee of the balance or harmony of a wine. Too much alcohol or an excess of glycerol will also help the formation of very fine 'legs'. A poor wine which is weak both in

extract and alcohol will be too fluid to develop 'legs'; in contrast, a Grand Cru Burgundy, because it is legally obliged to attain a high level of alcohol to qualify for its *appellation*, will always form very marked 'legs'.

The vocabulary relating to the **fluidity** or **viscosity** of a wine is more limited: **watery, liquid, fluid,** as opposed to **heavy, syrupy, unctuous, high on glycerol, forming 'legs', forming 'tears', weeping.** The terms **oily, viscous** and **thick** are used to describe sick wines, especially those attacked by 'ropiness', a rare bacteriological ailment.

Sparkling wines

Wines which contain less than 100 mg/l of carbonic gas are referred to as 'still wines'; wines which contain more are known by a number of terms ranging from **effervescent** to **sparkling.** The various intermediate degrees between still and sparkling wines are described as **bubbly, pearly, 'moustillant'** and **semi-sparkling,** since carbon dioxide can be traced from a level of 1.5–2 gr/l.

Wines which do contain carbon dioxide need special attention, as the presence of the gas may be either a fault or a virtue, according to whether or not it is supposed to be present in the type of wine to be considered. In the context of visual inspection, it effectively entails examination of the bubbles, their diameter, frequency and rapidity with which they recur. These bubbles can create a fine cream on the surface of the wine (Champagne Crémant) or a very thick 'head', likewise made up of small bubbles, all equal in diameter, but only lasting for a few seconds. The transformation of groups of small bubbles into larger bubbles only occurs in beer. Once the 'head' on the wine has disappeared, the cream forms a ring, called the *cordon*, around the side of the glass, which remains there as long as the bubbles are renewed.

The major champagnes are all better drunk mature than young and none should ever be drunk too cold. In the context of our visual examination, however, the taster will be looking for an attractive pale colour and a constant flow of bubbles. Old champagnes will display certain changes in their visual characteristics: the customary palish colour will deepen to something close to gold, while the actual 'bubbly' quality will be less vigorous and lively.

Tasting/The Nose 1

Once the visual stage of the tasting is over, it is the turn of the olfactory senses. There is obviously no need for the two stages to follow each other in separate sequence; after some practice, during a purely hedonistic tasting or in the course of a meal, eye and nose can go to work simultaneously and with the same glass of wine. For present purposes, however, let us imagine that the glass used for the visual examination has been put to one side and that a new glass has been poured for the next stage. In this way we can discuss the significance of the 'first nose' and then compare the condition of the wine in the two glasses.

The first nose
The newly filled glass is left to stand on the table. The taster expels the air from his lungs and then, nose in glass, inhales deeply.

The 'first nose', even though it is often only a pale reflection of the ensuing 'second nose', enables the taster to become aware of the presence of a number of highly volatile and fugitive chemical elements which quickly disappear into the surrounding air or are transformed by oxidation or combination. In many cases, the first nose is strongly influenced, or even dominated, by parasitic odours caused by the wine having been kept

in a bottle and by the presence of gas which the wine maker tries to eliminate before bottling; such odours may arise from sulphur dioxide (SO_2), from the fermentation process, the lees, mercaptan, hydrogen sulphide and other chemicals.

The second nose
The second phase of the olfactory examination of the wine begins with a familiar action. The taster takes the glass by its foot and swivels it to make the wine revolve inside. This is done in order to oxygenate the liquid and accelerate the process of oxidation. The oxygenation or aeration of the wine helps to get rid of the gases in solution and the oxidation opens up the various aromatic elements of the wine.

The third nose
Oxidation is a continuous process in that the complex chemical composition of wine is constantly changing through the loss of volatile elements, coupled with the oxidation of volatile products and the interaction of the remaining constituent elements. For this reason, we can now turn back to the first glass, which was served for the visual examination, to see how these various processes have

Opposite The 'first nose': the taster inhales deeply, nose in glass.

Tasting: the olfactory senses
The olfactory appreciation of a glass of wine takes place by way of the nostrils and also from behind the soft palate.

1. Front sinus
2. Olfactory bulb
3. Nasal cavities
4. Vapour rising directly through the nostrils
5. Roof of mouth
6. Upper lip
7. Soft palate
8. Vapour rising behind the soft palate

Tasting/The Nose 2

begun to affect the wine. Professional tasters may complete this part of the examination by testing the condition of the wine in the glass, which involves leaving it for twelve hours. Another method entails emptying the glass and then following the olfactory development of the remaining aromatic constituents, since they are then free from the influence of the alcohol. This procedure is especially useful in tasting wines with very high alcohol content, such as fortified wines, and *eaux-de-vie*.

The sense of smell plays an essential part in wine tasting in order to establish the nature and intensity of the wine's aromatic elements.

The intensity is expressed in terms of strength or weakness, and there are many words to describe the stages between two extremes. The most frequently used terms, in sequence of increasing approval, are **null, weak, small, poor, short, hollow, closed, medium, normal, strong, rich, developed, intense, ample** and **generous.**

Primary aromas refer to the fruity qualities of the grape and it is by these that the grape variety is most easily identified. Such aromas are especially noticeable in very young wines or wines made from very aromatic varieties for drinking young (e.g. Alsatian and German wines).

Secondary aromas (sometimes called fermentative) are those that refer more specifically to the wine itself; they are caused by the transformation of the must into wine, which brings into existence a number of elements not present in the must before fermentation, such as succinic acid. These aromas depend on the type of must (vines, soils), on yeasts and on the method of fermentation.

Tertiary aromas only begin to appear during the maturing period in cask or vat (oxidation) and/or after a period of ageing in the bottle. Such aromas are sometimes termed post-fermentative.

It would probably be true to say that the

Opposite *Swivelling the glass accelerates the process of oxidation and opens up the various aromatic elements of the wine.*

Odours and Aromas

There is likewise an accepted vocabulary for the various aromatic categories. Wine can never be defined in terms of one aromatic element, even if it is the dominant one; there are always several. For the sake of convenience, these elements have been classified into nine principal categories.

Animal odours: *game, gamey, venison, meaty, musk, musky, 'catty';*

Balsamic odours: all *resins, juniper, turpentine, vanilla, pine, benjamin;*

Empyreumatic odours: everything *dry, smoked, toasted bread, almond, hay, straw, coffee, wood;* also *leather* and *tar;*

Chemical odours: *spirituous, acetone* (nail varnish), *acetic, phenol, carbolic, mercaptan, sulphur* (and its deriva-

tives), *lactic, iodized, oxidized, yeast, ferment;*

Spicy odours: all spices, but most frequently *clove, laurel, pepper, cinnamon, nutmeg, ginger, rosemary, truffle, liquorice, mint;*

Floral odours: all flowers but most frequently *violet, hawthorn, rose, citronella, jasmine, iris, geranium, acacia, lime;*

Fruit odours: all fruits but most frequently *blackcurrant, raspberry, cherry, grenadine, gooseberry, plum, almond, quince, apricot, banana, nuts, fig;*

Vegetable and mineral odours: *herbaceous, hay, tea, dead leaves, truffle, mushroom, damp straw, damp moss, damp undergrowth, chalk, fern, ivy, green leaves.*

These terms do not differ greatly from those used for making qualitative judgments; and the more subjective the tasting becomes, the more this is reflected in the terminology. Thus, the nose may be described as **ordinary, vulgar, uninteresting, simplistic, lacking complexity** and **banal** or **refined, fine, sophisticated, stylish, distinguished** and **exemplary.**

The aromas are sometimes further subdivided into three categories.

taster will find most of the olfactory sensations he is likely to derive from a given glass of wine when he first passes his nose over it and inhales relatively lightly. Indeed, there is little point in lingering too long over the first nose of a wine, since too long an exposure to the initial bouquet will rapidly reduce its interest. It is better to pass on to the other stages of the olfactory examination which will then yield a much more rounded appreciation of the varied odours given off by the wine.

Tasting/The Mouth

It is not generally realized that the 'taste' of a wine depends more on the nose than the mouth. In other words, it is more of an olfactory than a merely gustatory experience. Expert wine tasters therefore rely heavily on the first purely nasal appreciation of wine in the knowledge that almost all its aromas travel to the mouth through the back passages of the nose. The effect is double-acting, since the olfactory glands, in addition to being stimulated directly when the nose is passed over the wine, are again alerted once the wine is actually inside the mouth, the vaporized aromas exciting one or more of the 50 million or so nasal nerve cells.

An understanding of this process helps to explain the logic of the tasting ritual and the reasons why the wine must always be distributed around the mouth. The taster takes a small quantity of wine into his mouth and, instead of swallowing it, allows it to lie on his tongue while slowly inhaling. The wine's aromatic vapours are released more strongly through being warmed gently in the mouth and by its evaporation in the air.

Some tasters prefer to 'chew' the wine, turning it round and round in the mouth, enabling the olfactory glands to confirm the sensations initially registered during the nasal phase. These sensations will not be identical, however, since the wine will have been warmed slightly inside the mouth, releasing a quantity of less volatile molecules that generate a complementary set of aromas; these are described in the same terms as those used for the purely nasal perception.

Taste in the mouth proper

The human tongue distinguishes four basic types of flavour: sweet on the tip of the tongue, salty just behind the tip and on either side of it, acidic on the sides, and bitter at the back. These four primary flavours are modified by sensations perceived by the tongue and the whole oral cavity: sensations of heat and temperature, touch, feel and consistency (fluidness, viscosity, etc.) and of chemistry, such as astringency and gas.

Aftertaste

It might be assumed that the taster, having looked at the wine, tasted it and analysed his oral sensations, would swallow it and pass on to the next sample. Not so, however, for there is one final factor that in itself can enable him to distinguish a great wine from an ordinary vintage. This is the wine's 'length' or persistence inside the mouth – on the face of it quite simple, yet in reality a rather complex phenomenon. After the wine is swallowed, its aromatic power tends to fill the mouth and then fade away gradually; the duration of this sensation determines the wine's persistence or ability to linger, and is measured in seconds. The longer or more persistent the aftertaste, the greater the wine will be; conversely, a short wine is never really acceptable.

Unfortunately there is one minor problem, namely that sensations are always mixed, since a wine's aromatic components are supported by its structure; and, in determining the wine's persistence in the mouth, sensation of structure plays no part. The structure of the wine is affected by acidity and by certain tannins yielded by the alcohol. To give just one simple example of how 'structure' and 'length' can be confused: vinegar leaves a persistent memory in the mouth but is not long in flavour, for it is only the acetic acid that is left behind. The length of more successful wines is, however, relatively easy to measure since their structure, body and aromas will be more evenly and equally balanced and so should provide an aftertaste that lingers and fades in perfect harmony.

Tasting: harmony and rhythm

The harmony that tasters expect of great wines presupposes an uninterrupted succession of positive impressions; in other words, the eye must herald the 'nose' that will be confirmed by the mouth. A red wine with a white wine flavour would never do, while a champagne that had a Bordeaux nose and a Blanquette de Limoux taste would be devoid of all interest.

The first in the sequence of sensations is the wine's 'attack', which should be clean, natural and precise. Many southern wines or wines made in very hot years have little or no attack. Secondly, the mouth should be wholly suffused with the wine's flavours and aromas. Finally, there is the aftertaste, the impressions of which must continue and prolong the original taste sensation without a break.

Comparative tastings presented in the Advanced Course (Course 3) will enable the reader to become acquainted with the techniques described here and with the terminology of tasting.

Tasting/Balance

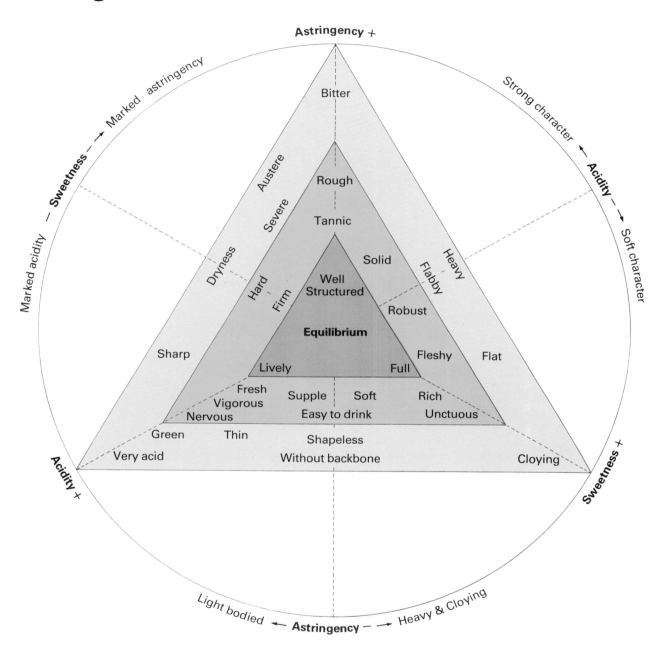

Tasting: balance

Tasting wine is like appreciating good music. Just as we can derive additional pleasure from reading the score, identifying the instruments, recognizing changes of key and so forth, we can enhance our enjoyment of a wine by seeking out the essential elements, determining which are complementary and which incompatible. A wine of quality imparts a sense of balance, created by a harmonious merging of constituent factors.

The diagram above, taken from *Le goût du vin* by Emile Peynaud (Bordas, second edition, 1983) explains the components and mechanics of this balancing process in red wines.

The Vine/Life Cycle

Right *The life cycle of the vine – from new leaves to ripe grapes.*

The vine is a humble plant, simply a domesticated creeper that happens to thrive well in a number of different soils, even poor ones, provided the climate is temperate and its roots do not rot with excessive dampness. The vine's most interesting feature – at any rate from our viewpoint – is that it bears fruit, the grape, that can be turned into wine. Here we are immediately confronted by a paradox, for experience shows that the best wines come from vines that in a sense, are made to 'suffer'. It is a fact that rich, well irrigated soils which get a lot of sunshine do not produce really great wines. At the opposite extreme, soils that are excessively wet and deprived of sunlight are equally unsuitable for growing vines. Scientific research has shown that the finest wines come from vines planted around the northern boundaries of areas given over to particular grape varieties. Of course, not every geographical region will be suitable for all the different varieties of grape, if only because their life cycles tend to vary. These matters are dealt with in greater detail in the Intermediate Course.

The life cycle of the vine is such that the grower must give it his constant, unflagging attention. Like all plants, the vine lies dormant in winter, and revives in the spring when the soil starts to warm up. This is true at any rate of temperate climates; in the tropics the various phases of a plant's life cycle may occur simultaneously, so that the vine will bear blossom, green grapes and ripe grapes all at the same time, in which case only rigorous pruning can establish a logical sequence. In Europe, winter cold and frost suspend the vine's growth but normally – since it is a hardy plant – do not kill it. Only if very cold conditions persist, as in 1956 when there were protracted frosts of $-20°C$, will it be finished off.

In spring, when the temperature starts to rise to around $11°C$, the sap rises and can be seen running from pruned shoots, when the vine is said to be 'weeping'. This is the moment when the buds develop and burst, breaking the soft down that protected them from the cold. The buds split open at different times, depending on the variety of grape. Early-budding varieties may still be threatened by late frosts, and therefore extra protection must be provided either by heating the surrounding air or by watering the vines,

Below The vine needs careful protection from adverse weather conditions: anti-frost stoves in California's Napa Valley.

since the resulting layer of ice insulates the buds (Chablis, Champagne).

Another risky moment for the vine comes in June when the plant flowers. Fertilization is essential if the blossom is to give way to grape berries, but in poor atmospheric conditions this will not happen and the plant will yield little fruit. Sometimes small grapes without pips will form, indicating a partial crop failure, known as *millerandange*. The annual harvest yield is often decided at this particular stage.

One hundred days elapse between flowering and harvesting, and during this period sunshine is of prime importance. Temperatures of around 30°C are ideal, especially if accompanied by a little rainfall from 15 to 20 August. Too much rain, of course, is detrimental to the vine and will never produce a great wine even though all other requirements may have been met (Bordeaux 1974 is an example). After harvesting, the leaves redden and fall and the vineyard returns to its winter slumbers.

The vine has a need for constant attention if it is to fulfil its role in the delicate chain from individual vineyard to wine bottle.

The Vine/Cultivation

Vines are usually discarded between the ages of 40 and 50 years, but the grower is faced with a dilemma. Although the vine's grape yield diminishes with age, the quality of the wine improves, and so a choice has to be made between quantity and quality. The older the vineyard, the less plentiful and more expensive the wine, as is the case with all Bordeaux first growths. In practice, however, things are not quite so simple, and the vines are replaced piecemeal in order to keep the quality consistent.

A vine has to be at least four years old before its grapes can legally be made into *appellation contrôlée* wines. The great châteaux wait as much as eight years before permitting grapes to go into their *grands vins*, so wary are they of unsuitably light wines from young plants. Replanting will depend on the variety of grape grown and the cultivation density, which may range from 5000 to 10,000 vines per hectare. It will also depend on the type of stock that is to be planted, since all post-phylloxera vines comprise a root (*porte-greffe*) to which the plant's aerial branches are grafted. The grafted scions produce the grapes.

Cultivation and treatment

Although, as mentioned, the vine thrives in poor soils, it stands to reason that enormous amounts of fertilizer, both natural and manmade, have to be applied to the vineyard. To begin with, each hectare is treated with 25 to 30 tonnes of natural manure together with about half a tonne of phosphates and, at time of planting, one tonne of potassium. The soil is treated in similar fashion approximately every four years. The vineyard requires constant attention: earthing-up in autumn to protect the base of the vine, de-earthing in spring to free the base, turning over the soil between the rows of the vine, tamping down the earth in May and finally topsoil dressing and hoeing in summer.

Some growers prefer natural cultivation, allowing grass to grow amongst the vines, though most make use of grass- and weed-killers. All, however, are engaged in a constant battle against vine diseases, which may either

Below The vines of Châteauneuf-du-Pape growing in characteristically pebbly soil.

Below right Vines need repeated spraying to combat the ravages of bacteria, fungi and insects; hand-spraying in a vineyard of Jurançon in south-west France.

be due to soil deficiencies, to bacteria or to fungi (mildew, oidium, blackrot, botrytis) and combated by means of fungicides, while others are animal in origin (weevils, mealy bugs, cochylis bugs, caterpillars, phylloxera and spiders). All diseases require a specific treatment and some – botrytis, for instance – need repeated spraying.

Pruning

The quality of the wine depends on the quality of the grape. As Jean-Paul Gardère, director of Château Latour, says: 'Give me good grapes and good vats and I will make you a great wine.' The fight against vine diseases does much to protect the grape's health, and pruning is equally valuable. Lack of pruning causes the shoots to grow too long and the yield to drop, since the older branches will cease to bear bunches of berries; incorrect pruning, on the other hand, may produce huge yields but the grapes may turn out to be weak and insipid.

Winter pruning Not all grape varieties are pruned in the same manner. There is, for example, the 'goblet' cut, used in the south of France, in the Rhône Valley, in Beaujolais, Burgundy and the Champagne region. According to this method, the stock or stem supports three to five branches each bearing one or two spurs dressed to form loops.

The Chablis cut is a variation of the 'goblet' system (four arms radiating directly from the main stem) and is the method used in the Champagne region for white-grape vines.

Then there are the Royat cordon cut (Pinot Champenois) and the single or double Guyot (Bordeaux) in which one arm of the stem (or both in double Guyot) follows the training of the plants and includes 6 to 8 loops (2×3 or 2×4 in the double Guyot). Whatever the method employed, the purpose of pruning is to expose the vine to as much sun as possible, to simplify cultivation and finally to facilitate mechanized harvesting.

Spring and summer dressing This includes disbudding – removing unwanted buds – topping to remove the uppermost branches, clipping to take off the ends of the twigs and, finally, thinning out of leaves.

Below Pruning vines in Champagne.

31

The Vine/Soil & Climate

Experts agree that the quality of wine depends on four factors and four factors alone: geology, climate, vine stock and vinification (method of wine-making) under which heading we must include growing and maturing. It could be argued that conditions of tasting are also important, but as far as the Académie du Vin is concerned these are the main areas of interest and research.

Subsoil and topsoil

Geology is for our purposes virtually synonymous with soil. It is not always easy to decide where the subsoil ends and the topsoil begins. The vine will often put down its roots to great depths in search of sustenance; for instance, cellars cut into the rock 10 to 15 metres beneath the Saint-Emilion vineyards at Château Ausone and Château Pavie reveal the roots of very old vines. As mentioned, the vine does poorly in very wet soil, but like any other plant it does need water and will probe deep down to find it. Thus the best soil for the vine is one with good natural drainage and free from obstacles likely to impede the roots. Such conditions are met by deep gravel and, to a lesser extent, by asteriated limestone of the type found in the Médoc and Saint-Emilion regions. In gravelly soil, where water cannot collect, the vine roots are free to grow and develop; in limestone soils, they burrow deep into the fissures between the solid blocks of rock.

Sandy and siliceous soils frequently produce wines that are fine but over-light, whereas limestone and clayey soils yield

Right The vines of Châteauneuf-du-Pape frequently grow on scree slopes; the pebbles improve the aeration and drainage of the soil and also store daytime warmth for release during the night.

vintages which are more robust than sophisticated. The actual presence of pebbles improves the soil's aeration and drainage as well as acting as a 'storage heater', releasing at night the warmth accumulated during the hours of sunshine. This is the case at Châteauneuf-du-Pape where the vines grow on a virtual scree slope. The actual colour of the soil also plays a part, since pale soils such as marls, chalks and tuff are better for white varieties, while the darker soils are more suited to red wines.

Climate

The four principal interactive elements of climate are sunshine, rainfall, temperature and wind. Areas that enjoy an abundance of sunshine will produce grapes that are rich in sugar but low in acidity. Regions with too much sun tend to yield wines that lack breeding. Too little sunshine, on the other hand, leads to wines that are over-acidic but low in alcohol and hence thin and feeble.

The vine requires from 16 to 24 inches of rain a year, though not at random: rain is welcome in winter and early spring but potentially harmful in summer and early autumn.

Wine-growing becomes a problem when mean annual temperatures fall below 10°C, and the quality of the vintage is usually decided in the months of August and September, when temperatures above 30°C enhance the prospects of the new season's wine.

North winds are favourable in hot regions as they cleanse and purify the vineyard, but excessively strong winds cause damage.

Left Close inspection of the dusty soil in a Napa Valley vineyard in California.

The Vine/Grafting

All the diseases mentioned previously will have a detrimental effect on the wine's quality, but there is one more that very nearly exterminated the vine for good in the 19th century. This disease was caused by the phylloxera bug (*Dactylosphera vitifolii*), an aphid brought across the Atlantic from America in the early 1860s, possibly on vine scions or table grapes. In 1863 phylloxera appeared in the extensive vineyards of the *département* of Gard, in Languedoc, and subsequently moved northwards to Orange, in Vaucluse, and Drôme; by 1868 the vineyards of Bordeaux and Portugal had been attacked. American vines were fortunately immune to phylloxera, but within half a century it had destroyed all of Europe's vineyards, since the only treatment found against it – carbon disulphide – proved difficult to apply, being highly flammable and giving off a foul odour, besides having toxic effects on humans.

The *vignerons* hit on the idea of replacing their defunct European vines with phylloxera-proof American ones, but the latter on their own proved incapable of producing wines of sufficient quality and distinction for European tastes. However, when European *vinifera* scions were grafted on to them the grapes – and hence the wines – took on the characteristics of the scions. Nowadays, quality vines the world over are grafted in this way. Only plants grown in sand can be left ungrafted because phylloxera cannot survive in this element.

Ever since this major replanting exercise – from 1¼ to 1½ million hectares were reconstituted in this way – experts have discussed and argued the various merits of grafting and its effects on the quality of the wine. Comparisons are difficult because pre-phylloxera vines are by now very old. The last quality vineyard to preserve ungrafted plants was Romanée-Conti, until the end of World War II; and at the moment the well known champagne firm Bollinger is cultivating two small plots of ungrafted Pinot Noir (so-called 'old French vines'), by way of experiment.

Any valid opinion must take into account the fact that the ungrafted vine has the great advantage of longevity – it survives for almost a century. As already mentioned, a wine's quality improves with the age of the vine, the bouquet becoming more refined and the structure more complex.

So what, apart from their resistance to phylloxera, are the benefits and drawbacks of grafted vines? Whereas ungrafted varieties grow in just about any type of soil apart from ground that is too wet, clayey or salty (chloride), the American vines that constitute the basis of present-day vineyards do poorly in limestone, which etiolates them (turns the leaves yellow); furthermore, grafted vines have a shorter life. On the other hand, they are many and varied; in France a grower has the choice of some 30 different vine stocks (including hybrids) which enables him to find exactly the right kind for the scions, depending on the particular type of soil and the type of grape he wants to cultivate. Factors such as strength, sugar, yield and resistance to disease, all vary according to selection of the stock for a particular environment.

Wine growers everywhere periodically come up with new stocks which they hope will be better suited to their particular soil, especially limestone, and yield even more fruit. The most recent is called Fercal, and great things are expected of it in Saint-Emilion and Champagne. In France alone, over 4000 hectares are devoted to the production of vine stocks for replenishing purposes.

Above *The phylloxera bug (*Dactylosphera vitifolii).

Right *Vine twigs for grafting, showing the W-form 'join'.*

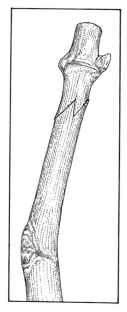

Top *The modern U-form vine graft, which can be done with a stamping machine.*
Above *The more traditional W-form.*
Right *Cutting and joining American root stock (dark twigs) to the desired French variety (pale twigs).*

The Vine/Mechanized Cultivation

Mechanization made its first appearance in vineyards just after World War II. The recently invented straddler tractor has transformed the lives of the growers, making possible a wide range of different treatments and processes. These vehicles have an adjustable track and the more sophisticated types are equipped with hydraulic levellers for safe working on hillside vineyards where rows of vines do not evenly follow the slope.

Winches are used on steeply inclined hills with rows that follow the line of the slope; and these have proved highly effective in reclaiming vineyards abandoned because of the difficulty and cost of manual labour (e.g. Sancerre and Switzerland). Trials are currently being conducted to test new tractors for the more precipitous, inaccessible slopes. These machines have articulated legs and feet in place of the normal wheels and are able to cope with any gradient while remaining in a horizontal position. This type of tractor is particularly suited to terraced vineyards thus far wholly reliant on manual labour.

The straddler tractors can be fitted with a range of attachments for various functions,

Below Manuring a vineyard in Savoy, using a tractor specially designed for this purpose.

such as earthing up and de-earthing, including sensor-controlled ploughs that till between the rows of vines without damaging the precious plants. The machines are also used for treating the vines, notably for spraying them with the innumerable fungicides and insecticides so essential for modern vineyard practice.

No machine has so far been invented for automatic pruning; nevertheless, pneumatic and hydraulic secateurs minimize physical effort and increase individual productivity. There is, however, a machine that collects and breaks up the pruned twigs and branches, incinerating them or burying them in the soil as additional fertilization.

Topping has also been mechanized, and rotary toppers and dressers mounted on the tractors help give the vineyard the ordered neatness and regularity of a formal garden. Dressing, of course, must be done with extreme care, for photosynthesis of the leaves determines the grape's sugar content.

Finally, and particularly if the grape harvest itself is automated, the straddler tractor can be converted into a pneumatic stripper which separates the bunches and eliminates unwanted leaves.

Mechanical harvesting

These machines are being used to an increasing extent. The bunches of grapes, provided they are correctly dressed, should develop and grow at specific heights above the ground, and so it is a simple matter for harvesters to drop the berries and grapes onto a moving conveyor where residual leaves are removed by powerful air blowers; under normal conditions the machines operate as well as, if not better than, teams of pickers.

Machines also have the additional obvious advantage of needing no sleep and so can work round the clock if there is a threat of bad weather. Last but by no means least, machinery enables the *vigneron* to start and finish the harvest when the grape is fully ripened. Note, however, that mechanical harvesting is prohibited in Champagne.

Below A mechanical harvester at work in a vineyard at Cahors.

Vinification/Introduction

Vinification is the collective term for all the operations and processes which turn grapes into wine. Authoritative books on wine written before World War II make no mention of vinification, but since then the art of wine-making has made great strides and a new kind of expert has emerged, the oenologist. The oenologist's mastery of vinification techniques is just as important as the grape variety, the soil and the climate. Not only is he a technician who must be versed in physics and chemistry, but he is also something of an artist, and a great wine represents his masterpiece. A good oenologist can stamp a wine with distinction; a bad oenologist can produce a bad wine even from excellent grapes.

Gifted oenologists tend to divide into two types, some being pure technicians, others more aesthetic. The technicians produce correspondingly technical wines, that is to say wines which, though faultless, are devoid of charm; the more artistic oenologists can also be further subdivided into those who impose their personality on the wine, 'signing' it, often to the detriment of the distinctive local or native tang, and those who, more self-effacingly, allow the characteristic qualities of the grape to speak for themselves.

Vignerons have repeatedly confirmed that the method of vinification is at least 50% responsible for the final quality of a wine. Naturally, therefore, the Académie du Vin attaches great importance to the various problems involved.

The same red grapes are capable of producing either a wine that is light, fresh and fruity rather than full-bodied, which should be drunk young or even very young, or a wine that is rich, dark and generous, heavy on extract, of great aromatic complexity and not to be drunk in the first ten years of its life. The grapes could even be used to make a light rosé for summer drinking or a fine and vinous white wine.

The same applies to white grapes. The wine maker can use them to create a fruity wine with an alluring primary bouquet, a somewhat facile dry white wine to accompany hors d'oeuvres, a truly great white wine with highly evolved secondary aromas from which the grape flavour has quite disappeared, or finally a sparkling or slightly sparkling dry white wine.

The type and quality of the finished product are thus dependent on the vinifier; and at the Académie du Vin it is our business to determine, simply by tasting, the method chosen by the wine maker and to compare wines, which, although they come from the same village or commune, possess different properties because they have been made on different estates. A knowledge of the principles of vinification is essential for this rather more sophisticated approach to wine.

Right *The quality of a wine depends greatly on the ability and taste of the vinifier: tasting wine from the cask in Beaujolais.*

Opposite *Pesage at Margaux, Bordelais.*

Vinification/The Cuverie

Adjoining the actual fermenting room – where the must is transformed into wine – is an area that usually features a *fouloir-érafloir* (or *égrappoir*) which simultaneously removes the stalks from the grapes and crushes them. After fermentation, the wine is aged and matured in storage vats and casks. The wine is then fined, filtered and bottled; and finally the bottles are labelled and packed into cases.

Each of these operations has led to the invention of special equipment. The crusher, as its name suggests, is used to squeeze the grape, thereby bursting its skin and releasing the juice. Crushing was once done by 'treading' the wine in huge casks, but nowadays the berries are passed between two rollers which are close enough to burst the grape but not to crack the pips. This is important, for the pips contain substances that give the wine an unpleasant taste.

The *érafloir* or *égrappoir* is a machine that separates the stalks and stems from the berries, although certain estates, e.g. Château Palmer, still carry out this work traditionally by hand.

The fermenting vats themselves may be made of wood, cement, plastic, enamelled metal or stainless steel, and can be open (Burgundy) or closed (Bordeaux). Vat capacities range from just a few to several thousand hectolitres; some white wines ferment in 2-hectolitre barrels! The temperature of the grape must has to be monitored and controlled, and fermenting temperatures are regulated by means of water cooling systems, heat pumps or heat exchanger coils. The pumps circulate the wine around the vats, conveying it from the base to the surface of the liquid, a process known as *remontage* and highly important for the quality of red wines. Pumps are also used to transfer the wine from one vat to another, and this is called *écoulage*. The 'cake' *(marc)* or residue collected inside the vat is transferred to a press, but since

Above right *Old-style press still in use for producing fine Sauternes at Château d'Yquem.* **Right** *A modern drum press at Château Beychevelle in the Médoc.*

there is no *écoulage* for white wines these are routed directly to the press.

Most modern presses are pneumatic or electrically operated horizontal machines with pressure control. As mentioned, it is essential never to crack the grape pips because they contain a bitter oil fatal to the quality of the wine. Inside the press, two screw-driven plates compress the 'cake' of skin, pips and sometimes stalks. A new model of press known as a balloon press has a rubber bag that presses the grape against a cylindrical grid when inflated. Pressing is done several times and between each pressing the 'cake' is broken up by removal of the plates and a system of chains or, in the balloon press, by deflating the balloon and rotating the cylinder. Once all the juice has been expressed, the press is emptied and the dried 'cake' is turned into fertilizer or supplied to a distillery for conversion into *marc* brandy.

The wine is then put into an insulated vat which may be artificially heated to encourage malolactic fermentation or cooled to promote the precipitation of bitartrate. Finally it will be stored in huge vats pending bottling or pumped to the maturing cellars where it will rest in wooden casks.

The following sections take a fairly detailed look at the various vinification methods and their respective effects on the taste of the finished wine.

Above Stainless steel tanks in a modern Californian winery can be used for both fermentation and storage.

Left Oak casks in the maturing cellar of a French négociant; the age and method of manufacture of a cask can have an influence on the eventual taste of the wine.

Vinification/Red Wine

Red wine is obtained by fermenting red grapes, although some white berries may be added to the process – something that is tolerated in Burgundy, common practice in the Rhône Valley and a tiresome obligation in Chianti. For the wine to be red, the pigments that give the grape skin its characteristic colour must dissolve in the colourless grape juice and this occurs under the influence of heat or alcohol, or both.

Sorting and pressing

When the grapes arrive at the fermenting room, they may be more or less sorted: in Champagne the sorting is thorough, in the Rhône Valley it is compulsory (at Châteauneuf, for instance, 5% are discarded), and this has an initial effect on quality. The harvest may also have been pressed and/or de-stalked, and manual de-stalking, as practised at Château Palmer, may necessitate additional sorting. Although all harvests are pressed (except in the special cases described on pages 54–55), de-stalking is a more complex issue, for the retention of stalks may actually be beneficial in certain grape varieties, harmful in others. The stalks of Pinot or Merlot, for example, make a positive contribution to the quality of the fermented wine, while those of the Cabernet or Carignan varieties give rise to disagreeable features. Generally speaking, the removal and elimination of the vine stalks will enhance the distinction and breeding of the wine, but in certain cases good stalks may strengthen its tannin and make it longer-lived.

Fermentation

Pressed grapes – whether or not partially or wholly de-stalked – are placed in the fermenting vats and at this point the vinifier has three parameters to consider: fermentation, temperature and *remontage*.

Fermentation ceases at temperatures below 15°C, while above 35°C the yeasts are killed off by the heat. Lower temperatures encourage primary aromas that are the attributes of wine which must be drunk young; hot fermentation tends to extract the polyphenols and tannins so essential for making great vintage wines. Similar criteria govern the actual fermenting time – short fermentation (24 to 36 hours only) produces light, so-called 'overnight' wines. Lengthy fermentation, as much as one month, produces more ambitious wines.

In deciding the fermenting period, the *vigneron* must take into account the potential of the vintage, the grape variety and his own personal taste. He may even increase the wine's degree of alcohol by adding sugar during the fermenting process. This practice, known as chaptalization, is the subject of much controversy but is nevertheless regulated (2°). In mediocre years the fermenting time has to be increased, although if the grape is unhealthy fermentation will have to be cut short.

The influence of the grape variety is very important. The fermenting period for Bordeaux varieties is, for example, two times longer than for the Pinot. It sometimes happens that the *vigneron*, when tasting the wine, feels the need for a little extra fermenting; yet to prolong it may be dangerous since risks of bacteriological disease (volatile acidity, etc.) are always present.

Remontage

The wine-maker also has to decide how many times to carry out *remontage*. During fermentation, the solids tend to float to the top of the vat, forming a thick crust called the 'cap' which floats on or just below the surface of the wine. This cap, buoyed up by the rising carbon dioxide gas, has to be kept immersed, or at least constantly pressed under (a process called *pigeage*); alternatively, it may be sprayed with wine pumped from beneath and back again over the cap, which is thereby kept wet. These essential operations increase extraction.

Vin de goutte and vin de presse

Next comes the process of running off the fermented wine from the vat (*écoulage*). This wine is the *vin de goutte*, of fine, sometimes great, quality. The solids taken from the fermenting vats are then pressed two or three times to yield the *vin de presse* (first pressing, second pressing and so on) which constitutes some 20% of the total volume. This is a very dark, extremely tannic wine which is slightly lower in alcohol and rather more acid. It is less refined and very unpleasant to taste on its own; some or all of it will eventually be added to the *vin de goutte*, depending upon the latter's constitution and the vinifier's preferences. In any event, both *goutte* and *presse* will first undergo malolactic fermentation, in which malic acid is converted to lactic acid under the action of lactic ferments.

The black grapes are first crushed before removal to the fermenting vat; red wine takes its colour from the pigments present in the skins.

The solids taken off from the fermenting vat, about 20% of the total volume, are pressed two or three times to yield the vin de presse.

The fermented wine is run off from the fermenting vat straight to the storage vat or barrel; this is the vin de goutte.

A certain amount of the vin de presse may be added to the vin de goutte, depending on the type of wine preferred by the vinifier.

Wine run off for storage in oak barrels takes on different characteristics from the wood; other wine may be aged in the bottle.

Vinification/Rosé Wine

In Europe, one region apart, rosé wines cannot be made by blending red wines with white. The exception is in Champagne where *vignerons* may legally tint their white wine by adding red wine from the same area of *appellation*. Otherwise there are three types of rosé, each the product of a special vinification technique: they are the pressed rosés, the 'bled' rosés (*saignée*) and rosés made from pink grapes.

The pressed rosé is made from red grapes but using the white grape method, bearing in mind the fact that good-quality red grapes are filled with colourless juice. These grapes are crushed, strained and pressed, and in very hot weather some of the pigments that give the skin its characteristic colour are dissolved, encouraged by alcoholic fermentation. Subsequent pressings will be increasingly coloured, and the first pressing is normally used to give the wine its pink hue. These relatively pale rosés are frequently sold as *vin gris* (grey wines), and are similar in taste to white wines (*vin gris de Toul, vin gris d'Orléans*). The Cabernets of Anjou and Saumur are vinified in this way to make the famous Rosé d'Anjou.

Unlike the must of white grapes, the two kinds of must, *goutte* and *presse*, are mixed in the vat without their solids having been removed, and allowed to ferment under the same conditions as white wine musts, i.e. at low temperatures and heavily protected from oxidation. Like white wines, they may or may not undergo malolactic fermentation, as the individual wine maker eventually chooses.

The rosés *de saignée* are in fact red wine grapes that are partially macerated or fermented for a short period. Unlike the pressed rosés, therefore, they result from the vinification of red grapes by the red wine method whereby maceration is restricted from a few hours to two or three days according to the final colour desired; after this time the vat is 'bled' or tapped to remove a quarter or a third of its contents, and the rest made into standard red wine. The tapped amount continues to ferment but is no longer in contact with the grape skins and so cannot be additionally coloured. These rosé wines are superior in quality to pressed rosés, and all undergo malolactic fermentation.

The third type of rosé is also the least common and found almost solely in the Jura region. It is produced by the red vinification of a very special grape, the Poulsard, special because of its pink skin and pink juice. This means that the grapes can macerate at length, the extraction of colouring and aromatic agents being extremely important. It is vinified in exactly the same way as a red wine, and is even referred to, if somewhat superficially, as a very light red. Another characteristic of the Poulsard rosé that gives it a resemblance to reds is its longevity, for its quality improves with age. Pressed rosés, on the other hand, should be drunk quickly, if possible within 12 months, while the rosés *de saignée* can wait a little longer but will hardly improve with age.

Opposite *Some of the thirteen grape varieties used in the preparation of the Tavel rosé, Côtes-du-Rhône.*

Vinification/White Wine

White wine is made by the direct pressing of white grapes or black grapes with colourless juice, although the great white wines – apart from champagne – are always made with white grapes.

Crushing and pressing

Once the grapes are harvested, they are immediately crushed and strained, mechanically or naturally, then pressed. Mechanical strainers can extract 75% of the must, which will be of a high quality. Subsequent pressings will be of lesser quality and the final 10–15% will be low in acidity, containing much tannin and iron; they are, in any event, coloured and so will not be used to make the wine.

At all stages of vinification the must has to be protected against oxidation, and this is done by sulphuring, i.e. treating the must with sulphur dioxide (8–10 gr/hl) which is both an antioxidant (a reducing agent) and antioxidasic. Oxidases (oxidation enzymes) are harmful to white wines and are capable of destroying them altogether (oxidasic breakdown); they attack the phenol components, giving bitterness, harshness and colour. Since they attach themselves to the solid matter of the berries, these solids have to be removed by a process known as *débourbage* and the juice allowed to ferment by itself. *Débourbage* may be natural – by means of sedimentation with the must cooled to prevent fermentation (−10°C) – or forced by filtration (bentonite), flocculation or centrifuging. These traditional techniques all help to improve the quality of white wines.

Fermentation

The clear grape must now begins to ferment and selected yeasts are added to the wine inside the vat or tank. Depending on the type of wine desired and the size of the estate, these fermenting vats may either be shaped like wooden barrels, to contain about 2 hectolitres, or be huge cement or stainless steel tanks of up to 1000 hectolitres.

The wine maker must, of course, pay particular attention to the fermenting temperature, since experience shows that anything over 19–20°C can jeopardize the potential aromas. White wine is best fermented in relatively small quantities: the process of fermentation gives off much heat and in large vats there is always a tendency to overheat, whereas in small ones the surface area of the walls is relatively greater, causing less trouble. The problem of vat size can be overcome by the use of internal refrigeration to regulate the temperature.

Low-temperature fermentation may take up to one month and the wine is considered to be dry when laboratory analysis shows it to contain only 2 grams of sugar per litre.

Malolactic fermentation

This is the moment when the wine maker is faced with a crucial decision: whether or not to allow malolactic fermentation to take place. Malolactic fermentation is triggered by heating the vats; otherwise the wine is sulphited (10 gr/hl) to destroy the lactic bacteria. The decision depends on the overall acidity of the young wine (and hence on the grape variety and year) as well as on the type of wine the vinifier wants to achieve. Malolactic fermentation is practised in Burgundy, where a degree of suppleness is sought, and in Switzerland, despite the Chasselas grape's lack of acidity. In Germany, the Bordelais and most of the Champagne region, however, it is avoided. It is worth noting that the conversion of malic acid into lactic acid reduces the wine's acidity, since 10 grams of malic acid produce 6.7 grams of lactic acid plus 3.3 grams of carbon dioxide which escapes as gas. Generally speaking, a standard dry white wine with 11–11.5° of alcohol is judged successful when its acidity reaches 4–5 grams per litre.

Below Sorting Chardonnay grapes at Cramant for the production of crémant, *or lightly sparkling champagne.*

A crusher-stemmer: both black and white grapes can be used in the making of white wine; if black grapes are included they must be pressed immediately to avoid contact between the skin (containing colour pigments) and juice.

Pressing: a horizontal press contains hoops to break up the caked grapes and solid discs at each end to apply gentle pressure to release juice without crushing the pips.

Fermentation: the length of this stage depends on the style of the wine being made; some fine white wines are fermented in the cask.

Maturation: this can take place in cask or vat, during which time the wine will undergo all necessary treatments, such as racking, fining and filtering, before bottling.

Vinification/Elevage

We have so far described the ways in which grapes are transformed into wine. But the tasks of the *vigneron* do not cease until the wine is actually bottled, and this may be early or after a period of one or two years. We have therefore to consider two types of wine, those that 'see wood' *(faire du bois)* and the rest. 'Seeing wood' means being left to mature, for a fairly long time, in wooden casks (usually 225 litres) or tuns, instead of being placed in neutral tanks – neutral because, being made of metal or enamel, they have no effect whatsoever on the wine, regardless of how long it is stored.

The wooden cask, on the other hand, has a considerable effect on the wine, depending on the type of wood, its age, its cut and the period of storage. Two main factors are influential: first, the wood releases tannins which pass into the wine (200 mg per litre in the first year with new casks), second, the wine oxidizes because the wood is slightly permeable, unlike metal. Researchers have measured the annual amount of oxygen that passes through the wood as between 2 and 5 cc per litre, more than offset by the 15 to 20 cc per litre that enter the wine through its upper surface. In addition, the wine is racked *(soutirage)* four times a year to separate it from its deposit and lees and to aerate it. Each time this is done, 3 or 4 cc of oxygen per litre are dissolved in the wine. It is this process, together with a slight loss of alcoholic potency, that helps to transform primary aromas into secondary aromas and to develop the wine's colour: the violet-red of the anthocyanes which disappear by precipitation is gradually replaced by the brownish-yellow-red of the tannins.

The wine maker controls the maturing process according to his taste for wines that are more or less woody, selecting new or used casks depending on the year, varying the number of *soutirages* and leaving the wine inside the casks for as long as he wishes.

Actual bottling is prefaced by a number of processes designed to clarify or fine the wine. White wines will be drastically cooled over a period of eight to ten days down to below 0°C in order to precipitate the cream of tartar. This lends the wine softness, causing it to lose its acerbic properties, and also prevents the formation of *gravelle* or crystalline deposit.

All wines, red, white and rosé, are fined. This is done by adding a coagulant (fish-glue, ox-blood, casein, gelatine, white of egg, bentonite, etc.) to remove impurities by flocculation and sedimentation. After fining, and

Right *Heating dampened barrel staves, which have been hooped at one end so that the other end can be shaped by pulling on a looped hawser.*
Far right *New oak barrels at Château Lascombes, Margaux.*

sometimes instead of it, wine may be filtered through meshes of varying grade (cloth, cellulose, mineral substances). The more modern estates employ sterilized filtration followed by bottling under sterile conditions.

Certain *maîtres de chai* claim nowadays that they prefer to reverse the order of these operations, filtering prior to maturing in cask (Château Cos Labory, for instance), but it is too soon to make any definite pronouncement on the advantages of this method. It is worth noting that wines matured in small quantities (in cask) over long periods, say three years, will self-clarify through sedimentation, although it is rare for a wine never to be fined or filtered.

Left The practice of 'thieving': using a velenche *(pipette) to inspect and taste wine as it ages in barrels at Château Grand-Puch, Entre-Deux-Mers, Bordeaux.*

Vinification/Special Methods 1

Right *Turning the grapes over in a press used specifically for making champagne; many of the grapes are still whole after the first pressing.*

Wines are basically still or sparkling: the former contain a few milligrams (75 per litre) of carbon dioxide in solution, undetectable to the palate and the eye, while in the latter the presence of CO_2 creates pressures inside the bottle that can reach 6 atmospheres. This is only found in whites and rosés, since gas and red wine go badly together (although this rule is successfully defied by certain Italian Barberas).

Slightly sparkling wines

Some white wine labels, bearing the words *mis sur lie* or *mis en bouteilles sur lie*, recommend that the bottle should be drunk while young, and a slight prickling sensation on the tongue will indicate that the wine contains a little carbon dioxide gas. This is not a defect of vinification but is done deliberately to give the impression of crispness, making up for a lack of acidity (Swiss white wines). Wines that are *mis sur lie* are bottled the moment they leave the fermenting vat while it is still 'on its lees' and before it has been de-gassed by repeated *soutirages*. The process offers certain advantages: re-casking a wine increases its oxidation and is harmful to white wines, but the lees act as a reducing agent and are antioxidant (Muscadet, Vin de Savoie, etc.). Sparkling rosés are made for the same reason.

Sparkling wines

Very different techniques are used to make sparkling wines, which occupy a special position by reason of their history, their taste and their usage. Some wines are carbonated artificially, but these are usually rough, coarse varieties without interest or *appellation*. More distinctive are wines that have been made to sparkle by the *méthode rurale*, by closed vat vinification or by the *méthode champenoise*. In all cases the carbon dioxide given off by the fermentation of the grape sugar or added sugar has to be dissolved.

The *méthode rurale* is undoubtedly the most ancient method, and is used for making what is perhaps the world's oldest sparkling wine, Gaillac – a title it contests with the Blanquette de Limoux. This was the method used by Dom Pérignon, and it was not until the first half of the 18th century that the *vignerons* of the Champagne region perfected a new technique of putting the bubbles into wine.

The *méthode rurale* is simplicity itself: the wine is bottled before fermentation is complete. Once fermentation is over, the bottle will contain carbon dioxide and fermentation residues – the deposit known as *lie*. This deposit may be removed by expelling a minute quantity of wine after the process of *dégorgement*, whereby the bottle is stacked on its neck or by decanting at low temperature in a vat under pressure, then filtering and re-bottling at the same pressure.

The *méthode champenoise* also works on the principle of carbon dioxide being dissolved after fermentation; but this fermentation is not natural, being induced by the addition of sugared liquor and yeasts in a mixture known as the *liqueur de tirage*. The wine ferments in very small quantities (by the bottle, in fact) and very slowly at low temperatures (10°C) to guarantee best results. The bottles are clari-fied by *dégorgement*.

The *closed vat* sparkling wines are made by adding sugared liquor and yeasts to a vat capable of withstanding high pressures. This brings about a second fermentation, followed by filtration and bottling under pressure. Such wines may prove satisfactory provided their second fermentation is slowed down by the cold. Asti Spumante is a sparkling wine produced in closed vats from which nitro-genous matter has been removed by filtration and centrifuging, then sterilized (filtration or pasteurization) to prevent further fermen-tation of the residual sugar it contains.

Left *Giving the bottles their daily twist and shake (remuage) in the cellars of a champagne house; since the bottles are stored sloping downwards towards the neck, remuage causes sediment to be dislodged from the glass on to the cork.*

Below *Sediment in a champagne bottle after second fermentation.*

Vinification/Special Methods 2

White wines are said to be dry when they contain under 4 grams of residual sugar per litre. Above this level, the wine may be medium (20 gr sugar/litre) or sweet (40 gr/l); and thereafter it is a fortified wine.

The presence of residual sugar, i.e. sugar that has not turned into alcohol, poses problems for the vinifier, since the yeasts that transform the sugar into alcohol cannot withstand high alcoholic concentration. They multiply in sugared liquids at moderate temperatures (approx. 10–35°C) with an alcohol content up to 15–16°, but beyond this they are killed off by the alcohol itself.

Since it is a fact that 17 grams of sugar produce one degree of alcohol, musts that are rich in sugar should in theory be capable of producing wines with a strength of 20° or more. But because the yeasts die at over 15° alcohol, the *vigneron* is left with 5° of potential alcohol in the form of unconverted sugar, and the wine is said to have 15° of actual

Right Vendange *on the Premières Côtes de Bordeaux for sweet white wines.*

Far left *Rotted Sémillon grapes going into the press to make the finest Sauternes at Château d'Yquem.*
Left *Tasting a Barsac by pipette.*

alcohol and 5° of potential alcohol – or 85 grams of residual sugar.

For many years fortified wines were only made from exceptional vintages that were unusually rich in sugar. Over the last two centuries – longer in Hungary (Tokay) – growers have allowed the grapes to desiccate (*vin de paille*, Jura) or have picked overripe berries attacked by *pourriture noble* or noble rot (Sauternes) in order to enrich the sugar content of their harvests. Even so, the sugar content is seldom high enough, and except in a rare year or on the occasional estate (Yquem) the wine maker has to interrupt the fermentation process artificially in order to strike an acceptable balance between sugar and alcohol. In general this balance is found at 14° of actual and 4° of potential alcohol; the process of halting fermentation is known as 'muting'.

There are several ways of killing or removing the yeasts, the simplest being to raise the alcohol level by adding more alcohol. This artificial fortification (*mutage*) is prohibited in the production of wine but permitted for making *vins doux naturels* (VDN wines include port, sherry, Banyuls, etc.). The second, commoner way uses sulphur dioxide

(SO_2) to kill the yeasts. In order to work well, this method requires a massive quantity of SO_2 which contravenes current legislation and in any event ruins the taste. Only the best wine makers manage to use it properly, and generally in conjunction with other procedures such as:
- eliminating the nitrogen on which the yeasts depend, accompanied by filtration and centrifuging;
- sterile filtration to eliminate the yeasts;
- refrigeration or cooling, which halts fermentation but only renders the yeasts dormant.

Other techniques include thermolization (partial pasteurization at 45°), flash pasteurization at 70°, and normal pasteurization at 70° and over, all somewhat drastic processes that are never inflicted upon the great wines.

Muting a wine is a tricky business; the fermentation of fortified wines is also hazardous, because the large amount of sugar present leads to botryticine, an antibiotic produced by botrytis. Since *débourbage* is practically impossible, there is always the risk of oxidation and volatile acidity. Fortified wines enjoy very rich and highly complex aromas but are the most difficult to vinify.

Vinification/Special Methods 3

Whole-grape vinification

We have so far discussed what are usually referred to as 'traditional' wine-making techniques, the methods used everywhere to make the great vintage wines. Yet a substantial portion of wine is vinified in other ways, one of which is whole-grape vinification.

It is possible that all wines were once made in this manner, to be superseded later by the 'traditional' method. This would imply, for example, that the *vignerons* of Beaujolais, rather than inventing a new and special technique, were continuing an ancient practice.

The great advantage of whole-grape vinification is its ability to extract powerful aromas, but its major drawback is its failure to endow the wine with the structure so vital for good maturing and ageing. The method derives its name from the fact that whole grapes (even whole bunches) are carefully placed inside a closed fermenting vat, being neither de-stalked nor crushed. The vat is saturated with carbon dioxide (hence 'carbonic maceration') supplied from another vat or gas bottle. Fermentation cannot take place in an atmosphere that lacks oxygen, but intracellular fermentation does occur inside each separate berry: two degrees of alcohol form inside each grape, while half the malic acid disappears and the juice takes on colour. It is to this enzyme fermentation that these first-pressing wines (*vins de primeur*) owe their unmistakable aromas. After one week oxygen is supplied to the vat and the yeasts do their work. Malolactic fermentation takes place, *vin de goutte* and *vin de presse* blend together.

This type of vinification has spread to the Rhône Valley and has even extended its range to certain *appellation* wines around Crozes-Hermitage and Châteauneuf. It is possible to blend carbonic wines with those macerated in the traditional manner (Château Beaurenard) so as to combine the aromatic exuberance of the former with the structure and roundness of the latter. Broadly speaking, *vins de primeur* are vivid and very fruity mild wines for quick consumption, since they do not improve with age.

Vin jaune

There is another type of oxidized wine – *vin jaune* – which truly defies all the laws of oenology. It is actually a white wine left for six years in an open 225-litre cask, without *ouillage*, i.e. topping up of wine lost by evaporation. As a general rule, wine left in this

way turns sour to become, at best, vinegar, but with *vin jaune* a crust forms on the surface to protect it against oxygen. This *fleur du vin* consists of yeasts (*Saccharomyces oviformis*) that cause part of the alcohol in the wine to oxidize into ethyl aldehyde, contributing to the famous 'yellow flavour', a taste reminiscent of walnuts.

The *vin jaune* method is rare, costly and not always successful. It is practised mainly in the Jura, the most famous exponent being the Château-Chalon which produces a strong, dry yellow wine that may be drunk as soon as it is bottled. It is somewhat similar to sherry, and it is interesting to note that the latter, which is a fortified wine, also depends on the magical effects of the *fleur du vin*.

Heating the maceration process

All maceration is hot because fermentation heats up the grape must. This 'natural' heat is sometimes artificially boosted to 50–80°C; the grapes may or may not be crushed. At these temperatures the extraction of colour is reinforced (almost double the number of anthocyanes are developed); this high-temperature maceration is followed, after cooling, by the fermentation of the now deeper coloured must. The wine is then matured in the traditional manner.

This method has three distinct advantages: it destroys the oxidases, makes it easier to vinify rotten grapes and stimulates the extraction of the anthocyanes, which disappear after two years. The aromatic implications of this method have been much debated. At Château de Beaucastel (Châteauneuf-du-Pape) it has been employed for some 50 years, and the principle itself has been known for at least two centuries.

Vintage/Introduction

The year in which a wine is made is of tremendous importance, and if a year is not declared it must be with good reason. The quality – and price – of a wine may vary enormously from year to year; and in bad years even great *appellation* wines will not be marketed because they are considered unworthy of their domaine or château.

Not every wine-growing region is equally reliant on the concept of year or vintage or on the success – or failure – of a harvest. Certain regions benefit from a very even climate, but whether such a climate creates average conditions and hence unvaryingly average wines, or ideal conditions conducive to perennially perfect vintages, is a debatable point.

We at the Académie du Vin feel that the difference in vintage years only stresses the diversity of the wines themselves, underlining certain aspects and characteristics of the wine as a consequence of capricious weather conditions. The vintage adds an extra dimension to a wine, instantly appreciated by the connoisseur.

There is no way of guessing at the quality of a wine unless it is seen and tasted – 'experienced' – and a particular vintage cannot be selected or recommended without some personal knowledge or recollection of it. Quality ratings by region and by year can help to refresh hazy memories; and, generally speaking, such ratings are agreed by experts, even if sometimes disputed by wine merchants who have to sell the 'little' years as well as the great ones. In any event, the development of the wine memory is of paramount importance in this context and great emphasis is placed on this in these courses.

An understanding of the interplay between climatic conditions and quality is essential when choosing a wine, for regions, grape varieties and types of wine all react differently to changing weather conditions.

It is obvious, for example, that a region close to the sea will be much influenced by the ocean's thermal fluctuations. Temperature, however, is only one climatic factor, and the sea offers no protection against rain, nor does it guarantee sun. A thorough understanding of these three factors, *temperature, rainfall* and *sunshine*, affords a sound basis on which to approach and evaluate a year, although they are insufficient on their own. It is vital to have accurate information on hourly distribution and incidence, to know that the sun shone towards the end of the summer, that it did not

rain before or during the harvest, and that temperatures were sufficiently high.

Distribution is the essential question. Annual statistics of temperature, rainfall and sunshine are virtually useless, since they do not reveal whether it rained a little every day or if there were just two weeks of pouring rain during the whole year. Nor will they indicate whether it was too mild in winter or too cool in summer. To ascertain this, figures would have to be provided only for the growing period from March to October, taking account of the vine's very specialized requirements. In fact, studies for collating all this information, including hourly variables and time factors, are currently under way. It may not be long before it is possible to predict the likely effects of climate on each vintage and to use this as a standard wine rating.

Above The year of a wine is part of its unique individuality: one of the prime factors in determining quality and price.

Left White wine ageing in the cellar of a négociant (Calvet) of Bordeaux.

Vintage/Principal Influences

Weather conditions affect the grape in two ways. Firstly, they can accelerate or impede the growth and ripening of the grape; secondly, they may create conditions favourable or detrimental to the proliferation of parasites. Both contingencies affect quantity and quality.

It is often assumed that quantity and quality are incompatible, although this is not always the case. Certainly, when yield per hectare tends to be excessive, quantity is harmful to quality, and the distinctive characteristics of the wine become 'diluted'. This always happens if there is rain just before the harvest when the vine plant is still actively growing: the berries fill with water pumped up from the roots and the result is almost certainly a wine lacking in colour, substance and density, irrespective of previous weather conditions. Such rainfall may have even more drastic consequences if it has been preceded by a succession of very dry months, if the grapes are small and if, as sometimes occurs, the skin of the grape lacks suppleness. Because the berry cannot swell, it cracks and the harvest is lost.

Rain does not always have the same effect. Cold rain will increase the hectare yield, whereas warm, mild rains will create ideal conditions for the development of grey rot –

fatal to wine, especially red wine, which has to macerate to extract colour. Spring rain can threaten the very existence of the wine, washing away the pollen from the flowers so that there are no grapes.

Premature growth of the vine is another cause of anxiety, for spring frosts can destroy pollen and buds. However, if the vine survives this ordeal, its chances of success are much higher. Since the grape is harvested 100 days after the plant flowers, the sooner the flowers fade and die, the earlier the grapes can be picked. It often rains at the autumn equinox – around 21 September – and if the grapes are harvested before then, it augurs well for the wine.

Until 1978, all the great vintages were the result of early harvests; recently, however, the vine has become a much tougher plant, capable of withstanding the attacks of parasites following in the wake of bad weather. This increased resistance on the part of the vine is the consequence of successful treatments which are discussed later.

Too much heat and sunshine are not necessarily good for the vine; although this gives a red wine more colour, it reduces acidity (red and white) and impairs finesse. Furthermore, vintages exposed to excessive heat frequently fail to develop or last well.

Right Young vine shoots are especially vulnerable to frost in spring. One means of protecting them against the frost involves the use of rapid burners to heat the atmosphere around the shoots.
Opposite Syrah grapes growing in the strong sunshine of the Côtes-du-Rhône area.

Vintage/Choice

Right *The vine is a pampered and cosseted plant: hand-spraying in Burgundy against parasites.*

Whereas the year is an important consideration for southern vineyards, it is absolutely vital for those farther north, where the climate is more extreme. Another significant factor is the grape variety, since not all grapes are equally capable of resisting climatic catastrophes. Each region, in fact, has discovered varieties best suited to its own particular climate. The Cabernet Sauvignon, for example, needs intense heat, and is thus not found north of the Loire; and both the thin-skinned Grenache and the Merlot, being prone to rot, are vulnerable to rain.

In choosing a wine it is a help to know something of the vine's idiosyncrasies as well as the age of the vineyard. Young vines react strongly to climatic conditions, so much so that in 1976, during the very long, dry summer, the youngest vines all but died. The older vines, capable of pumping up much-needed water through their longer roots, and generally adapting to changing weather conditions, had no difficulty in surviving.

Geology also provides a guide, especially in the case of difficult years. A soil's permeability and capacity for drainage will affect its absorption of heavy rainfall, and the advantage of deep gravel (10 to 15 metres) is obvious. The presence of impermeable layers of soil, as, for instance, at Château Haut Bailly (Graves), prevents good drainage and hinders root growth, so that the wine is highly sensitive to the year.

Apart from the direct consequences of climatic conditions, there are the indirect effects of parasites, although much progress has been made in recent years, notably systemic preventive sprays for saving harvests and vintages. Proper treatment enables the vine to come through the dangerous periods unscathed, and so allows the grape to ripen fully. The excellent late vintages in Bordeaux in 1978 and 1979 bear witness to this success.

Such treatments have greatly improved the strength of white and red grapes but are difficult to apply to vineyards producing fortified wines since these are harvested late. Autumn is the important season, and although some years may be average for a red wine because of a mediocre summer, they may be highly rated for a fortified wine thanks to autumnal morning mists and sunny afternoons. This happened in 1967, though more often it is the other way round.

Below Nylon filaments are sometimes draped over vines to protect them from the ravages of birds.

Wine Buying & Transport

Wine can be bought through many channels, directly from the producer, from a wholesaler, in a grocery or supermarket, or in a wine shop. Yet it is likely that the same bottle of the same wine will vary in quality or flavour in each of these establishments. Wine is a living thing that improves or deteriorates according to how and where it is stored, and the wine lover must remember this when purchasing.

The ideal way is to buy straight from the producer, for this is where the wine is born and raised, and the maker has a reputation to safeguard. You can also taste beforehand. A word of advice on this. Do not be tempted by accompanying small pieces of cheese or nuts since these will mask possible defects in the wine.

Wholesalers are usually well equipped to

Above left Buying from the producer: a grower's sign at Chinon on the Loire.
Below left Direct sales by the producer: Maurice Gousset, l'Aiglerie, Anjou.

Right The wines of the Bergerac region displayed in a wine shop in Périgueux.

store wine correctly but sometimes refuse to sell retail. Grocers will not necessarily have a good cellar for storage and the wines may be kept too warm. Nor are they likely to have the time or expertise to select the best suppliers.

Supermarket wines are generally overexposed to both heat and light. White wines in particular are liable to deteriorate by photosynthesis, which is why champagne bottles are always protected by an opaque sheet of paper. The specialist wine merchant or cellar will offer the best guarantee of good wine, with a greater selection of the better vintages and estates.

Travelling

Transporting wine after purchase demands as much care as any other aspect of handling. If you buy your wine straight from the pro-

ducer, whether in bottles or in quantity (barrels, 'bonbonnes' or cubitainer), load it carefully into your car and make sure that it will not be exposed to too much heat either from the sun or the heater. Try to avoid sudden changes in temperature. Wine will be damaged if transferred from a cellar at 11°C to a car at 25°C, and vice-versa. Buying from a shop poses the same problems, though not so serious because the distances will probably be shorter.

If the wine is for early consumption the bottles should be transported and stored upright; always allow the bottles to stand for a day or two following a journey, even a week or more when the wine is worth it. A good bottle taken to friends for drinking the same day can often turn out to be a considerable disappointment.

Wine Storage

If circumstances permit, bulk buying for home bottling is a worthwhile investment. Wine that is transported in plastic containers should be bottled as soon as possible; if purchased in a barrel it is best left for up to two weeks, preferably in the place where bottling will eventually be done, and set up with an air space to aid ventilation.

Bottling should be done when the weather is dry and fine and atmospheric pressure high – rain and thunderstorms are fatal. The process should never be interrupted for any reason; leaving a half-empty barrel will destroy all the remaining wine. Before starting, therefore, make sure there is an adequate reserve of clean bottles and suitable corks. The bottles must be filled by siphoning the wine and allowing it to run down the sides to avoid frothing which will lead to oxidation. Corks must be long (38 to 52 mm) if the wine is to mature, and previously softened by soaking for ten minutes in very hot, but not boiling, water or, even better, in steam. Corks must be rinsed in cold water before being inserted far enough into the neck to leave little or no air between cork and wine. Once the cork is dry, the bottle may be capped or waxed, then labelled – a very important detail in the practical life of wine.

The cellar

The cellar, preferably with a solid door and strong locks, must afford the wine the best chances of development and improvement, and all bottles should be sensibly arranged so that they are accessible for supervision and consumption. Ready-made wine racks can be bought anywhere and are ideal.

A good cellar should protect the wine from outside odours, vibration and light. Never use a room that smells, for example, of domestic heating oil or one exposed to regular vibrations (as from a nearby underground railway). The cellar should be quiet, with a relative humidity of around 90% and a constant temperature as near as possible to 10–11°C. Minor variations in temperature are permissible provided it never exceeds 16°C, since sudden changes will ruin the wine, and a cellar that is always warm will accelerate ageing and deprive the wine of its very best quality.

The cellar register

A cellar register is essential if the wines are to be enjoyed at their best. Besides recording the contents of the cellar, the register should also contain notes, made after each tasting, on how the wine is developing and maturing.

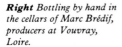

Right *Bottling by hand in the cellars of Marc Brédif, producers at Vouvray, Loire.*

Left A mechanical bottling line in the champagne house of Pommery & Greno.

Below A range of traditional bottle shapes for different wines; left to right: Tokay, Verdicchio, Chianti, Alsace/Rhine, Claret, Burgundy and Champagne.

The Chemical Composition of Wine

Components and effects

SUBSTANCE	WEIGHT	WINE	REMARKS
SWEET			
Sugar	1–4 g	Dry white Red Medium white Sweet white Fortified	Sugar has not fermented
Ethanol (alcohol)	70–120 g	All wines	Preserving agent. Gives body
Glycerol	5–10 g up to 18 g	Quality wines Fortified	Gives density, though some deny this effect
BITTERNESS (and ASTRINGENCY)			
Tannins (leucoanthocyanes) (phenolic)	1–4 g 0.1–0.3 g	Red wine White wine	Colour structure, falls off with age Supports but hardens white wines
Anthocyanes (phenolic)	0.1–0.5 g	Red wine	Colour of young wines Disappears in 2 years Monoglucide in European wines Diglucide in American wines
Malic acid	0.1–5 g	White wines (not all)	Apple-greenness, acerbic, not found in the grape
Succinic acid	0.5–5 g	All wines	Product of fermentation
ACIDITY			
Succinic acid	0.5–1 g	All wines	Breakdown of malic acid
Lactic acid	2–8 g		Product of fermentation
Tartaric acid			Precipitates in cold (deposit)
Citric acid	traces		Disappears during vinification
Acetic acid (volatile acidity)	0.6 g 0.9 g	All wines Fortified	Too much indicates disease and careless vinification
SALTY			
Succinic acid	0.5–1 g	All wines	Product of fermentation
Mineral and organic acids	2–3 g	All wines	Enhance sense of freshness
Trace elements	traces		

Components without flavours or aromas

SUBSTANCE	QUANTITY	
Water	850–900 g	Pure water, biggest component by volume
Nitrogenous substances	1–3 g	Feed the yeasts; becoming rarer in modern wines
Vitamins	Traces	Helpful to yeasts
Gums	0–3 g	Becoming rarer in modern wines
Carbon dioxide Sulphur dioxide	2–3 mg	Irritate the mucous membranes CO_2 is unacceptable in tannic red wines, but is capable of improving certain whites and rosés SO_2 is always a mistake as soon as it becomes noticeable

Aromas

The aromatic components of wine run to several hundreds, including acids, alcohol, aldehydes and cetones.

AROMAS	SUBSTANCES	
FLORAL		
Geranium	Hexane dienol	
Rose	Geraniol Phenyl alcohol Phenyl acetate	
Iris	Irone	
FRUITY		
Banana	Acetates of isoamyl, methyl, ethyl, butyl, isobutyl, isobutyl amyl, hexyl	
	Butyrates of isoamyl, butyl amyl	
	Various alcohols	methanol ethanol propanol butanol pentanol hexanol
Cherry	Benzaldehyde cyanhydride	
Strawberry Raspberry Blackcurrant	Various acids, alcohol, aldehydes and cetone	
Bitter almond Almond	Benzoic aldehyde, acetoin, (cetone)	
Hazelnut	Diacetyl (cetone)	
Apple	50 components!	
Peach	Undecalatone (alcohol)	
SPICES AND OTHERS		
Cinnamon	Cinnamic aldehyde	
Liquorice	Glycyrrhyzine	
Honey	Phenylethyl acid	
Rancid butter	Excessive diactyl (cetone)	
Sour wine	Ethyl acetate (ester)	

2
INTERMEDIATE COURSE

Wine is a complex business, its harmony and balance being matters of extreme delicacy. Each component exerts an influence upon another, which is why any blinkered study of a single constituent must be doomed to failure. Nevertheless, the Académie du Vin has decided to devote a special course to the varieties of wine grape, in the belief that this subject is fundamental to the better understanding of all other branches of the business and art of wine-making. For the grape, in its diversity, its sensitivity to different soils and climates, and the potentialities it offers to the wine producer, is an extraordinary fruit.

Our investigation of the principal grape varieties will be followed by a tour of France and indeed of the whole world, for each region and each country possesses its own stocks which it nurtures, improves and crosses with other stocks to create hybrids with the aim of modifying, both directly and artificially, the biological genotypes. Having

described these varieties and the ways in which they are affected by soil, climate and vinification, we shall be ready to go on to the Advanced Course in Appreciation, which deals with the wine itself, in all its marvellous diversity.

In accordance with the established principles of the Académie du Vin, we shall try to identify some causal relationships between the conditions in which wine is nurtured and developed, and the wine itself.

Quite apart from the intrinsic interest of this study, we are convinced that the wine lover who knows how a wine comes into being is better equipped to appreciate it, to remember it and to choose it wisely. Wine, after all, is more than a casual, pleasant diversion. If, as we must surely believe, the art of living is a cultural phenomenon, it follows that the knowledge and use of wine are cultural activities, part and parcel of a civilized and satisfactory existence.

Grape Varieties/Introduction

The study, description and classification of grape varieties is called *ampelography*. Though ancient, this science is nevertheless imprecise, and differences of opinion often occur. For example, in the texts of ratifications published by the French Institut National des Appellations d'Origine Contrôlée (INAO) in the *Journal Officiel* (French law gazette), Chardonnay is always referred to as Pinot-Chardonnay. Now it is well known that there is no connection at all between the Pinot and the Chardonnay, that they do not belong to the same family, that the white grape close to the Pinot is the Pinot Blanc, and finally that it has to be called Pinot Blanc Vrai in order to indicate its true affiliation. The term Pinot-Chardonnay can thus breed confusion.

Below Merlot grapes growing in Saint-Estèphe.

Correct nomenclature is important because varieties are designated and regulated for each *appellation*. The wine grower buys his grapes from nurserymen, and when he plants Cabernet, he has no more desire to pick Sémillon grapes than a tree grower wishes to see an oak when he has planted a cherry tree! Ampelography aims to define the varieties of grape and to classify them family by family. The task, however, is not made easier by the fact that the science must deal only with pure varieties; and they cannot be judged pure before they are defined. Many systems of definition have been suggested. Some are based on the particular date of budding, flowering, ripening, maturing or defoliation, while others are related to the type of vine shoots, roots, flowers or even leaves. This last

system, extremely meticulous, is based on the angles of the veins in the leaves, and it originated a branch of the science known as *ampelometry*. The latest classification, based on phenotypes, takes account of all the visible hereditary features of the vine.

A serious study of grape varieties must embrace both the scions and the stocks. Whereas the variety of scion determines the variety of grape, the quality depends on the stocks that bear the scion. For example, the stock known as SO4 (Berlandieri-Riparia No. 4, selected at Oppenheim) increases the hectare output and reduces the grape's sugar content.

The grape's quality is also modified by selection. Mixed selections have long been the rule, but more recently cloned selections have come into fashion, raising the prospect of vineyards being nothing more than an infinite reproduction of a single vine stock, which would greatly impoverish the wine. Selectors who tend to promote quantity at the expense of quality are therefore to be treated with circumspection. In addition to the selectors, nurserymen and research centres can also influence grape varieties.

Since the vine is a sexed plant it can be cross-bred. First cross-fertilizations give hybrids, sometimes directly productive, of two different species, while second cross-fertilizations, using varieties of the same species, yield hybrids with remarkable characteristics. Thus the most popular variety in Germany is the Müller-Thurgau, a cross between Riesling and Sylvaner.

Left Gamay grapes in the Beaujolais.

Grape Varieties/Influence

The influence of the grape variety on the finished wine cannot be over-stressed. It gives it colour, of course, but much more than that, as is testified, for example, by the wines of Germany and Alsace, which are derived from the same soil, the same vineyard and the same vinification processes, yet bear the names of individual grapes. There is no confusing a Riesling with a Gewürztraminer. The effects of soil and climate must not be underestimated, but it is the historical connection over many centuries between specific grapes and specific regions that has created the ideal growing environments.

Three distinct techniques of wine-making have emerged over the years. The first, and the simplest, produces wine from a single grape variety. The wines of Germany, Alsace, Burgundy and the Loire illustrate this process.

The second is more sophisticated – several varieties of grape are simultaneously introduced into the *cuves* (wine vats) and ferment together. This is the process employed in the Rhône Valley and a number of Italian regions, and it is suitable for producing both red and white wines; furthermore, both white and black grapes can go into the vat to make red wines. Châteauneuf-du-Pape, for instance, comes from the in-vat fermentation of between one and 13 varieties of *Vitis vinifera*. It is obvious that only white grape varieties are vatted together in the case of white wines.

The third method of processing different varieties of grape into a single wine is known as blending. Two, three or four grape varieties are vatted separately, and each produces its own wine. During February-March, after the harvests, these wines are blended in proportions specified by the cellar-master after tasting. The wines of Bordeaux and south-western France, both white and red, are produced according to this principle.

The pros and cons of blending grapes and wines are topics of endless discussion. The

Below An impressive array of grape varieties awaiting pressing at a wine producer's in the Pays d'Aude.

partisans of grape blending assert that mixed fermentation causes interactions among the particular components of each variety, and the complexity of chemical reactions during fermentation may indeed give some credit to this theory.

Nevertheless, the method has its drawbacks. Not all the varieties of grape will achieve full maturity at one and the same time, but if each is vinified separately they can be harvested at exactly the right moment. On the other hand, it is impossible to alter the contents of the vat, whereas blending, by definition, facilitates precise, proportional adjustments. Once adopted, methods are not necessarily permanent. In Champagne, for instance, grapes used to be blended in the lifetime of Dom Pérignon, but today it is the wines that are blended. Mixed methods are also practicable. In the Rhône Valley some wines are produced by blending the grapes in the vat and then blending its contents.

Left and below Tasting for blending at the champagne house of Moët & Chandon; the chef de cave, Dominique Foulon, is working on the cuvée before second fermentation takes place.

Grape Varieties/International Reds 1

The Cabernets

This is a large and well-bred family which includes the Cabernet Sauvignon, the Cabernet Franc and the closely related Petit Verdot and Carmenère.

Cabernet Sauvignon

The origins of this patriarch of the Cabernet family are obscure, but it is assumed to be derived from a wild vine of the Bordeaux region. This is a late ripening variety, with buds that also open late, best suited to warm climates. The Sauvignon is an expanding variety, grown in Europe, the Americas, Africa, Australia, New Zealand and elsewhere.

In the south of France, it covers an area extending from the Loire to the Pyrenees. Its tiny spherical black berries with their colourless juice produce wines that are very tannic, astringent and highly coloured, of moderate alcoholic strength and with complex aromas, including cedar, but more often of a fruity blackcurrant type. This harsh wine is long-lived and continues to improve with age. It plays a major role in the blending of Médocs (50–80%) and a minor one in the Graves and Saint-Emilion. It produces reds and rosés in Anjou and Saumur wines.

Cabernet Franc

This is the Bouchy of the Pyrenees and the Breton of the Loire. It is a late ripening variety, budding just before the Cabernet Sauvignon and rather eclipsed by the latter's showy splendour. Its wines are less tannic, have a greater 'nose' (violet, raspberry, black-currant, gooseberry, liquorice) and are more refined. It is always blended in the Bordeaux region but is nevertheless the basis of the Chinon, Bourgueil and Saumur Champigny of the Loire. Its finest wine is Château Cheval Blanc (Saint-Emilion), accounting for two-thirds of the constituents.

Below Cabernet Franc.

Petit Verdot

A very late variety of Médoc which does not always ripen. It produces wines that are highly coloured, tannic and with a respectable alcohol content.

Carmenère

An excellent Médoc variety which has disappeared. It is currently being re-selected in the experimental plantation of the Château Dillon (Médoc).

Far left Cabernet Sauvignon.

Merlot Noir

Yet another expanding variety of wine grape, occupying more surface area in the Bordelais region than the two Cabernets together. It extends to southern France and is much prized in Italy, the Americas, Africa and many other countries.

The Merlot Noir is an early-budding, second-vintage variety which often falls victim to spring frosts. The thin skin of its berries is susceptible to rotting; the rather small black berries have colourless juice and are very numerous. Yields can be substantial (100 hl/ha). The wines of Merlot are stronger than those of Cabernet but of low acidity – often too low – supple and velvety with animal and truffle fragrances, and should be drunk fairly rapidly.

In France, Merlot wine is rarely pure (as it is in Italy and on other continents). As a blender grape, it is used up to 20–40% in the Médoc, 40% in the Graves, 60% in Saint-Emilion and up to 85% or higher in Pomerol.

Merlot Blanc has been grown for about 75 years and yields a weak wine of poor quality.

Pinot Noir

This very old traditional grape of Burgundy, perhaps originating there, used to be called Morillon or Auvernat. It is also known in Germany by the names of Noirien and Burgunder.

The Pinot Noir is an early ripening grape which can be planted anywhere from south to north, although nocturnal warmth impairs the finesse of its wines. It buds very early and is thus susceptible to spring frosts, which may cause total or partial crop failure. Its finest wines are produced on limestone soil, and in more northerly regions. The blue-black berries are small, spherical, compact and thick-skinned, although their very compactness encourages mould. The juice is colourless. The Pinot wines are usually more acid than those of the Cabernet, but less tannic, rich ruby in colour with aromas of the red soft fruits. The Pinot grape is always vinified on its own, except for the Bourgogne Passetoutgrains (⅓ Pinot and ⅔ Gamay).

The Pinot thrives best in Burgundy. In Champagne the grape is vinified into a white wine, and in Alsace it makes light-coloured wines, and is particularly successful as a rosé. In Germany and farther east it is used to make a variety of light coloured wines. Pinot Noir wines from California tend to be fatter and richer.

Above Pinot Noir.

Pinot Meunier

A variant of the Pinot, dating from the 16th century. It buds and ripens after the Pinot Noir, etiolates (turns white) in limestone soils and is resistant to frosts. Its bunches are large with round, compact, blue-black grapes that give good yields. Its wines are less acid, less vigorous and less sophisticated than those of the incomparable Pinot Noir. These versatile wines mature quickly and have found their true place in Champagne.

Grape Varieties/International Reds 2

Zinfandel

This grape is most probably of Austro-Hungarian origin, or possibly Italian, but it has found its adopted soil in the United States where it was imported in 1851 by Baron Agoston Haraszthy, who first planted it at San Diego.

Zinfandel buds late and is very late ripening with a life cycle that is even later than that of the Cabernet Sauvignon. Its long bunches of blue-violet, compact and medium-sized grapes give very varied hectare yields. It does not thrive in flat, open country or strong heat, preferring chalky-limestone, slightly sandy soil of dry hillsides.

Well situated vines that are over 25 years of age produce highly coloured wines with spicy, black pepper and raspberry aromas. They are long-lived and the best of them come from the high hillsides of the Napa Valley in California.

Cot or Malbec

This variety is said to originate in the Bordeaux area, although each region gives it a different name: Malbec in its supposed place of birth, Auxerrois around Cahors, Cot in the Loire Valley, Pressac towards Saint-Emilion. Despite so many names, it is a vanishing variety, although it continues to form the basis for the Cahors vine stocks. One reason for its gradual decline is its high failure rate, a tendency accentuated by its life cycle, since it buds very early and is thus susceptible to winter frosts. This early ripening variety bears medium-sized bunches of grapes that are round, small to medium in size, fleshy, black with a colourless juice. Yields can be high.

The wine of the Malbec is highly coloured and markedly tannic. It is well constituted but the aroma is somewhat feeble, which is why preference is often given to the Cabernets and Merlot. It is grown in the south-west and on the banks of the Loire where it goes into the making of rosés and uncomplicated reds.

Gamay Noir

Reputed to originate in the Côte d'Or, having taken its name from a village where, ironically, only Pinot grows today, this grape is so closely associated with Beaujolais that it is sometimes called Gamay-Beaujolais. It is, in fact, the most fashionable variety of red grape, precocious, early ripening and suitable

for planting practically anywhere; indeed, it has already invaded the foothills of the Lyonnais, Jura and Savoie, lined the higher banks of the Loire and Rhône, and even extended south-west as far as Gaillac. Its progress is only resisted – at least for the time being – by Alsace in the east, the Bordelais region and the Midi in the south. The warmer climates do not seem to suit its attractive bunches of medium-sized, oval berries (the juice is colourless) with their high yields (100 hl and more). This early-budding variety thrives best in granite soils, and although it may succumb to spring frosts, it is fairly resilient, with second buds appearing to bear grapes.

Above *Gamay Noir.*

To give of their very best, the grapes have to be vinified whole (semi-carbonic maceration). Good Gamay wines are light, fresh, and with a pleasant bouquet, provided they have not been subjected to over-zealous 'chaptalization' (sugaring of the wine during fermentation). They should be drunk while still young. Gamay grapes planted in clayey limestone soils (Côte d'Or, for instance) produce uninteresting wines.

There are a number of *teinturier* Gamays, so called because the juice of their berries is coloured. These wines lack finesse although they may be used to give colour to others.

Syrah

This is a high-quality grape provided its yield never exceeds 40 hl/ha. Recent developments in this variety reflect the errors of ill-advised cloned selections. Its low yield, rarely exceeding 30 hl/ha, has been forced up to 100 hl/ha, resulting in wines of little or no quality.

It is a late ripening variety that has been grown in the Rhône Valley for over 1000 years. Nowadays, it has spread abroad to California, South Africa and Australia, and other regions. The grapes are small, oval, purple-violet and bloomy, in medium-sized bunches.

The quality of the Syrah grape is such that for a long time it improved the great wines of Bordeaux, including Château Latour, which was called 'hermitaging'. Needless to say, the system of *appellations* has put paid to this practice.

The wine from the Syrah grape is strong in colour and alcohol (11–13°), tannic, and endowed with the bouquet of violets highlighted by cherry and blackcurrants. Syrah shows at its best in the wines from Hermitage.

Left *Syrah.*

Grape Varieties/Local Reds

Grenache Noir

As its name might suggest, the Grenache, a round, medium-sized grape with colourless juice, is Spanish in origin and is one of the principal varieties in the wines of Rioja. It is a very late-ripening grape requiring much warmth, and therefore valued on the west coast of the Mediterranean. It is also extensively used in Australia and California to make a number of rosés.

It is not, however, without faults: it buds early, thus exposing it to spring frosts, it often suffers from irregular flowering and, like many varieties, it is prone to rot. Moreover, the wine it produces lacks acidity and oxidizes extremely quickly. How then to account for its popularity and success? The answer is that when it is planted *en coteau*, grafted onto a not too vigorous rootstock, and when one is satisfied with half its yield from the plain (130 hl/ha), it forms the base wines that are high in alcohol, fleshy, with a rich, round flavour. It is blended in the vat with other grapes (Cinsault, Mourvèdre, Syrah, Carignan, etc.), constituting as much as 70% of the make-up of Châteauneuf-du-Pape and the Côtes-du-Rhône.

There is a Grenache Blanc in the Roussillon but this variety produces no great wines since it is too strong in alcohol, oxidizes too rapidly and lacks acidity.

The Grenache Gris, i.e. pink, produces the fortified *vins doux naturels* (VDN) in the Roussillon.

Carignan

This variety takes its name from the Aragon town of Cariñena in Spain, where it probably originated. It occupies nearly 220,000 hectares of French soil, making it the most widely grown grape, but quantity is not necessarily conducive to quality. The grape only ripens with plenty of sunlight, and for this reason is chiefly found along the Mediterranean coastline. A late-budding, late-ripening variety, it does best near the Pyrénées Orientales provided it is grown on hillsides and the vines are fairly old, thus giving a low yield. On the plain it is capable of producing over 150 hectolitres per hectare.

Its usually large, compact bunches consist of medium-sized, spherical berries that are black-skinned with a colourless juice; the skin is thick and highly astringent.

The wine of Carignan averages 9 degrees on the plain and 13 on the hillside; it is dark coloured, very harsh in its youth and frequently bitter even when mature. Its participation is always limited in AOC wines (40% or less) falling to nil in the better wines. It is very seldom made as a single variety wine. In Languedoc tests have shown that Carignan would require at least 20% Cinsault to refine it and 20% Grenache to lend it body and softness.

Cinsault

This is both a table grape and a wine grape, good for eating because of its large, thin-skinned berries. It hails from southern France, the Midi, but is being more widely cultivated as growers come to appreciate its versatility, for it can go into *primeur* wines and even rosés (Tavel). Cinsault lends finesse and softness to the great *appellation* wines (Châteauneuf-du-Pape, Gigondas, etc.) but is also capable of high yields (100 hl/ha). This late-ripening variety should never be grafted onto over-vigorous stocks nor be planted in the plain, where yields tend to be too high.

Its bunches are large, the berries black, elliptical and compact (with colourless juice), bloomy and fleshy.

The Cinsault wines are usually full-coloured, very soft, low in tannin, with a medium alcoholic strength, maturing very quickly. Its floral aromas are elegant and sophisticated. In red wines it makes an excellent complement to the great varietals, but should not be used on its own.

The fact that it is sometimes called Hermitage in South Africa causes confusion, all the more since the world-famous original *appellation* comes only from a single variety, the Syrah.

Mourvèdre

This important variety, of Spanish origin, was widespread in the south of France in the days before phylloxera. It was not replanted because no suitable stock could be found. This problem, however, has been solved since World War II, and Mourvèdre is now increasingly found improving Côtes de Provence, Châteauneuf-du-Pape and other wines of the Midi.

It is a contradictory plant since it needs a lot of warmth but is susceptible to drought, and because it likes hillsides yet needs rich soils. This is a late-budding, very late-harvest grape with medium-sized bunches bearing very small, black and compact berries with thick skins and an unbearably tart taste if eaten. Yields are low to medium. Mourvèdre wine is usually average in alcohol, highly coloured, well constructed and very tannic, with a spicy bouquet that has a hint of violets. The grape has the unique characteristic of being anti-oxidant (very useful when blended with Grenache).

Tannat

A robust grape of ancient origin, from the Béarn region, it buds late and ripens correspondingly very late. The compact bunches with their tightly packed, small round berries, give good yields.

Tannat wine is highly coloured and very tannic, a characteristic to which it probably owes its name. It is a long-lasting wine which softens only with time.

Tannat used to be blended with Bordeaux wines to give them body and colour. Nowadays, it is blended where harvested with other quality grapes of a gentler nature, such as Bouchy, alias the Cabernet Franc. This is the way in which Madiran is made.

One also finds the Tannat in other wines: Tursan, Béarn, Irouléguy and Côtes de Saint Mont.

Poulsard

This is a very ancient grape from the Jura, being some 2000 years old and known by its present name since the 14th century. It appears to thrive only in the clayey schists and blue marl of the Jura.

It is an early-budding, but latish-ripening variety with large, loose and oval grapes with thin skins of a pinkish-violet colour. Its juice is slightly rosé. Poulsard is a table and wine grape that produces naturally rosé wines.

Trousseau

Another variety from the Jura, recorded by Olivier de Serres. It buds late and ripens during the autumn. The bunches bear very black, thick-skinned ovoid grapes of medium size. It produces wines that are highly coloured, firm, tannic and strong in alcohol, best when old.

Negrette

A grape from the south-west which buds late but ripens relatively early. It is widespread in the Middle Garonne basin where it produces fruity, soft and highly coloured wines for drinking within two years. Its finest example bears the AOC label of the Côte du Fronton-Villaudric. This is the wine drunk in Toulouse.

Jurançon Noir

This south-western variety is often called Folle Noire. It buds late and ripens in mid-October. Bunches are large, and the grapes round, medium-sized and bluish, giving respectable yields.

Its wines are light in colour, pleasant but of little character. It forms a make-up grape for certain lesser *appellations* of the south-west (Lavilledieu, etc.).

Mondeuse

This is a typical medium quality, late-budding grape from the Savoie producing large bunches of small, blue-black, oval berries. Yield per hectare is high. The wines of the Mondeuse are rich ruby in colour. They are clean, honest and uncomplicated, firm and rather harsh in youth, although they soften with age. Good Mondeuse wines can be found under the Vin de Savoie Chantagne label.

It is, however, a vanishing variety, being gradually superseded by Pinot Noir and Gamay.

Grolleau

In the Loire Valley, its birthplace, this grape bears several different names: Gros Lot de Cinq Mars or Pineau de Saumur, but its nick-name seems to describe it exactly: Aramon du Val de Loire, an allusion to the southern variety of Aramon, a table-wine grape that produces a 'gros rouge qui tache' (literally 'a coarse red wine that stains' – a polite name for 'plonk'). The Grolleau wine hardly stains at all because it is weak in colour and frequently vinified into rosé (Anjou and Touraine). Its bunches are large with medium-sized, bluish, round and compact berries full of colourless juice that gives substantial yields (120 hl/ha).

Pineau d'Aunis

This is an authentic black variety of the Loire sometimes called Chenin Noir. It is a late-ripening grape that produces good-quality yet light coloured wines that are delicate with a raspberry fragrance (Coteaux du Loir).

Grape Varieties/International Whites 1

Chardonnay

This is the grape of the world's greatest dry white wines, probably Burgundian in origin, or perhaps from the Mâconnais, if we believe the story that it was selected close to the village alleged to be responsible for its name.

It is, in fact, known by different names, Beaunois in Chablis (an allusion to the town of Beaune), Melon Blanc in Arbois (Jura) and, quite stupidly and misleadingly, Pinot-Chardonnay.

This relatively early-ripening grape buds and ripens a little after Pinot. It is not surprising, therefore, that it is found in the same areas, especially since it has the same preference for poor, rocky, clay-limestone soil.

These strains of Chardonnay are carefully selected, for the grape is highly vulnerable to *court noue*, a viral disease that has greatly impaired the quality of Montrachet and other wines since the war.

Its small spherical yellow berries colour slightly at maturity; yields can be high in fertile soil (100 hl/ha). The Chardonnay wines excel by their delicacy, their balance of acid with alcohol, their aromatic richness and their capacity for improvement with age.

The pink Chardonnay is an anomaly, while the musky Chardonnay with its odd flavour offers little interest.

Colombard

The life cycle of this grape is similar to that of the Folle Blanche, which it resembles in many different respects. Like Folle Blanche, its wine can be drunk as it is or may be distilled into Cognac or Armagnac. Colombard brandies are slightly inferior in quality to those made from the Folle Blanche grape, more or less on a par with brandies made from the distillation of Ugni Blanc wine (Saint-Emilion) but better than those made from the Baco 22A.

The Colombard may be blended together with grapes of the great classical varieties to make Bordeaux wines such as Entre-Deux-Mers; by itself it produces Côtes de Blaye.

This is a quite late-ripening grape variety. Its medium-sized bunches bear light golden, oval-shaped grapes, a centimetre in diameter, with substantial yields exceeding 100 hl/ha.

The Colombard grape has its own particular character. Quite a full yellow in colour, it has a pleasant bouquet, a good alcohol-acid balance, but should be drunk young to be at its best.

Riesling

Riesling is to Germany what Chardonnay is to France. Originating along the banks of the Rhine, it spread to Alsace and Luxembourg before extending into Italy, Yugoslavia and Hungary, and then abroad to the United States, South Africa and Australia. It is a late-ripening grape (15 October) and a late budder, thus escaping the rigours of early frost; all the same, it needs a clement autumn, and is best suited to the continental climate.

Its bunches are small, compact and plentiful; the small round berries are golden yellow, tinged with green. Yields are high (100 hl/ha). The grape is susceptible to *Botrytis cinerea* (*pourriture noble*) which develops favourably thanks to the dawn mists of the Rhine, in which case the yield may fall by as much as 90%.

Riesling can therefore produce both dry and sweet wines, and is the most delicate of all the German-Alsatian aromatic varieties.

Below Riesling.

Apart from its delicacy, Riesling wine is clean, honest, precise, distinguished and elegant, with excellent acidity-alcohol balance. It is free from the fault that other aromatic varieties display of being over-exuberant.

If harvested late and vinified into a sweet wine, it becomes more complex.

Its wines are among the best in the world; whether sweet or dry; the acidic strength of the grape allows them to age and improve over long periods.

Gewürztraminer

This grape is a native of Germany and more specifically of the Palatinate (Pfalz). Its popularity has since spread to neighbouring Alsace, Austria, etc. and its range has extended abroad to the United States, South Africa and elsewhere.

The life cycle of the Gewürztraminer precedes that of the Riesling, alongside which it is often grown. This is an early-ripening and early-budding variety and is therefore best suited to continental climates.

Its small bunches of equally small, oval and loosely spaced berries are easily recognized by their pinkish hue. Hectare output is moderate. Although thick-skinned, it is a prime target for *pourriture noble*, when yields can drop drastically. The still, soft, golden Gewürztraminer wine is immediately recog-nizable. Its musky, spicy, rose-scented aromas are well sustained by average acidity, giving an impression of richness on the palate which may be supported by residual sugar in a late-picked wine.

Chenin Blanc

This is, in every sense, a universal grape, firstly because it is found in Europe, the United States, South Africa, Australia and other areas, and secondly because it forms the basis of dry, semi-sweet, sweet or sparkling wines. In France, except for a few plants which have migrated towards Aveyron (Entraygues and Fel), it is found only in the Loire Valley, apparently its birthplace, where it is known as Pineau de la Loire.

It is a late-ripening grape with a regrettably early budding that can pose problems with spring frosts.

The medium-sized bunches of golden, oval grapes, over one centimetre in diameter, can produce yields of up to 100 hectolitres, although such yields are not achieved in the better vineyards on the *tuffeau*, i.e. chalk.

Without sufficient sunshine Chenin wines will suffer from unbearable acidity, but in sunny years they can offer aromas remin-iscent of lemon-apricot, acacia honey and quince, while the sparkling wines that improve with age – unlike champagne – take on the aromas of lime and honey.

Left Gewürztraminer.

Grape Varieties/International Whites 2

Ugni Blanc – Trebbiano

Originating in Tuscany, this is the most commonly grown white variety in Italy and in France (100,000 hectares).

It needs much sun to ripen since it is a very late-ripening vine and a late budder. In France, it produces drinkable wine only in the south and in Corsica, although growers from the Cognac and Armagnac regions plant numerous specimens to make so-called *vin de chauffe*, i.e. wine intended for distillation.

The wine is thus nothing special, acidic and sharpish, with 7–8° of alcohol. Ugni Blanc, which is known locally as Saint-Emilion, achieves yields of 150 hl/ha. Its bunches are very large and the round, golden grapes darken when fully ripe.

In the south of France and Italy – especially in Tuscany, where the grape is called Trebbiano – the wines, a very pale yellow, are stronger in alcohol and more acidic, something that is often lacking in warm regions where white wines are often too soft. Ugni Blanc is unfortunately rather poor in aroma. It is blended to make that well-known red wine, Chianti. This is a pity, as it does nothing for it!

Pinot Blanc

Pinot Blanc is itself a mutation of the Pinot Noir. Although Burgundy is its birthplace, it is hardly found there today. In Alsace it is known as Clevner (Klevner); in Italy it is made into a dry sparkling wine, while in California it is sold under its proper name. Pinot Blanc is a productive variety of grape that forms the basis for well-rounded, well-balanced wines which are nevertheless far less sophisticated than those from the Chardonnay.

Pinot Gris

Yet another derivative of the Pinot Noir, the Pinot Gris is found in small quantities in Burgundy, where it is called Pinot Beurot; in Alsace it is known as Tokay and in Germany as Ruländer. This pink-graped variety gives well-constructed and full-bodied wines of moderate acidity and a respectable alcohol content.

Right Pinot Gris.

Sylvaner

The Sylvaner grape is grown all over central Europe, having originated in Austria. In Germany it is second in importance, or first if Rheinhessen is considered separately. In California it is sometimes called Riesling, confusingly so, for the banal Sylvaner does not bear comparison with that noble wine.

This is a variety that buds neither early nor late, with grapes that ripen late in autumn. Bunches are medium-sized, as are its grapes, which are round, compact and light yellow. Like many other grape varieties, Sylvaner is prone to excessive yield (over 100 hl/ha), and then the faintly scented, pale, thin Sylvaner wine lacks charm.

The grape loosely resembles the Chasselas, and may be eaten as a table grape.

The best Sylvaner vinification takes place in Germany. German Sylvaner is a great wine which unfortunately underlines the insignificance of many Alsatian Sylvaners.

Muscat

Muscat varieties, genuine or false, black or white, are found all over the world, though originating in Greece. The grapes can be distilled, turned into dry wines like those of Alsace, sparkling wines such as Clairette de Die, Asti Spumante, or even 'natural sweet wines' like Rivesaltes, Beaumes de Venise, Lunel, Frontignan, etc. The Muscat from Hamburg is a large, black table grape. Drinking varieties include the Muscats of Frontignan (these small grapes are the best), Alexandrie and Ottonel. Bunches ripen fairly late, but the buds open early. Its small to medium-sized round grapes are amber, tinged with red. Once grown in Alsace, its late maturity is causing it to be superseded by the earlier-ripening Muscat Ottonel. The Muscat d'Alsace is, in fact, the only Muscat-based still, dry wine produced in France. It is very delicate, very aromatic and must be drunk young.

The Muscat d'Alexandrie produces wine comparable to those made from the Frontignan grape but are rather less refined. This is a variety that ripens very late indeed, best suited to very warm, very dry regions (Aude-Pyrénées Orientales). Its medium-sized bunches bear huge, elliptical, yellow and thin-skinned grapes that are fleshy and musky. This is an all-purpose grape used for making aromatic sparkling wines in Italy.

Left Chardonnay.

Sauvignon

This variety enjoys universal, almost excessive popularity. It is known by different names, including Blanc Fumé, which is found under the *appellation* of Pouilly Blanc Fumé. It is a relatively early-flowering grape that ripens quickly.

Its numerous small bunches of musky, golden yellow, little oval-shaped berries give respectable yields of up to 100 hl/ha. In a relatively cool climate, limestone soils enhance the floral bouquets of the wine, while gravelly or siliceous soils tend to moderate it.

Until quite recently, in the Bordeaux region, the Sauvignon merely played a supporting rôle in the great sweet wines based on the Sémillon; but since the vogue for dry white wine, it is gradually replacing the Sémillon, even though the latter is still the most widely planted white grape in Bordeaux.

In other parts of the south-west it is displacing the local grapes, and already reigns supreme on the banks of the Loire around Sancerre, Pouilly-sur-Loire, Quincy, Reuilly, etc.

Its often accentuated aromas are reminiscent of spices, straw, blackcurrant leaves and gooseberries. On the palate it is aggressively fruity, with excellent acidity.

Grape Varieties/Local Whites

Sémillon

The Sémillon grape, occupying nearly one-quarter of all Bordeaux vineyards, is thus the principal variety of this region, even though on the decline. Many Bordeaux growers have uprooted Sémillon and replaced it with Sauvignon. This is because of the fashion for dry white wine (for which Sauvignon is better suited) and the declining popularity of sweeter wines based on the Sémillon.

It is a middle-budding variety which ripens fairly late. Its round berries, a centimetre or so in diameter, range from greenish-yellow to yellowish-pink. Sémillon lacks a little fruit on the palate and the aroma, especially of young dry white wines, is somewhat reminiscent of green apples. Once bottled, it must wait five years to attain rich and complex tertiary aromas.

It is largely affected by *pourriture noble* and used for the greater Sauternes, almost always supported by a little Sauvignon (20%).

The Sauternes-Barsac Château Doisy-Daëne is made from Sémillon alone (Lafaurie Peyraguey 98%).

Its prime example as a dry wine is the Laville-Haut-Brion (60% Sémillon); this admirably dry, golden and soft Graves is full-bodied, with a superlatively rich aroma.

Muscadelle

Muscadelle is one of the three varieties used for the great Bordeaux white wines, albeit the least popular and least widely grown. Yet despite a slight decline, Bordeaux growers stick by it and it gives them good yields in return. The plant itself is frail and is invariably the first to be affected by disease in a vineyard, sounding the alarm for growers to treat the other varieties. Though frequently sick, it is very consistent, yielding relatively few grapes, but giving them every year, whatever happens.

It is a late budder that ripens correspondingly late. Its large bunches bear round, medium-sized, pinkish-yellow berries that take on colour as they mature, and with a musky flavour which is transferred to the wine. Output per hectare is modest.

Chasselas

Chasselas is grown far more as a table grape than as a wine grape, but nevertheless forms the basis of *appellation contrôlée* wines such as Crépy, Ripaille, Marignan (AOC Savoie) in the Haute-Savoie, Pouilly-sur-Loire, Gutedel – the Alsace name for Chasselas – and more especially the white wines of French-speaking Switzerland, where it is known as Fendant or Dorin.

It is an undistinguished early-ripening variety able to withstand the very varied climates of Languedoc, Alsace and the sub-alpine plains. Bunches are medium sized, and the grapes hardly exceed one centimetre in diameter, being greenish-yellow, very juicy and thin-skinned. Hectare yields can attain 100 hectolitres.

Aligoté

This grape, probably a native of Burgundy, and cultivated since ancient times, cannot compete in that region with the incomparable Chardonnay. It has been given an *appellation* that prevents any confusion with the latter, since it is the only Burgundy wine to bear the name of the variety – Bourgogne Aligoté.

Folle Blanche

This variety goes by several names. In the Nantes region it is called Gros Plant, and has also given its name to a VDQS wine (*vin délimité de qualité supérieure*), the Gros Plant du Pays Nantais, which is a sort of sub-Muscadet.

In southern France it is called Picpoul, where it is the basis of another VDQS wine, the Picpoul de Pinet. It is best known in Cognac and Armagnac, whose finest brandies come from the distillation of the lean, light and acidic wines of Folle Blanche.

The plant itself is very vulnerable to cryptogamic attack and is being gradually superseded by its descendant, created by a cross with the Noah grape – the Baco 22A.

Mauzac or Blanquette

The Mauzac is a very ancient variety from south-western France. In the Aude, known as Blanquette, it has given its name to the Blanquette de Limoux *appellation*, generally known as a sparkling wine made according to the *méthode champenoise*, although probably better still is the Vin de Blanquette, which is made to sparkle by the *méthode rurale*. It is also used to make the still and sparkling white wines of Gaillac.

This middle-budding variety ripens late. Its largish bunches are laden with spherical, thick-skinned grapes containing large pips, making them unsuitable for eating. In flat, open country, yields are high (100 hl/ha) but the quality suffers, while on hillsides output falls off and quality improves. Mauzac can be harvested over-ripe or mouldy with noble rot, when they produce rich, sweet wines.

Clairette

Clairette has given its name to a number of *appellations* and hails from southern France, where it has been grown for centuries. The high sugar content of its grapes, and hence the alcoholic strength of the Clairette wines and their ability to maderize, once made the grape an ideal raw material for aperitif wines. Nowadays, however, the Clairette grape, if well tended, is reserved for AOC wines, provided yields do not exceed 50 hl/ha. In fertile alluvial soils the yield doubles at least, and Clairette produces only table wines.

Clairette wine is excellent, provided it is not over 12.5°; the aromas are flowery, it oxidizes quickly and is low on acidity. Poorly made, it is heavy and strong. Clairette may be either vinified alone or blended. In the former case, the grape produces the Clairette de Bellegarde, the Clairette du Languedoc and the sparkling Clairette de Die made by the *méthode champenoise*. When blended, it is used to make Côtes-du-Rhône and Châteauneuf-du-Pape (white) as well as the sparkling Clairette de Die Tradition (with Muscat).

Melon or Muscadet

The Melon de Bourgogne is indeed a native of Burgundy and has only been called Muscadet since it was first planted around Nantes, in the Loire Atlantique and in Anjou during the 16th century. It is said to have replaced the local varieties in these regions that were killed off by very cold winters.

The Melon de Bourgogne is undoubtedly hardy and resistant to frost, as was proved in the winter of 1956 when the vineyards were ravaged and decimated by cold.

No longer grown in Burgundy, where because of its susceptibility to rot (*pourriture grise*) it earned the nickname *pourrisseux*, it seems better suited to the crystalline schists of the Nantes region. It is an early-ripening, early-budding variety; its medium-sized bunches bear small, round berries with thick golden skins. Yields are respectable though not excessive. The wine made from Melon de Bourgogne, i.e. Muscadet, is pale gold with a green lustre. Its delicate, accentuated floral aromas, though not very full or complex, are nevertheless clean and light. In the mouth, a musky flavour accounts for its name.

Other White Varieties of Grape

Viognier

Otherwise known as golden Viognier, from the northern Rhône Valley. An extraordinary, late-ripening grape with a low yield but with very rich and complex aromatic powers (Condrieu, Château Grillet).

Roussanne

An excellent, low-yield grape from the northern part of the Rhône Valley, it ripens late. Its wine is very refined and improves with age (Hermitage, Saint-Joseph). Unfortunately the greed of some growers is causing them to replace it by Marsanne. It is called Bergeron in Savoie.

Marsanne

A productive, very late-ripening variety, with large bunches and round grapes. Gives same wine as above (Roussanne) though less refined and not so intense.

Traminer–Savagnin

Otherwise known as Naturé. The only variety from the celebrated Château-Chalon (Jura). Low in yield, late-ripening. Compact bunches of small berries. An unforgettable wine.

Jacquère

A typical Savoyard variety that is late for the region. Productive plants produce round, compact and thick-skinned berries. Makes for moderately good local wines, the most representative being the AOC wine of Savoie, Apremont.

Bourboulenc

A white grape used to blend Châteauneuf-du-Pape. Grapes are reasonably compact, of good aromatic strength, delightfully fresh and persistent.

Maccabeu (Maccebeo)

A late budder, ripening very late, for dry regions only. Wine is golden, full-bodied, strong and fruity but lacking in finesse. Well suited to fortified wines. Grown in Roussillon.

Ondenc

A grape from the south-west of France with early budding and early ripening. Yields are low but the wine is well balanced, strong in alcohol and in most instances blended with others.

Baroque

A good variety from south-west France (Tursan) that is growing in popularity. Late-maturing; the wine is balanced and strong in alcohol.

Wine Producing Regions/France/Bordeaux 1

The Bordeaux *appellation* area comprises 100,000 hectares of vines, and is the world's largest producer of fine wines.

There are three types of soil: the Graves soil, limestone soil and sandy soil, although these may overlap and mingle. The region roughly coincides with the *département* of Gironde, and can be further subdivided into three sections:

the left bank of the Garonne and Gironde;

the right bank of the Dordogne and Gironde;

the centre between the Garonne and the Dordogne.

In each of these areas there are at least a dozen sub-regional or local *appellations*. The latter, the commune *appellations*, are the cradle of the *crus*, the Châteaux, the Clos and the smaller properties so typical of the Bordeaux vineyards. The great wines are made from three red varieties (Cabernet Sauvignon, Cabernet Franc and Merlot) and three white varieties (Sémillon, Sauvignon and Muscadelle). All fine Bordeaux wines are blended.

In order to simplify the commercial side of their activities, the Bordelais invented a system of classification by quality – in fact, by price – for their growths (*crus*). The first official classification came in 1855, covering five different classes of Médoc and Sauternes-Barsac (plus one Graves) only. In 1973 it was revised to allow Château Mouton-Rothschild to move up from Second to Premier Cru. Allowing for all the various divisions and groupings, 87 châteaux are currently classified.

In 1953 and 1959, 14 Graves châteaux (white and red) were classified without any specific placing, while the Saint-Emilions were classed in three categories in 1955 and 1958. This particular classification at present covers 84 châteaux.

The wines of Pomerol and the other regions are unclassified, although Château Pétrus (Pomerol) is included in the innermost circle of greats which also encompasses Margaux, Latour, Mouton-Rothschild, Lafite Rothschild (Pauillac); Haut-Brion (Graves); Yquem (Sauternes); Cheval Blanc and Ausone (Saint-Emilion).

Left bank of the Gironde

Médoc This is divided into Haut and Bas Médoc. Haut Médoc is in turn subdivided into six communal *appellations*:

Margaux (R) This *appellation* extends beyond the Margaux commune into the neighbouring parishes of Soussans, Arsac, Cantenac and Labarde. Here, in gravelly soil, we find the finest Médoc wines with *sève*, grace, softness and distinction. One Premier Cru, five second, ten third, three fourth, and two fifth *crus* are classified.

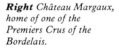

Right *Château Margaux, home of one of the Premiers Crus of the Bordelais.*

Saint-Julien (R) These are great wines of balance, elegance and mellowness. There are five classified second, two third, and four fourth *crus*.

Pauillac (R) An AOC that spills over the communes of Saint-Estèphe, Cissac and Saint-Julien. These great wines are tannic, full-bodied with plenty of *sève*, taking time to mature. There are three Premier Crus, two second, one third and twelve fifth *crus*.

Saint-Estèphe (R) Well-structured, powerful wines but less refined than Pauillac. Two second, one third, one fourth and one fifth *cru* are classified.

Moulis (R) Well-made, supple wines but with neither the finesse nor the ambition of the *crus* mentioned above.

Listrac (R) Close to Moulis in style but perhaps a shade more rustic.

Haut-Médoc (R) This is the *appellation* on the labels of five classified *crus* from communes not mentioned above.

Médoc This AOC encompasses all the *appellations* so far mentioned plus those wines produced in the northern part of Médoc whose rough and less gravelly terrain tends to impair their finesse.

The *crus exceptionnels, crus bourgeois exceptionnels* or *supérieurs*, and the *crus bourgeois* number 117 in all, some equivalent to a kind of 'sixth *cru*'. The (rare) white wines produced in the Médoc region are only entitled to the *appellation* Bordeaux or Bordeaux Supérieur.

Wine Producing Regions/France/Bordeaux 2

Left bank of the Garonne

Graves (R & W) A distinction is made between the northern Graves from the ancient district of Bordeaux and the southern Graves with their less distinguished wines. The red Graves can claim to be as great as the Médocs. They improve over 10 to 15 years.

Sauternes, Barsac (sweet white) These regions are bordered by the Graves to the south, some 50 kilometres from Bordeaux. In theory, the grapes are only harvested one by one when they have been affected by *pourriture noble*.

The fact that this noble rot develops irregularly means that harvesting must sometimes be done piecemeal, each picking being a *trie* (or *tri*). The harvest is sometimes split up into as many as ten *tries*, each being separately pressed, vinified, then reassembled or blended before bottling.

The sweet wines are very aromatic (honey, quince, acacia, lime, almond, etc.), and have a particular and complex balance, the sugar and alcohol being offset by the acid and the bitterness.

Right bank of the Dordogne

Saint-Emilion (R) An AOC comprising the commune of Saint-Emilion and eight others adjacent to it. A distinction has to be made between the Saint-Emilions from the slopes close to the town itself, with their limestone soil, and those of the more sandy *graves* terrain which include two great Saint-Emilions, Château Cheval Blanc and Château Figeac. Of the 12 Premier Grand Crus Classés, these are the only ones grown on the *graves* soil, the ten others coming from the *côtes* grown on limestone. They are as fine as the best classified *crus* of Médoc, but more round and with more vinosity. While lamb is the perfect partner of Pauillac, beef goes beautifully with Saint-Emilion. Some of the neighbouring communes are allowed to add the distinction of 'Saint-Emilion' (Saint Georges-Saint-Emilion, Lussac-Saint-Emilion, etc.) after their name, although their wines are less substantial than the real thing.

Pomerol (R) Separated from Saint-Emilion only by a few yards, Pomerol brings out the

Below Château d'Yquem, producer of the finest Sauternes.

best in the Merlot grape. The richness and generosity of these wines has earned them the nickname of 'the Burgundies of Bordeaux'. The communes of Néac and Lalande de Pomerol produce wines that are less rich and less rounded.

Fronsac, Canon-Fronsac (R) A firm, well-built wine offering an excellent introduction to the classified Bordeaux *crus*.

Côtes de Bourg, Côtes de Blaye (R & W) A vast region producing wines that are generally well made and for the most part inexpensive.

Bordeaux Côtes de Castillon (R) Honest wines typical of the communes surrounding Saint-Emilion, offering a good value for money.

Bordeaux Côtes de Francs (R & W) AOC Bordeaux in character, but sometimes lacking definition. The white wines may be made dry or sweet.

Between Garonne and Dordogne

This is a huge triangle with ten or so *appellations* of red, dry white and sweet white wines.

Entre-Deux-Mers (W) A crisp dry white wine with finesse but not much body. Very agreeable.

The red wines are only entitled to be called Bordeaux or Bordeaux Supérieur.

Premières Côtes de Bordeaux (R & W) An honest, uncomplicated wine. The white may be dry or sweet.

Cadillac, Loupiac, Sainte Croix du Mont (sweet W) Sauternes style with less richness and not so rounded. The Sainte Croix du Mont are often very sophisticated, with a rich smoothness.

Côtes de Bordeaux Saint Macaire (W) Dry or sweet. Similar to the Premières Côtes de Bordeaux.

Saint Foy de Bordeaux, Graves de Vayres (R & W) Again, similar to the Premières Côtes. The Graves de Vayres are quality wines that are certainly worth looking out for.

Neighbouring regions

These regions, with the town of Bergerac at their centre, are extensions, both geographically and in terms of grape variety, of the Bordelais.

Monbazillac (sweet W) A sweet wine, historically perhaps older than Sauternes, with

Above Château de Monbazillac, where a sweet white wine similar to Sauternes is produced.

the same varieties of grape and the same vinification. Honey, violet, plum and crystallized apricot. Sweetness compensated by good acidic backbone.

Haut Montravel, Côtes de Montravel, Rosette (sweet W) Lighter than the Monbazillac, same style.

Montravel (dry W), **Côtes de Bergerac, Bergerac Côtes de Saussignac** (R & W)

Above Château La Jaubertie produces wines under the Bergerac appellation.

The reds are reminiscent of the light Bordeaux, while the whites are nearly always on the dry side.

Côtes de Duras (R & W sweet or dry) Red wines in the Bergerac style. The dry whites are legally obliged to state 'sec' on their labels.

Pécharmant (R) This is the best of all the reds in the region. It can be considered a sort of Bergerac Premier Cru.

Wine Producing Regions/France/Burgundy 1

The wine-growing part of Burgundy starts 120 kilometres south of Paris and extends almost as far as Lyons. This is a distance of 350 kilometres but that in itself is misleading on three counts. In the first place, the northern vineyards of Burgundy stop at Chablis and only continue after Dijon, a break of 100 kilometres; secondly, because Burgundy proper does not extend beyond the southern boundary of the *département* of Côte d'Or, above Chagny, another 50 kilometres, and finally, because the vineyard is narrow, with widths ranging from a few hundred metres to several kilometres.

Six separate zones may be distinguished: Chablis, the Côtes de Nuits and de Beaune, followed by the Côte Chalonnaise, the Mâconnais and Beaujolais. All these vineyards are based on a handful of grape varieties. The more serious wines are all single varieties: i.e. the white of Chardonnay, the reds of Pinot Noir and the Beaujolais of Gamay. The less ambitious Bourgogne Aligoté wines are made from the white Aligoté variety.

Chablis (W) A truly world-famous white wine *appellation*. One should separate four *appellations* according to their soil and exposition.

Petit Chablis (W) These are not quite authentic since the *appellation* covers an area of soil that is not Kimmeridgian (i.e. limestone marl), an essential prerequisite for true Chablis.

Petit Chablis is nevertheless a pleasant and drinkable wine when still young.

Chablis, Chablis Premier Cru, Chablis

Grand Cru These are the real Chablis, in order of increasing quality. There are seven Grand Crus and eleven Premiers Crus. They achieve a really high quality, being dry, rounded and full, without any sweetness; their colour is green or yellow golden.

They improve over 8–10 years, are excellent with shellfish, poultry and white meats.

Côte de Nuits Along the Côte de Nuits and the Côte de Beaune, there is an ascending hierarchy of quality starting with the *appellations communales*, the *appellations communales premier cru* and culminating with the Grands Crus, without naming the commune. Here are the more prestigious *appellations*:

Fixin (R & W) Mostly red, well-constructed, keeps well.

Gevrey-Chambertin (R) The best are the Chambertins, being full, well-structured, with great flavour and immense length, best drunk between the ages of 10 and 20 years.

Morey Saint-Denis (R & W) Has a raspberry and violet bouquet, with a full flavour. The five Grands Crus include the famous Clos de Tart and the Bonnes Mares which we come across again at Chambolle-Musigny.

Chambolle-Musigny (R) The most sophisticated and delicate of the Côte de Nuits. The exceptional wine here is le Musigny, of which a tiny amount is white.

Vougeot (R & W) Clos de Vougeot is the Grand Cru of this commune. The style is ruby-coloured with an aroma of truffles.

Echézeaux and Grands Echézeaux (R) Two Grands Crus from the commune of Flagey-Echézeaux. An aristocratic wine with a bouquet of violet and a hint of raspberries on the palate.

Vosne-Romanée (R) Both commune and wines are legendary, with five outstanding Grands Crus: la Romanée-Conti, a silky, suave and superbly elegant wine; la Romanée, the smallest AOC in France (only 8345 square metres), which is sometimes equal in quality to Romanée-Conti, but rather less silky; Richebourg, powerful and authoritative; La Tâche, the synthesis of all that is best in the *appellation*; and Romanée Saint-Vivant, elegant but less reliable.

Nuits Saint-Georges (R & W) There are some marvellous Premiers Crus: Vaucrains, Saint-Georges and Boudots are powerful, with a hint of strawberries, while Les Pruliers and Les Porrets are rounded and firm, but with great finesse. The wines of this commune tend to be full-bodied and age well.

Top First spraying at the Clos de Vougeot, Côte de Nuits, Burgundy.
Above A bottle of Chablis Premier Cru.

Wine Producing Regions/France/Burgundy 2

Côte de Beaune

Corton and Corton-Charlemagne (R & W) The red Grand Cru is clean, firm and full, with aromas of peach, blackcurrant and raspberry. The white Grand Cru is full-bodied, generous and rounded, with plenty of *sève*; a spicy cinnamon, floral bouquet and backed up by good acidity.

Pernand-Vergelesses, Savigny-lès-Beaune, Ladoix-Serrigny (R & W) In the style of the Corton but less full-bodied.

Chorey-lès-Beaune (R & W) More modest than those above.

Beaune (R & W) Fine, delicate wines which mature fairly quickly, with a floral nose of hawthorn and rose.

Pommard (R) A full, generous, virile wine. The Rugiens are the most potent while the Epenots are the most refined.

Volnay (R) The most refined and elegant of the Côte de Beaune. The Caillerets is the best vineyard.

Monthélie, Auxey-Duresses, Saint-Romain, Saint-Aubin (R & W) A firm, precise, straightforward red wine which is typically Pinot. The white is sophisticated, delicate and clean.

Meursault (R & W) A generous white *grand vin*, dry without being parched, hint of hazelnut on the palate.

Puligny-Montrachet (R & W) A great wine with a complex flowery aroma.

The Montrachets (W) These are the world's greatest dry white wines; they are potent, full-bodied and generous, with floral and fruity aromas and flavours reminiscent of almond, hazelnut and honey. They have a long, lingering aftertaste and keep well (15 years).

Chassagne-Montrachet (R & W) The white is fruity, full of vigour and keeps well, while the red is well-built and full-bodied.

Santenay (R & W) The red Santenay is well-

N

5 miles
5 kms

o Montagny

Tournus

MACONNAIS

□ Cluny

Saône

Mâcon

Pouilly O
Fuissé o   o
              Vinzelles
Saint-Véran o
              o Saint-Amour
Juliénas □
          □ Chénas
          □ Fleurie
    o Chiroubles
       o Morgon
    o Brouilly

Saint-Julien □

Villefranche-
sur-Saône

BEAUJOLAIS

Lyon

constructed although rather less virile than the Pommard. White Santenay is a rarity.

Côte de Nuits-Villages, Côte de Beaune-Villages, Hautes Côtes de Nuits, Hautes Côtes de Beaune (R & W) These are wines of somewhat less sophistication, without aromatic intricacy and lighter in structure.

Côte Chalonnaise

The Côte Chalonnaise has no Grands Crus although it does possess a few Premiers Crus that are outstanding, though little known.

Rully (R & W) Although less floral, the white wines of Rully can compare with the Savigny-lès-Beaune and Pernand-Vergelesses.

The red Rully wines are reminiscent of Volnay but without the latter's finesse and complexity.

Mercurey (R & W) Mercurey is highly successful. It resembles the wines of Beaune, but is a little rougher and has less finesse. The whites are floral, quite rich, yet occasionally a little dull.

Givry (R & W) Close in style to Mercurey, Givry is less generous and open. The very rare white Givry is similar to Rully, but lighter.

Montagny (W) A light, fresh white wine for summer or afternoon drinking.

Mâconnais

The 50 kilometres that separate the Côte Chalonnaise from the Beaujolais region are filled with vineyards planted with Chardonnay, Pinot Blanc, Pinot Noir and Gamay, this last *cépage* forming the transition to Beaujolais itself.

Wines made from the Chardonnay, Pinot Blanc and Pinot Noir grapes are allowed to bear the Burgundy label – the whites are generally better than the reds. They can all have the following labels, in order of improving quality: Mâcon, Mâcon Supérieur and Mâcon followed by the name of the locality; the white can also be Mâcon-Villages. Both the white and red Mâcons preserve their quality and refinement well, but should not be over-aged owing to their relative lack of substance and fullness.

Pouilly-Fuissé, Pouilly-Loché, Pouilly-Vinzelle, Saint-Véran (W) are four different wines all made from the Chardonnay. Pouilly-Fuissé is undoubtedly the best, with its pale golden colour tinged with emerald, its violet and acacia-honey nose and flavour of honey and almonds.

Beaujolais

True Beaujolais wine is a product of the Gamay grape granitic soil and, let it be admitted, some aggressive marketing. Only the northern part of the *appellation* region is actually granitic, so that southern Beaujolais wines are really 'illegitimate'. The range includes Beaujolais Primeur, sold in the shops from 15 November onward, Beaujolais, Beaujolais Supérieur, Beaujolais-Villages (red, rosé and white) as well as the Beaujolais *crus* (red only). Only the *villages* and the *crus* grow in ideal soil.

Moulin-à-Vent is the finest and most full-bodied and can keep up to five years, while the **Fleurie** is its elegant cousin. **Saint-Amour** is fruity, light and pleasant. **Chénas** is robust yet smooth, **Juliénas** fruity and more showy, while **Chiroubles** is soft and ideally light. **Morgon** has a violet nose and is best enjoyed when a year or more old. **Brouilly** is luscious and rich in alcohol; **Côte de Brouilly** is full-bodied, well-rounded and strongly flavoured.

Opposite left Courtyard of the Hôtel-Dieu, Hospices de Beaune.

Below The hill of Solutré towers over the vineyards of Pouilly-Fuissé in the Mâconnais.

Wine Producing Regions/France/Champagne 1

Contrary to what one hears all the time, Dom Pérignon (1639– 1715) did not invent champagne; neither did he make it nor even drink it. What he did make were outstanding country-style sparkling wines. True champagne is produced by a second in-bottle fermentation, a method first employed after the death of the famous monk from the abbey of Hautvillers.

Dom Pérignon is also said to have invented the art of blending, the second principal char-

Right *Statue of Dom Pérignon outside the headquarters of Moët & Chandon, Epernay.*

acteristic of champagne. The truth is that he blended grapes, never wines, and only Pinot grapes, whereas nowadays 80% of champagnes are the result of blending Chardonnay with Pinot Noir and Pinot Meunier.

According to the modern pressing procedure, the black grapes are put in a specially designed press that is broad yet shallow, and the colourless juice is rapidly squeezed out of the whole grapes without allowing them time to discolour. The wine produced from fermenting this clear must is a Blanc de Noirs as opposed to a Blanc de Blancs, resulting from the pressing of white Chardonnay grapes.

Generally speaking, champagne is a two-thirds/one-third or three-quarters/one-quarter blend of Blancs de Noirs and Blancs de Blancs respectively, and it is the way the wine is elaborated and blended that gives each champagne its personality. Champagne is usually a *vin de marque* or brand, made by *négociants* who buy the grapes from the grower and press and blend them into cham-

pagne. They are called *négociants manipulants* (NM), as opposed to *recoltants manipulants*, who both grow and process the grapes. Other champagnes are made by cooperatives (CM) whose members supply the grapes for vinifying, blending and processing (i.e. turning into champagne). These abbreviations are important because they must be shown on champagne labels to identify its origin. The letters MA mean that the champagne has been bought from a merchant, grower or cooperative to be marketed under a *marque auxiliaire* (secondary brand) or *marque d'acheteur* (buyer's own brand).

To be entitled to an *appellation*, champagne must come from a specific area, chiefly from the *départements* of Marne or Aube, east of Paris, and be made from the Chardonnay, Pinot Noir and Pinot Meunier grapes. Because vineyards produce grapes of varying quality, communes have been classed and quoted in percentage terms (80%–100%).

Nine communes in the Montagne de Reims and two in the Côte des Blancs are quoted 100% and so are entitled to be called Grand Cru. Premier Cru identifies communes quoted between 90% and 99%.

The grapes themselves are pressed several times; and each stage in the process is traditional and strictly controlled. Every 4000 kg (four tonnes) of grapes yields 2050 litres of top-quality grape-must called the *cuvée*[1], 410 litres of *première taille* and 205 litres of *deuxième taille* (subsequent pressings). The finer champagnes are made only from the *cuvée* and the *deuxième taille* is never used by serious *manipulants*.

The champagne *appellation* cannot be used for more than one hectolitre (100 litres) for every 150 kilograms of grapes.

The *cuvée* is colourless and refined, with good acidity, the first *taille* lacks finesse and a little acidity, while the second *taille* is inferior still, being harsh and rather coloured.

The final blend is born from these wines, from grapes of different varieties and various origins and even by the addition of reserve wines, i.e. wines held over from previous years. In the latter case the champagne cannot be 'vintaged' but can be sold 12 months after bottling, unlike vintage champagnes which stay in the cellars for at least three years.

[1] The word *cuvée* has two meanings:
a) first pressing, *vin de cuvée*
b) the blending of wines.

Epernay

Chalons-sur-Marne

Marne

Aube

Bar-sur-Aube

Bar-sur-Seine

les Riceys

Ville-Dommange

Verzenay

*MONTAGNE
DE REIMS*

*COTEAUX
CHAMPENOISE*

Bouzy

Damery

Mareuil-le-Port

Marne

Mardeuil

Ay

Epernay

Pierry

N

Cramant

OTES

Avize

DES

BLANCS

miles

kms

Wine Producing Regions/France/Champagne 2

Coteaux Champenois (R, W and rosé)

This is the second *appellation contrôlée* of the Champagne region and only came into being in 1974, the AOC Coteaux Champenois replacing the old Vin Nature de Champagne which in turn replaced Champagne Nature from 1953 onwards.

Since the word 'Champagne' is exclusive to the celebrated wines of the area, the new Coteaux Champenois *appellation* was created because the qualifying word *nature* somehow implied that the other wines were 'artificial'. These wines may be red, white or rosé and their very existence is erratic since the Coteaux Champenois are only made when there are 'too many' grapes, in other words more grapes than can be vinified into champagne, which was not the case in 1978, 1980 or 1981.

The white Coteaux Champenois are historically interesting inasmuch as they resemble the Champagne wines that existed before the age of Dom Pérignon. The pale rosé wines of the 16th and 17th centuries were probably much like today's white Coteaux Champenois.

These are dry, fresh and moderately fruity wines, light and relatively simple in character; like champagne itself, they may be made from a single variety of grape or blended. The Blancs de Blancs – the Chardonnay wines – are the best and finest, though less typical because the grape's character does not come out so much in Champagne soil, something that the *vignerons* positively appreciate. A more pronounced influence would mark the *cuvée* too much during blending.

It is therefore pointless to compare wines made from Champagne Chardonnay on the one hand and Burgundy Chardonnay on the other.

The best red Coteaux Champenois come from the Pinot Noir grown in the commune of Bouzy (100% Grand Cru). This is a wine vinified *à la bourguignonne*: it is clean and well-structured without ever attaining the complexity, roundness or richness of its Burgundian counterpart. Coteaux Champenois rosé wines are rare.

Rosé des Riceys

This is the only *appellation d'origine*, apart from Tavel, reserved exclusively for a rosé. Riceys, a little commune in the *département* of Aube, has been making rosé for over 1000 years and once used Gamay as an ingredient. Some are bottled straight from the vat and resemble the rosé wines of Sancerre, while others are kept for a year in *pièces champenoises*, wood barrels containing 205 litres. The taste of the Riceys is unmistakable and only appears during fermentation after a variable lapse of time, requiring great expertise on the part of the *vignerons*. It is a very rare wine, a mere 60 hectolitres being produced each year, and is every bit as expensive as champagne.

Above Remuage *of champagne bottles in the Heidsieck cellars.*

Left *Removing the sediment from a bottle of champagne (dégorgement); a wrist guard is worn for protection against bursting bottles.*

Vinification

Once the *cuvée* has been blended (February-March) the wine is bottled with the addition of *liqueur de tirage* (24gr sugar dissolved in wine and yeast). This is the second fermentation in the bottle, called *prise de mousse* (March to May); the bottles are laid horizontally on *lattes* for about one year at 10°C, then stored on their *pointes* (neck down) with the fermentation deposit (stored at 10°C from a few months to several years) to enable the sediment to rest on the cork. The process by which this sediment is removed is called

dégorgement. The expert *dégorgeur* takes each bottle and removes the cork with one hand to let the sediment fly out. After a fraction of a second he prevents further loss of liquid by placing his thumb over the neck of the bottle, then deftly inserts a fresh cork. The lost liquid is made up by the so-called *liqueur d'expédition* or *liqueur de dosage* which consists of pure cane sugar adjusted to suit the champagne's intended market (dry, medium or sweet). The illustration above shows how cork and sediment are removed with the aid of 'lobster' pincers.

Wine Producing Regions/France/Rhône

The Rhône vineyards occupy the hillsides on the left and right banks of the Rhône a little below Lyons, extending to and beyond Avignon. They can be split into two types of wine corresponding to distinct plant families and geological categories. The two zones, with nothing in common except the river and a hot to very hot climate, more or less correspond to the northern and southern Rhône respectively.

Northern Côtes-du-Rhône

These remarkably steep, terraced vineyards have always been worked by hand, being virtually inaccessible to machines. The heat is stifling, magnified as it is by the reflection from the Rhône itself and the narrowness of the river valley.

The white and red wines of this region are some of the best in the world, although they no longer enjoy their former immense reputation. The vineyards date back to Roman times when the wines produced around the town of Vienne graced the tables of the imperial capital. The glory of the Rhône wines has, for about a century, now been somewhat overshadowed by the Bordeaux and Burgundies. Hardly surprising, since the great Rhône wines are rare and the vineyards cannot be expanded, making their wines the prerogative of the lucky few who have discovered them.

Côte Rôtie (R) As its name suggests, this region is literally 'roasted' by heat and sun. These rich ruby wines with their violet aromas derive their vigour and luxuriance from the admirable Syrah grape, assisted by the no less respectable white variety, Viognier. They are tannic, well-built wines that require years of maturing, and go perfectly with game. There are differences in style between the top-quality wines from the Côte Brune and Côte Blonde.

Condrieu – Château Grillet (W) Two white wines which are very similar both in soil and taste, produced by the Viognier vine planted in the thin mica soil of the region. These golden wines are distinguished by their exuberant floral and fruity aromas, and go excellently with fish and shellfish. Must be drunk very young, and do not travel.

Hermitage (R & W) A red wine made only from the Syrah grape, and one of the greatest in the world. This dark ruby wine is rich in tannin, well-balanced and with aromas of violet and hawthorn; it keeps well, and is best enjoyed with red meat or game.

The greatest white Hermitage wines are made from the Roussanne grape, while the rest are blended with Marsanne. This very distinguished wine is complex, with clean aromas of wild flowers, and great finesse. It perfectly complements the better fish dishes.

Crozes-Hermitage (R & W) Similar to Hermitage but not quite so distinguished. Should be drunk before it is five years old.

Saint-Joseph (R & W) Not unlike the Crozes-Hermitage and occasionally better.

Cornas An imposing red wine made from Syrah with an extrovert, virile character; it resembles Hermitage but is less complex.

Saint-Péray (still white and sparkling) Made from the same grape variety as Hermitage, with a pale yellow hue and bouquet of violets and hazelnut. More often produced as a sparkling wine by the *méthode champenoise*.

Southern Côtes-du-Rhône

This vast area of the Côte-du-Rhône *appellation* is also the home of a great wine which is gradually regaining the quality that once made it so celebrated: Châteauneuf-du-Pape. Taken all together, the wines of this region including the more modest, are constantly improving.

Châteauneuf-du-Pape (R & W) These warm, rich, full-bodied and spicy wines are produced in extensive vineyards, often on a bed of round pebbles, and planted with Grenache, Cinsault, Mourvèdre, Syrah or other varieties (13 permitted in all, including some whites) set out in broad rows. These are winter-evening wines designed to accompany red meats and cheeses; their very potency often detracts from their finesse, and they should be drunk between 4 and 8 years old. Some domaines are making wine by *macération carbonique*; these have some finesse but are not typical Châteauneufs.

Above Château des Fines Rochers, Châteauneuf-du-Pape.

Gigondas (R, rosé) The best of these are comparable to the Châteauneuf-du-Pape in quality and style.

Tavel (rosé) Ten different varieties, including some white, go into the making of this wine, long claimed to be the best French rosé. This is a wine for summer evenings, complementing poultry and white meats.

Lirac (R, W, rosé) The rosés fall somewhere between the Tavels and the Côtes-du-Rhône rosés, while the reds are as good as the best Côtes-du-Rhône-Villages. The white tend to be short on finesse and vigour.

Côtes-du-Rhône-Villages (R, W, rosés) Seventeen communes, all renowned for their quality, are entitled to use this *appellation* in conjunction with their own name. The absence of such a name indicates that the wine originates from more than one commune. The reds are the best known, with their deep ruby colour and nose of blackcurrant and raspberry. They are well-rounded, full and spicy to the taste, with more body than finesse.

Côtes-du-Rhône (R, W, rosé) Everyday wines; many are made by *macération carbonique* and sold *en primeur*.

Opposite left Vines on the banks of the Rhône, Côte Rôtie.

Wine Producing Regions/France/Alsace

The vineyards of Alsace lie on the left bank of the Rhine in the French *départements* of the Bas-Rhin and the Haut-Rhin, stretching from Mulhouse to Strasbourg. It is an extremely picturesque region of valleys dotted with ancient hamlets that have preserved their character quite successfully by resisting modern development. The soil is varied but mostly limestone, and the climate is pre-continental with low rainfall and plenty of sunshine.

Alsace has frequently been at the heart of wars between France and Germany and has been occupied several times, even annexed to Germany from 1870 to 1918. These disputes have had lasting side-effects, not the least of which is that the system of *appellation d'origine contrôlée* in use since 1962 – the year in which the Alsatian vineyards were elevated to AOC status – much resembles customs still practised in Germany itself. As in Germany, the variety of grape takes precedence over the *cru*; as in the German Palatinate or Rheingau, the cooperatives turn out a large proportion of the total production; and finally, like many German wines, the wines of Alsace come in a 'flute' bottle so typical of hocks and Mosels.

The shape of the bottle has been laid down and regulated since 1972 by the Comité Interprofessionel des Vins d'Alsace. Yet there is no rule that dictates the shape of bottle for any particular *appellation*, except for Château-Chalon; and a Bordeaux may theoretically grace a Burgundy bottle (or vice versa). In reality, of course, this never happens, although specially designed bottles are not hard to find. Château Haut-Brion, for instance, is a Bordeaux wine but is never sold in a classic Bordeaux bottle.

The Comité Interprofessionel has another apparently beneficial rule, that no Alsace wine (AOC) may leave the region before being bottled. It is unlikely that this type of regulation offers the same sort of guarantee as 'château bottling'. At most, if the wine does not satisfy the consumer or fails to live up to its label, it can be traced back to Alsatian soil.

The appellations and the wines

The wine can be sold as a *vin d'Alsace* pure and simple, or as a *vin d'Alsace* made from a specific and identified grape; a commune may also be mentioned, and an Alsace Grand Cru category has existed since 1975, although the wines that have applied for admission are still being evaluated. The yield per hectare for

Below Young vines at the village of Turkheim, Alsace.
Opposite left Vineyards on slopes facing the Rhine, Alsace.

these Grands Crus is low (70 hl/ha) but the degree of alcohol is required. Only the very best grapes have a right to the *appellation* (Gewürztraminer, Riesling, Pinot Gris, Muscat).

Riesling (W) This is the best, most refined of Alsace wines, aristocratic and full of character. It goes excellently with chicken, fish and even sauerkraut.

Gewürztraminer (W) The most aromatic. Not easy to enjoy with meats, and goes better with foie gras and spicy dishes.

Pinot Gris (Tokay) (W) A round, mouth-filling wine best suited to white meats.

Muscat (W) An extraordinary wine that successfully expresses the aromas and finesse of the variety. It is the perfect aperitif wine and should be drunk without fail while still young and fresh.

Sylvaner (W) Pleasant and dry, but has little finesse. It can be drunk with hors d'oeuvres but does little for them.

Clevner (Pinot Blanc) (W) Minor version of a Tokay, with a good price/quality level.

Edelzwicker (W) Mixed varieties of noble grapes. Nothing special, but agreeable.

Pinot Noir (R) A very light red, or rosé, wine. Clean, fruity, not very complex.

Wine Producing Regions/France/Loire

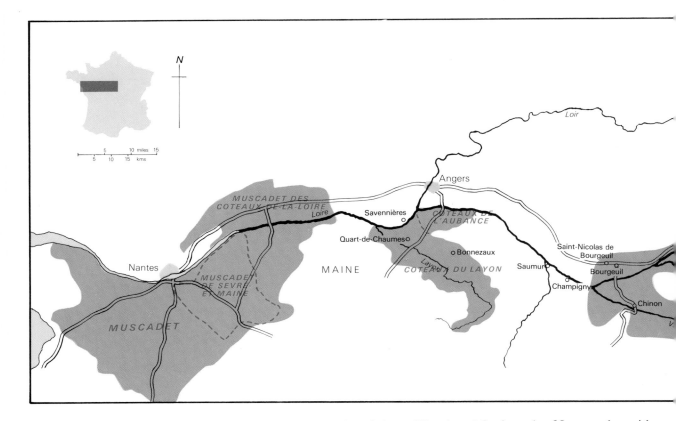

The Loire is a very old wine region. Saint Martin founded a religious order and an abbey in AD 372. It was he who, so the legend goes, first made wine here. The vineyards flank the River Loire and its tributaries for over almost 1000 kilometres. For simplicity, the middle and lower Loire is here divided into five sections, corresponding to five styles of wine and to specific grape varieties.

Sauvignon
Pouilly Blanc Fumé (W) A dry white wine with strong floral aromas. This is a summer wine that owes its freshness and finesse to the clayey-limestone soil where it is grown. Not to be confused with the lesser *appellation* of **Pouilly-sur-Loire**, an everyday carafe wine made from Chasselas grapes.

Sancerre (R, W and rosé) Sancerre illustrates the almost over-emphatic characteristics of Sauvignon wines that are derived from clayey-limestones, marls and chalk soils. Much like Pouilly Blanc Fumé. The red is made from Pinot Noir grapes and is half-way between a light Burgundy and an Alsace Pinot Noir.

Quincy (W), Reuilly, Ménétou Salon (R, W and rosé) In the style of Sancerre but with less pronounced qualities.

Wines of the Orléans Region
Strictly for the record and as a reminder of the past, France's largest vineyard, until the 17th-18th centuries, produced a Gris d'Orléans, a pale rosé wine made from the Pinot Meunier grape.

Wines of Touraine
From Blois to Vouvray we find a number of AOC Touraine wines, red, white, rosé and sparkling, all based on Burgundy grapes and varieties native to the Loire.

Great Wines of the Loire
Vouvray and Montlouis (W) Until 1937 these two AOC white wines, mellow-sweet or sparkling, belonged to the same *appellation*. They are very typical of the Chenin grape from which they are made, and the dry wines can be over-acidic in poor years. They have a long lifespan, up to half a century.

Bourgueil and Saint-Nicholas de Bourgueil (R, rosé) A sturdy red wine made from the Cabernet Franc grape; when the soil is limestone rock, the wine is tannic and firm, while the more sandy, or even pebbly soil (*graves*) yields a gentler red wine.

Chinon (R, W and rosé) Grown on the left bank, opposite the last two. The same soil with the same grape variety yields a very similar though often softer wine with a bouquet of violets.

Jasnières (W), **Coteaux du Loir** (R, W and rosé) The Jasnières is a Chenin wine close to the Vouvray, with a nose and aroma of peach and apricot. Coteaux du Loir wines are soft and friendly, and there are even a few red wines with a raspberry aroma. These are made from the Pineau d'Aunis.

Saumur (sparkling, R & W) The white Saumur is made from Chenin, the red from the Cabernet Franc varieties. They are clean, firm and straightforward.

Saumur Champigny (R) The true *cru* of Saumur, with a dark ruby colour. It has a nose of violet and raspberry and is subtle in the palate. The great old vintages are outstanding.

Rosé d'Anjou is a medium light rosé; Anjou Gamay is characterized by the Gamay grape, Cabernet d'Anjou; Rosé de Loire is a mediocre rosé; Coteaux du Layon, Coteaux

de l'Aubance, Bonnezeaux and Quart de Chaumes are mellow, even luscious white wines from the Chenin grape. The last two *appellations*, equivalent to the Grands Crus of Layon, are complex, rich and even sublime in a good year.

Anjou Coteaux de la Loire (W), **Savennières** (W), **Savennières Coulée de Serrant** (W), **Savennières Roche aux Moines** (W) There is very little to distinguish these wines from each other, although the last two are the Grand Crus of Savennières, the best commune in the area.

The Chenin grape finds its best expression in the Coulée de Serrant, a truly great and generous dry wine.

Muscadet

Three wines make use of the Muscadet or Melon de Bourgogne grape: first upstream is the rather solid Muscadet des Coteaux de la Loire, then Muscadet de Sèvre-et-Maine, which is the finest and best balanced, and finally Muscadet, a *vin de carafe* without much complexity, crisp, fresh, to be drunk young. Slightly more acid is the VDQS le Gros Plant.

Wine Producing Regions/France/Jura, Savoy & Provence

Jura

This rocky and mountainous region produces one of the world's really great white wines, the Château-Chalon, so long lived that outstanding pre-revolutionary bottles still exist. The vineyards of the Jura cover the same area – 1200 hectares – as those of the neighbouring Savoy region, and are special in that they produce all types of wine (except for sweet white) including 'straw' or dessert wine, as well as reds, rosés, whites, *vins jaunes* and sparkling wines.

The Côtes de Jura regional *appellation* comprises all the various types of wine produced in the area. White wines are made from the Chardonnay, and especially the Savagnin grape, the reds from Trousseaus, Poulsard and Pinot Noir, alone or blended, while the best rosés come from the Poulsard variety on its own.

Vin de paille is made by a special process, and is so named because the grapes were once dried on straw, although nowadays they are dried on mats or hung up. After drying for some two months, the grapes are pressed and the resulting must, very rich in sugar, ferments slowly. *Vin de paille* is not unlike white port, but is richer and more complex.

The best still Jura wines are labelled Arbois and Arbois Pupillin, while the best sparkling wines are from the Etoile *appellation*.

Red Jura wines made from Trousseau grapes are richly coloured, robust and long-lived, going well with grilled red meats.

The white Arbois wines are full, dry and well-rounded in good years. As for the *vins jaunes*, their extraordinariness surpasses comment!

Savoy

Savoy possesses no great wines but has some excellent ones which are true examples of their grape variety.

The region of Savoy makes the best Chasselas wine, Crépy. The vineyards rise above Lake Geneva and lie facing those that produce the Swiss Fendant (also from Chasselas). This is a golden-yellow wine of medium acidity and with a hazelnut aroma. It

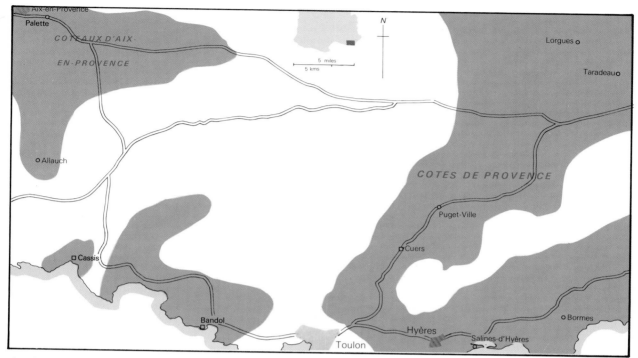

should be drunk young, ideally with fresh perch or dace from the lake.

The Roussette de Savoie is named after its grape, which should not be confused with Roussanne. Altesse is another name for this delicately structured, well-balanced wine with its pale golden hue. It is best enjoyed with trout freshly caught in Lake Bourget which is overlooked by the Roussette vines.

The Seyssel and Seyssel Mousseux dominate the *départements* of Savoy and Ain.

Great wines of Provence

Four wines have always stood out beyond and east of the Rhône corridor, namely Palette, Cassis, Bandol and Bellet.

Palette (R & W) Palette is the only one of the four not to have a piece of Mediterranean coastline, being situated close to the city of Aix-en-Provence. They are truly remarkable wines: the reds, based on the best Rhône grapes: Grenache, Cinsault and Mourvèdre, are highly coloured, tannic, full-bodied and keep well; the whites are made from the Clairette grape and are unusually sophisticated for this variety, a contradiction explained by their more northerly position.

Cassis (R, W and rosé) The whites are the best (Clairette, Marsanne, Ugni Blanc); these wines are floral and maintain their quality well, with good acidity.

Bandol (R, W and rosé) The reds are the best (60% minimum of Mourvèdre, Cinsault, Grenache), sometimes capable of rivalling the quality of some Bordeaux *crus classés*.

Bellet (R, W and rosé) The Bellet wines owe their quality to the fresh climate of the mountains overlooking Nice, planted with rare and original vines. The whites are dry and lively, the rosés are interesting and refined, while the firm, precise reds have none of the southern flabbiness. They are all perfectly suited to the very traditional and typical cuisine of Nice.

Corsica/Provence

Corsica (R, W and rosé) The authentic Corsican grapes are the Niellucio, the Sciacarello and the related Montanaccio, as well as the white variety of Vermentino, often called Malvoisie de Corse.

The best Corsican wine is without doubt the red Patrimonio. It is grown in limestone soils, is deep coloured and powerful.

Côtes de Provence (R, W and rosé) The whites are not particularly interesting since the sheer heat of the region is not conducive to the generation of subtle aromas. The well-known rosés are more successful, fresh, light and with a good bouquet. The red wines are improving, the mediocre Carignan grape being used less and less in their creation.

Wine Producing Regions/France/Languedoc & the South-west

Languedoc

Between them, the plain of Aramon and the Carignan grape manage to produce one of the most mediocre wines of France and the world. This is the land of 'plonk', the kind of mouthwash that blenders try to 'improve' with Italian wines. These table wines are sold

Right *Picking white grapes in Languedoc.*

in bulk and do not concern us here.

Nevertheless, the very same region does produce the Coteaux du Languedoc VDQS wines, most of them robust and red.

The three exclusively white AOCs are the Clairette de Bellegarde, the Clairette du Languedoc and the Blanquette de Limoux. These bear the name of their grape (Blanquette = Mauzac), the first two being rich and heady to the point of being heavy, while the third is full, round and nearly always sparkling. All three must be drunk young.

The three red AOCs are Fitou, Collioure and Côtes de Roussillon.

Fitou, the best wine from Carignan grapes planted *en coteau* (+ Grenache + Lladoner), is kept in the barrel for at least nine months. It is a dense, full and semi-refined wine that forms an excellent accompaniment to wild boar and cheese.

Collioure (Carignan, Grenache, Cinsault, Mourvèdre) is a strong red wine reminiscent of Fitou but often more sophisticated.

Côtes de Roussillon wines combine the grapes of the last two *appellations* (mainly Carignan). There are several light Côtes de Roussillon wines; some are drunk as *primeurs*, others are best after a few years.

Their popularity is growing, and although they are light for the region, they have good body and fruit.

Corbières, Minervois and Costières du Gard are good quality VDQS wines, comprising three reds and an interesting white by virtue of its basic ingredient, the Folle Blanche grape (at least 70%), known locally as Picpoul de Pinet.

The South-west

A beautiful region of much interest to the student of wine because of its diversity of wines produced.

Cahors (R) An historic wine made with Malbec (at least 70%) known in the area as Auxerrois. This is the 'black wine' of the olden days, well-built, tannic and simple, ideal with goose *confit*.

Côtes de Buzet (R, W and rosé) Bordeaux varieties in good regional style.

Gaillac (R, W and rosé) Gaillac includes a vast range of wines: the Gamay red should be drunk young. There are other reds made from more local grape varieties (Braucol, Fer, Duras, etc.) which can be interestingly firm and balanced. The slightly sparkling Mauzac whites, best enjoyed when chilled and young,

are fruity but sometimes low on acidity; the wines can be mellow and include a very interesting full sparkling wine made by the improved *méthode rurale*.

Côtes du Frontonnais (R, rosé) A soft red wine based on Négrette that is fruity, light and simple.

Madiran (R) Madiran is an impressive dark red Pyrenean wine which is lively yet keeps well, a suitable accompaniment to the strongest flavoured dishes.

Jurançon (W) An original wine made with special varieties of grape (Courbu, Manseng). This dry wine is lively with a firm clean flavour. The *liquoreux* wines show an amazingly spicy bouquet. In the mouth they offer a rewarding aromatic mixture of cinnamon, ginger, nutmeg and clove.

Pacherenc du Vic Bihl (W) Another Pyrenean wine similar to the dry Jurançon. Sometimes mellow.

Irouléguy (R, W and rosé) Hails from close to the border with Spain – the red is the best known of the three colours, not unlike the Madiran but less impressive.

Béarn (R, W and rosé) Bears the name of its home province. This is a simple and unpretentious wine, the rosé highly successful.

Wine Producing Regions/Germany 1

It can be important when assessing wine to know by what standards its maker wishes it to be judged. The claim that German wine is unique can easily be understood, for no other wine-producing country in Europe has such an unlikely climate for vine-growing. Often the absence of real summer warmth can only be compensated by a harvest late in the season, in November or even December, when the maximum amount of sugar has been formed in the grape. This slow ripening period, from the flowering of the vines in June until the vintage towards the end of the year, produces wines with a high acid content and relatively little alcohol. The result can be great freshness, delicacy and length of flavour, and these are the qualities to look for in German wine.

Classification and control

In most years, about 5% of the total crop will be basic table wine, and the largest part of the harvest will be in simple-quality wine, or as the Germans call it, *Qualitätswein eines bestimmten Anbaugebietes*, mercifully shortened into QbA. Superior qualities of wine, (*Qualitätswein mit Prädikat*, or QmP), are made from grapes riper than those that produce the QbA, and these are known as *Kabinett* wines. *Spätlese, Auslese, Beerenauslese* and *Trockenbeerenauslese* are all terms used to describe wines of increasing degrees of excellence, deriving from a late gathering or special selection of grapes.

In some years, when the temperature drops well below zero in the early days of winter, it is possible to harvest grapes that have been left on the vine with the hope that they will be frozen solid. Pressed in this condition, the juice is wonderfully concentrated, rich and luscious, and from it *Eiswein* can be made.

Below *The vineyards of the Mosel near Bremm, with the ruins of the monastery of Stüben in the foreground.*

Wine Producing Regions/Germany 2

Riesling

To get the very best out of their northern climate, the Germans have become exceedingly skilled in producing successful new vine varieties, and in making sure that the quality and health of their traditional vines are as good as possible. Nearly half the area under vine has been rebuilt and replanted in the last 30 years. The construction of new service roads, the replacement of terraced vineyards by more economically worked slopes, and the improvement of drainage to reduce the risk of soil erosion have been given priority. At each replanting, only the best quality of vine is selected, and the vine variety today is as important as it ever was in influencing the quality of German wine.

The Riesling vine, whose origins are uncertain, but which is known to have been growing in Germany for over a millennium, produces the finest wines of the River Mosel and of the Rhineland regions of the Rheingau and the Nahe. Like the great Chardonnay, particularly associated with Burgundy, its flavour is concentrated and positive. It can be almost steely, but never overpowering or cloying, and a fine fruity acidity often ensures a long life in bottle. Some will say it makes the best white wine in the world. In vineyard sites which do not enjoy the good microclimate that the Riesling requires, the Müller-Thurgau vine is frequently grown. It provides the main constituent in many sound commercial blends, but seems incapable of true distinction when compared to a Riesling. Many of the new crossings of various forms of *Vitis vinifera* produce wines with a strong bouquet. In the Rheinhessen, and the Palatinate adjoining the French border, a crossing of Silvaner X Riesling, called the Scheurebe, produces scented wine with good acidity and fine style. Other vines, such as the Morio-Muskat and Siegerrebe, also make strongly scented wine.

Above The slate river banks of the Mosel provide the ideal conditions for the extensive cultivation of the Riesling grape.

Above Burg Cochem, partly concealed by the burgeoning vines of the Mosel.

more alcoholic, and, to the outsider, less typically German.

The Riesling wine of the Mosel-Saar-Ruwer, in a slim green bottle, and with a delicate, elegant style, often used to be called feminine, before sex discrimination became unacceptable. At the same time, the supposedly masculine virtues of firmness and strength could legitimately be attributed to Riesling from the Rheingau. A region whose considerable reputation does not for once depend on the Riesling vine is Franconia. Its climate is continental and can be extreme at the wrong time of year for vine-growing, so that drastically reduced crops occur quite often. Franconian wine, mainly from the Müller-Thurgau and Silvaner grapes, has an earthy, positive flavour, and is easily recognized by its flagon-shaped bottle – the 'Bocksbeutel'. For continuity of *Kabinett* and *Spätlese* quality, almost year after year, the northern part of the Palatinate near the villages of Forst, Deidesheim and Wachenheim is without equal. A good microclimate provides growers in the best vineyard sites with a degree of protection against the sometimes volatile weather found elsewhere. Stylish Riesling wines are made with their own individual rounded flavour, to which the soil makes a positive and noticeable contribution.

Buying German wines

Because of the different qualities of wine that each vineyard can produce, depending on when and by whom the grapes were harvested, there is an enormous variety available. There may well be a problem for somebody coming to German wine for the first time to know where to begin and what to buy. In principle, the very cheapest wines are probably best ignored. If you cannot get the advice of a specialist wine merchant, go to a source whose general reputation is sound and from whom, possibly, you would be happy to buy other products. To learn about fine estate bottled wine can be the absorbing hobby of a lifetime, but great knowledge is not a prerequisite to their enjoyment. The charm of German wine is nearly always obvious and accessible. Even fine Riesling wines of *Kabinett* quality and upwards are eminently drinkable when young, but subtlety of flavour and individuality need time to develop in bottle, and that can be from two to ten years or more. It pays to be patient.

Many of the vineyard holdings in Germany are too small to enable the owner to make a living from grape-growing, so much of the crop is delivered to cooperative cellars. They operate to a high technical standard, and make excellent wine. For examples of German wine at its finest, however, one should probably turn to the many distinguished estates, with a history reaching back to medieval times or even earlier. Inevitably, they are almost all found where the Riesling vine is most widely grown, for their *raison d'être* is fine wine production.

Wine producing regions

There are 11 individual vine-growing regions, and the best known of these abroad lie in the northern part of the viticultural area. Here the wine is at its crispest. In the southern state of Baden, that runs down to the Swiss border and where the sun shines more strongly, the wines are broader in flavour,

Wine Producing Regions/Italy 1

Italy is one of the oldest wine-producing regions in the world. The vine has been grown here for thousands of years – fossilized grape pips from the Stone Age have been unearthed near Venice – and wine has always played an important role in the life of the peninsula's inhabitants.

History

During the Greek Empire, the cultivation of the vine in Italy became increasingly important for both social and religious reasons. The cult of Dionysus, Greek god of wine, was particularly important in the south and in Sicily. There are still grapes growing in southern Italy with origins that date back to the Greeks (Greco di Tufo and Aglianico).

The Romans were accomplished vintners and the cultivation of the grape was encouraged both at home and in the outposts of the empire, notably in the Rhône and Burgundy areas of France and in Germany. Soldiers were rewarded with gifts of land on which they had to plant vines; since the vine takes four years to bear fruit, the emperor was thus guaranteed the loyalty of the new Roman territories while his soldier-farmers awaited their crops.

The pioneering spirit of modern Italians can still be found among its wine makers, many of whom have left their homeland to establish wineries in younger countries, notably in the United States, South America and Australia.

Geography and climate

The Greeks, who were the first to realize Italy's natural disposition as a wine-making area, named it Enotria or 'Land of Wine'. Apart from the flat, fertile, alluvial valley of the River Po, stretching from Turin in the north-west past Milan to Venice in the north-east, the terrain is broken by hills and mountains, making it ideal for wine grapes.

The Alps, forming the northern boundary of the country, slope gradually down to the Po Valley, criss-crossed by steep man-made terraces in the highest parts and carpeted with undulating vineyards on the gentler slopes. Italy's backbone is formed by the Apennine mountains which rise near Genoa in the west, and swing southwards near Bologna down to the tip of the boot-shaped peninsula. Apart from the highest, snow-covered peaks, these mountains, too, are covered with vineyards. Poor soil makes for good wine, and again Italy has an edge on other wine nations. Apart from the rich soil of the Po Valley, where rice and corn are the main crops, most of the country has fairly barren soil on which grapes thrive. The soil ranges from granite in the north-west with patches of clay and limestone in Trentino, to schistous clay and gravel in the centre, and volcanic soil in the south and in Sicily.

It is a popular misconception that the climate of Italy is perpetually sunny and warm. The truth is that there are several different types of climate: *continental* in the north and southward as far as Tuscany, giving bitter winters, hot summers and frequent rain and hail storms; *equable* in the central part with cool winters and warm summers; *Mediterranean* in the south and on the islands, with mild winters and hot dry summers in which drought can be a major

Right The terrain of much of Italy – mountain and hill slopes – makes it an ideal wine-producing country and every region produces some wine.

problem. The hills and valleys also give rise to individual microclimates which affect the wines made in these areas.

The tremendous variety of topographical, climatic and soil conditions in Italy result in a wider range of different types and styles of wine than in any other part of the world.

Italy's wine law

In 1963 the Italian government passed the DOC wine law. DOC stands for Denominazione di Origine Controllata or 'Controlled Place Name'. The law regulates the production of about 200 wines and controls the following:

- area of production;
- permitted grape varieties and percentage of each type;
- height above sea level and exposure of the vineyards;
- methods of training the vines;
- maximum yield of grapes per hectare;
- maximum yield of wine from grapes;
- ageing period in the winery before release;
- size of bottles or containers in which the wine may be sold;
- chemical analysis of the wine;
- organoleptic characteristics of the wine.

A step beyond DOC is DOCG – Denominazione di Origine Controllata e Garantita – which also guarantees the quality of a wine. Only four wines (Barolo, Barbaresco, Vino Nobile di Montepulciano and Brunello di Montalcino) have so far been promoted to this category. In addition to the controls for DOC wines, DOCG wines are tasted for quality at regular intervals by a panel of experts; if the wine of any producer is considered to be below standard all this wine is declassified to ordinary table wine. The DOCG law constitutes the strictest wine legislation in the world – for two reasons. In no other country is quality legally guaranteed, and nowhere else are so many aspects of wine production controlled by law. For example, if a wine maker makes more than the permitted quantity of wine from his vineyards, all his wine of that year is declassified to ordinary table wine. Compare this with France where over-production in Margaux is declassified to AOC Bordeaux.

Chaptalization, the adding of sugar to must in order to achieve higher alcohol, is illegal in Italy. Concentrated grape juice may be added instead to some wines.

Italian Wine Names

Wines may be named for:
1. *Geographical location* – e.g. Barolo (a village), Chianti (an area), Sangiovese *di Romagna* (a region). All DOC wines have a place name.
2. *Grape name* – *Barbera* d'Asti (grape + town), *Verdicchio* dei Castelli di Jesi (grape + area), *Pinot Grigio* delle Tre Venezie (grape + region).
3. *Brand or generic name* – Most non-DOC wines e.g. Corvo, Venegazzu'.

The wine regions of Italy

There are 19 autonomous regions in Italy – in the north, Val d'Aosta, Piedmont, Lombardy, Liguria, Veneto, Trentino-Alto Adige and Friuli-Venezia Giulia; in the centre, Emilia-Romagna, Tuscany, Umbria, Marches and Latium; in the south, Campania, Abruzzi-Molise, Apulia, Basilicata and Calabria, plus Sicily and Sardinia.

Unlike other wine-producing nations, where wine is only made in certain areas, Italian wine is made in every single region. It is important to remember that Italy has been a united nation for little more than 100 years; before then the country was a conglomeration of kingdoms, duchies and city-states that were frequently at war with one another. Because they were separated geographically and politically, each region developed individual customs and traditions which can still be clearly identified today. These differences also extend to wine-making practices.

The easiest way to learn about Italian wines is to divide the country into five sections – the north-west, the north-east, the centre, the south, and the islands. Each section has broad similarities with regard to climate and grape varieties, though styles of the wines can vary.

Equally important to bear in mind is that because Italian wines are made from grapes rarely grown in other parts of the world they should never be compared with wines from other countries. Different grapes give different tastes so the only true way to understand Italian wines is to make an extensive tasting of the good examples. A little effort will be amply repaid since Italian wines can be outstanding and are generally slightly lower in price than wines from other countries.

Wine Producing Regions/Italy 2

Below Dégorgage,
refilling and corking of
Brut Spumante, a
sparkling wine made by
the méthode
champenoise, *near Turin.*

1. North-west Italy

This section includes Val d'Aosta, Piedmont, Liguria and Lombardy and is known for its full-bodied reds and for its excellent *brut spumante* which is often made by the Champagne method.

Piedmont

One of the most important red wine areas in the world. Wines tend to be full-bodied and tannic and many require lengthy ageing to achieve their potential. About 90% of the production is of reds.

Barolo: full-bodied, tannic, made from the Nebbiolo grape grown near the village of Barolo in southern Piedmont. At its best after 10–15 years ageing, it possesses the typical garnet colour of wines from this grape and a rich bouquet which makes it one of the easiest wines to identify. DOCG.

Barbaresco: called Barolo's younger brother, also made from Nebbiolo, but the soil in Barbaresco produces a slightly more gentle, elegant wine. DOCG.

Barbera d'Asti and **Barbera d'Alba:** the Barbera grape is the most widely planted variety in Piedmont, accounting for 50% of the region's reds. Best wines are from the

south around Alba and Asti. Medium-bodied, fruity, good after 3–7 years. DOC.

Asti: most popular sparkling wine in the world. Made from Moscato di Canelli grapes around the town of Asti. Unlike other sparkling wines, Asti is only fermented once, in large tanks. After the harvest the must is refrigerated and stored at 0°C until fresh wines are needed. Then the must is brought to room temperature, inoculated with selected yeasts and fermented until an alcohol level of 7° is achieved. Fermentation is then arrested, the wine filtered and bottled. This method ensures that the fresh, fruity quality of the grape is captured in the wine. DOC.

Gattinara: also made from Nebbiolo, but in the north of Piedmont. Required ageing before release is 4 years and can be cellared for 10–15 years. DOC.

Carema, Ghemme: medium-bodied reds also from Nebbiolo grown in the north. Slightly lighter than other Piedmont Nebbiolos due to different soil. DOC.

Lombardy

Two main wine areas are Valtellina and Oltrepo' Pavese.

Valtellina: situated high in the mountains near Switzerland, has a tiny production of quality wines made from Chiavennasca grape (local name for Nebbiolo). All vineyards are on very steep, man-made terraces where all work has to be done by hand.

Sassella, Inferno, Valgella, Grumello: the main wines made here. Lighter in style than Piedmont Nebbiolos and suited to only moderate ageing. DOC.

Sfursat: from Nebbiolo grapes that have been dried for 2–3 months on special racks. A rich, lush wine with high (14–15°) alcohol and hint of residual sugar. DOC.

Oltrepo' Pavese is the hilly area south of the Po Valley. Main grapes are Barbera and Bonarda for red wines (**Gutturnio dei Colli Piacentini** is one of the best), and Pinot and Chardonnay for whites, many of which are used as base wines for *brut spumante*.

2. North-east Italy

This section includes Veneto, Trentino-Alto Adige and Friuli-Venezia Giulia and is characterized by the fact that most of the wines are labelled for the grapes which make them (varietal wines). Many of the grapes were imported from France and Germany during the 19th century.

Veneto

The two main areas are the Veronese and the Piave Valley.

Veronese is the area around the town of Verona and along the east shore of Lake Garda. Light, fresh wines are produced here.

Soave: perhaps Italy's best-known white wine, made from Garganega and Trebbiano grapes. DOC.

Bardolino and **Valpolicella:** light fruity reds to be drunk young. Smaller producers often make high-quality wines. DOC.

Amarone: made from the same grapes as Valpolicella which have been dried for 3 months on racks (cf. Sfursat from Lombardy). The wine is rich and lush and can stand lengthy ageing. DOC.

Piave is a large area where four varieties are grown – Cabernet and Merlot for reds and Verduzzo and Tocai (both local varieties) for whites. Most of these wines are drunk locally.

Another area of quality wines is the countryside around the town of Treviso where **Prosecco di Conegliano**, a semi-dry, aromatic sparkling wine, and **Venegazzu'**, a proprietary label made from a blend of Cabernet, Merlot and Malbec, are made.

Trentino-Alto Adige

The northern half of this region, Alto Adige, is also known as Süd Tyrol and was ceded to Italy at the conclusion of World War I. Wines are made from Riesling, Müller-Thurgau, Sylvaner, Pinot Grigio, Chardonnay and Pinot Noir, and they tend to be clean, fruity and crisp. Quality is universally high. The DOC is called *Alto Adige* and controls a number of wines labelled for the grape variety from which they are made.

The southern half of the region is formed by the province of Trento where similar grapes are grown and the wines also labelled for the grape variety. The DOC is called *Trentino*. Chardonnay grapes are being planted increasingly and are used to make *brut spumante*.

Friuli-Venezia Giulia

Some of Italy's finest whites are made here from Riesling, Müller-Thurgeau, Sauvignon, Sylvaner, Pinot Grigio, Tocai and Chardonnay grapes. Cabernet and Merlot make light, fruity reds for early consumption. The best DOC areas are *Collio* and *Grave del Friuli* and wines are labelled for their grape variety.

Wine Producing Regions/Italy 3

3. Central Italy

The third section is formed by Emilia-Romagna, Tuscany, Umbria, Marches and Latium. The main grapes are Sangiovese for reds and Trebbiano and Malvasia for whites.

Emilia-Romagna

Region known as the cellar of Italy due to its consistently abundant harvest.

Lambrusco: a semi-sweet or semi-dry, low alcohol, effervescent red made from grapes of the same name. Extremely popular in the USA and Japan.

Sangiovese di Romagna: a fruity red for early consumption. Ranges from fairly harsh and acidic to smooth and elegant.

Tuscany

Major red wine-producing area. Also famous for its olive oil, the typical Tuscan landscape comprising rows of vines separated by olive groves.

Chianti: perhaps Italy's most famous red wine and one of the most underestimated wines in the world. Made in two styles. The first produces a young wine, ready to drink by March following the harvest. This wine does not age well. The second style is intended for longer keeping and is called Riserva. It is aged for 3 years in wood in the winery, and good vintages can be held for 10–15 years. Wines labelled *Classico* come from the heart of the DOC area and are considered the best. The DOC area is the largest and has several geographical subdivisions. *Rufina* is regarded as second only to the Classico area.

Brunello di Montalcino: made from a clone of the Sangiovese grape, known as Brunello. A powerful, full red aged for 4 years in wood before release. One of the longest-lived wines, top vintages can take 25 years to reach their potential. DOCG.

Vino Nobile di Montepulciano: Similar to Chianti, though with a little more finesse. Can be aged for 10 years in good vintages. DOCG.

Vernaccia di San Gimignano: a quality white from the Vernaccia grape. Reputed to have been Michelangelo's favourite wine, it was also the first Italian wine to become DOC. The Riserva is aged in wood for one year.

Umbria

Known as the green heart of Italy and famous for its hill towns – Perugia, Assisi, etc.

Torgiano Rubesco: highly regarded red made from Sangiovese and other red grapes. The Riserva can age well for 10 years and becomes a very elegant, full wine.

Orvieto: two styles of this white are produced, *secco* and *abboccato* (dry and semi-sweet), both made from the Trebbiano and Malvasia grapes. The quality has improved during recent years thanks to newly introduced techniques for making white wines (cold fermentation, refrigeration). DOC.

Marches

Region famous for its Adriatic beaches and seafood.

Verdicchio: a crisp, dry wine with high acidity suited to fish dishes. Made from grape of the same name and traditionally sold in green amphora-shaped bottle. DOC.

Latium

Rome is the capital of Italy and of the region of Latium. Wines from this area are generally light; most are drunk locally by tourists.

Frascati and **Marino:** best known whites of the area, similar in taste and style. Both are made from Trebbiano and Malvasia grapes. Recent vintages have benefited from the use of new white wine technology which results in crisper, cleaner, more stable wines. DOC.

4. Southern Italy

The south-eastern half of this section is responsible for the majority of wines produced in the south. The rest of the region tends to be very barren and rocky with a tendency to drought.

Regions in the south are Campania, Abruzzi-Molise, Basilicata, Apulia and Calabria.

Campania

Despite its southerly latitude, some of Italy's most elegant quality wines are made here, high up in the mountains where altitude offsets the effects of the southerly climate.

Taurasi: a robust red made from the Aglianico grape (Aglianico = Hellenic, a grape of ancient Greek origins) grown inland from Naples on volcanic soil. Improves after 5–10 years ageing. DOC.

Fiano di Avellino: one of the few Italian whites to improve with moderate ageing, made from Fiano grapes. A rich wine with a very agreeable, honeyed bouquet. DOC.

Greco di Tufo: another excellent white which can also withstand some ageing. Made from the Greco grape near the village of Tufo, named for its tufaceous (volcanic) soil, evidenced by the steely characteristic of the wine. DOC.

Basilicata

Aglianico del Vulture: similar in style to Taurasi, since it is made from the same grape, though slightly less elegant. DOC.

Apulia

Region which produces vast quantities of wine, much of it shipped in bulk to northern Italy and France. Recent experiments have yielded successful results with varieties such as Cabernet and Pinot Noir.

5. The Islands

Sardinia

The Emerald Isle produces relatively little wine and most of this is consumed by tourists.

Sicily

A region which produces large quantities of wine, much of it shipped in bulk to France. Recently there has been an increase in the production of quality bottled wine, with heavy government investment in new winery equipment, research into irrigation systems for the vineyards and experiments with more suitable vine varieties for the island.

Wine Producing Regions/Spain & Portugal 1

Spain

Spain is the third largest wine producer in Europe, after France and Italy, although its vineyards cover a larger area than either of these countries. The history of Spanish vine-growing goes back well before the Christian era, but it is only in the last 20–30 years that high-quality table wines have been regularly produced. (The history of sherry is very different, fortified wines of the highest quality having been made in Andalusia for the past 200 years.)

In 1970, the Instituto Nacional de Denominaciónes de Origen was set up, similar to, although a little less strict than, the French AOC and Italian DOC systems. The fact that Spain, once known principally for its hearty but dull table wines, now has the reputation for producing some of the most interesting wines in Europe, is attributable to dramatic changes of policy: investment at vineyard level for higher yields of healthier grapes, much experimental planting of new grape varieties, installation of modern methods of vinification alongside the traditional wood-ageing, and constant commitment to quality by the producers.

Spanish table wines are produced in four major areas: Rioja, Catalonia, La Mancha and Levante, with scattered vineyards in the north-west and the south.

Rioja

This region, named after the Rio Oja, a tributary of the Rio Ebro, which runs through the whole of this wine-producing district, is the best known for quality wine. While there are some quite exceptional wines from the Penedés region of Catalonia, these are better known under the names of the producers (Torrés, Jean León), than by their geographical appellation. The Rioja region has a quality ring to it, rather like Bordeaux. Indeed, the histories of the two regions are interlinked: in the 1870s and 1880s, many Bordelais growers left their phylloxera-ravaged vineyards for nearby Rioja, introducing their wine-making techniques. Although they departed again at the end of the century, when phylloxera eventually reached Spain, the Bordeaux influence remained.

In terms of geography and quality, the Rioja is divided into three distinct districts: Rioja Alta, of which the capital is Haro, with a temperate climate that produces the finest

Above Cement fermenting vats in the bodega of Valdepenas, one of the major wine producing towns of La Mancha in central Spain.

wines; Rioja Alavesa, centred on Logroño, producing fine wines under a similar climate; and Rioja Baja, on the south side of the Rio Ebro, where a hotter and drier climate produces heavy wines with low acidity. Wines from the Rioja Alta and Rioja Baja are often used together in commercial blends.

The production of the Rioja is mostly red, although more white grapes are being planted now that modern vinification techniques produce a lighter, crisper style. The principal grape for the better red Rioja is the local Tempranillo, to which may be added some Garnacho (the Grenache, from the Rhône Valley). In the Rioja Baja, Garnarcho is planted almost exclusively. White Rioja is made mainly from the Viura, while minor grapes used are the Malvasia and Garnacho Blanco.

Opposite below Wine from the vineyards of Senorio de Sarría in Navarra can rival the best from Rioja in quality, although production is restricted.

The style of wines from the Rioja region is very varied. The younger and cheaper are deep-coloured *tintos*; as they mature, particularly if aged traditionally in small oak barrels, they lose colour, take on a touch of vanilla from the wood, and become more complex and slightly drier. Vintage dates are more reliable than they used to be, and only the good years are vintaged. Riojas often state on the label the number of years after the date of the vintage that the wine was bottled – 3° ano, 4° ano – and may be drunk immediately. White wines are dry, and a clean, fruity, more 'modern' wine is taking over from the less fresh, more mature style. Whereas the image of a red Rioja seems quite well defined, that of a white Rioja is not. A little rosé is made, best consumed on the spot.

Wine Producing Regions/Spain & Portugal 2

Catalonia

The vines of Catalonia grow in the north-east of Spain, just down the coast and inland from Barcelona. If the Rioja region is known for quality, Catalonia, and more specifically the Penedés region, is known for the variety of its wines. North of Barcelona, the Denominación de Origen Alella produces fine white wine from the Farnacho Blanco, Picpoul, Malvasia and Maccabeo (the same as the Viura in the Rioja), and may either be dry or sweet. From around the port of Sitges comes the sweet, white Malvasia de Sitges, a fortified wine. Farther down the coast, the larger town of Tarragona has given its name to a rich sweet wine from the Garnacho, Maccabeo and Pedro Ximénez grapes, while above Tarragona a powerful dry red wine is made from the Garnacho and Carineña grapes at Priorato.

These wines, however, are surpassed in quality and variety by the wines from the **Penedés** region. First in importance are the sparkling wines made by the *méthode champenoise*, which is distinguished from the *cuve close* process by the addition of the word 'Cava' to the label. These Cavas, especially the Brut Blanc de Blancs, can rival the best sparkling wines from other parts of the world. But perhaps the most innovative wines in Spain, certainly in Catalonia, are being made by the Torrés family. To the traditional white grape varieties of Parellada and Maccabeo, they have added Muscat, Riesling and Gewürztraminer from Alsace, and Chardonnay from Burgundy; alongside the classic reds, Ull de Llebre and Monastrel, they have planted Cabernet Sauvignon, Cabernet Franc and Merlot from Bordeaux and Pinot Noir from Burgundy. By matching these foreign grapes to the soil and climate, and allying ultra-modern methods of vinification to traditional wood-ageing, Torrés is making wines that break out of the Spanish mould. Another good grower in the Penedés, Jean León, has planted Chardonnay and Cabernet Sauvignon grapes.

La Mancha

The area of La Mancha, on the high plateau south of Madrid, produces the largest quantity per hectare in Spain. The wines of Valdepeñas are pleasant table wines, especially the reds. Much of the wine produced in the La Mancha region is used for blending or for distilling into brandy.

Levante

To the east of the La Mancha plateau, extending to the coast from Valencia to Alicante, the vine competes with other types of fruit in this Mediterranean climate. The districts of Valencia, Utiel-Requeña, Cheste, Almansa, Alicante, Jumilla and Yecla all benefit from Denominaciónes de Origen, but are seldom exported as such. The wines, produced mainly from the Monastrel grape, are high in alcohol and cannot rival in quality those from Rioja and Penedés.

Northern Spain

From Navarre, between the Rioja Baja and the Pyrenees, comes some solid red wine from the Garnacho grape, and from around Pamplona some firm but lighter reds and rosés from the Cerasol and Secano varieties. The region of León produces full-bodied reds and *claretes* (rosés), which have much in common with the wines of northern Portugal, while in the north-west corner of the country, Galicia produces rough, young wines, slightly acidic, even *spritzig*, in the Portuguese Vinho Verde style.

Southern Spain

The best known wine is Montilla-Moriles, a Denominación de Origen from south of Córdoba, which produces white wines more akin to sherry than to table wines. The principal grape is the Pedro Ximénes, grown on the same chalky soil as is found in the region of Jerez de la Frontera.

Below The wines of Montilla are fermented in earthenware tinajas *and then matured in a* solera *like those of Jerez.*

Portugal

Portuguese wines, with the exception of port, are not as well known as wines from Spain. Although wines from Portugal are exported all over the world, some 45% of this quantity comprises a handful of internationally known brands of slightly sweet rosé that are certainly better recognized by their brand name than for their origin.

In contrast to Spain and France, where the majority of vines are planted on the plain, Portugal is mainly mountainous, and the vineyards relatively scattered and divided.

Fine wine production is concentrated in the north. The coastal lowland vineyards give way to the terraced vineyards of the Sierras. Here the soil is rocky and schistous, excellent for the vines, but very hard to work. The climate is damp with very hot, dry summers.

Portugal has a system of regional Denominaçãos do Origem, under the control of the Junta Nacional do Vinho in Lisbon. There are already seven demarcated areas: Entre Minho e Douro, Douro/Tras os Montes, Dão, Colares, Carcavelos, Bucelas and Setúbal/Palmela. From these areas come the following wines:

Dão

Dão wines are the finest in Portugal. Vines are planted on hillside terraces in granite soil. The grapes used are Tourigo, Tinta Pinheira (related to the Pinot Noir) and Alvarelhão for the red wine; Arinto, Dona Branca and Barcelos for the white. The latter are straw-coloured and should be drunk young. The red wines have a deep ruby colour from long maceration of very ripe grapes, and a velvety richness on the palate.

Douro

The Douro is better known for its port than for its table wines. Nonetheless, the latter are produced in large quantity in this region situated to the north of Dão and to the west of the Minho. The wines from the heart of the valley are more alcoholic and lower in acidity than those from the borders of the Douro, which are fresher and livelier.

Colares

Colares, in the Sintra region on the Atlantic coast opposite Lisbon, is famous for its vines which are resistant to phylloxera, due to being planted on sand-dunes. Red wines are made from the Ramisco grape, white wines from the Malvasia. They are light, with a refreshing acidity; both improve with age.

Bucelas

Bucelas comes from the valley of the river Trancão, inland and to the north-west of Colares. Only white wine is made from the Arinto grape. It is light and crisp and has a high natural acidity.

Moscatel de Setúbal

Moscatel de Setúbal is a dessert wine made to the south of Lisbon.

Vinhos Verdes

These come from the north-west corner of Portugal, roughly between the Minho and the Douro rivers. Vines are trained high to provide shade for the bunches of grapes. The word *verde* signifies 'green' or young wines, low in alcohol, high in malic and tartaric acids, slightly *pétillant*. Three-quarters of the wine produced is red, the rest white. Both should be drunk young.

Vinhos Rosados

Portugal's *vinhos rosados* have no Denominação do Origem, although their methods of production are controlled. The colour comes from a short maceration of red grapes. They may be dry or sweet, still or sparkling, the most popular style being slightly sparkling and slightly sweet.

Below Springtime in the vineyards of Utiel-Requeña, in the hills west of Valencia. The region produces good red wines from the Monastrel grape and also a light and fragrant rosé.

Wine Producing Regions/Austria, Switzerland & Luxembourg

Austria

Wine-growing in Austria is concentrated in the eastern part of the country, the majority of table wines coming from near the Czechoslovak and Hungarian borders, and from the south, close to the Jugoslav frontier. One of the finest wine-growing regions of the old Austrian ·Empire, Tyrol, is now mainly Italian. Four-fifths of the wine produced is white, most of the remainder being red, with small quantities of rosé and sparkling wines.

The principal grape is the Grüner Veltliner, a variety particular to Austria, resembling a rather less aromatic version of the French Traminer, followed by the Müller-Thurgau, Wälschriesling (Italian Riesling), Rhein Riesling, Gewürztraminer, local versions of Pinot Blanc and Pinot Gris, a little Muscat Ottonel and the indigenous Rotgipfer. Red and rosé wines, almost all locally consumed, come from the Blauburgunder (Pinot Noir), Blauer Portugieser (Merlot) and Gamay.

Vines are planted in four main regions:

Lower Austria, in the north-east, is the most prolific, producing the country's finest white wines from the Rhein Riesling and the dominant Grüner Veltliner, as well as the charming and fruity Gumpoldskirchen from just south of Vienna.

Burgenland, in the south-east, produces some very fine dessert wine from botrytized grapes, and the only good Austrian red wines from the Eisenberg region.

Styria, on the Jugoslav border, produces attractive white wines from the Wälschriesling and the Müller-Thurgau, but in much smaller quantities than the other regions.

Vienna, the capital, would probably be merged with Lower Austria as a wine region were it not for the custom of serving *heurige*, the just fermented wine of the new vintage, direct from the grower's cellars or in the local Weinstuben.

With the exception of the dessert wines, white wines from Austria are generally drier than their counterparts from Germany.

Switzerland

Switzerland, being part French, part German and part Italian, can be expected, as a wine-producing nation, to exhibit characteristics from each of these countries. Vines are planted principally on the foothills of the Alps, around Lakes Geneva and Neuchâtel,

along the valley of the upper Rhône and in the canton of Ticino. French, German and Italian grapes, as well as many local varieties, produce over 200 different wines, two-thirds of them white. Most of the production is consumed domestically. Although there are no really great wines produced in Switzerland, the diversity of vines and the dedication of the growers are reflected in a wide range of deliciously fruity wines of fine overall quality. The major wine-producing cantons are Valais, Vaud, Neuchâtel and Ticino.

Valais This is the most important canton for quality, producing Switzerland's best red wine, Dôle, made from the Pinot Noir or the Gamay, either separately or blended. Dôle has a rich ruby colour, some of the bouquet of a Burgundy and the body of a Côtes-du-Rhône. The dominant white wine is Fendant, made from the Chasselas grape; light and fruity, with low acidity, it should be drunk young and fresh. Other wines of note are Riesling, Johannisberg, Hermitage, the sweet Malvoisie and the very rare Glacier.

Vaud The leading canton for quantity, Vaud produces mainly white wines from the Chasselas. The principal vineyard areas are La Côte, on the northern slopes of Lake Geneva between Nyon and Lausanne, and Lavaux, from Lausanne east to Vevey, where the Dézaley wine combines body with finesse and distinction. From the Chablais region, farther east, come the firm, flinty whites of Yvorne and Aigle.

Neuchâtel From the north-west of Switzerland, along the northern side of Lake Neuchâtel, close to France, the Neuchâtel white wines are crisp and dry, yet although they are made from the Chasselas, they can be rather acid in poor years. These wines are often bottled *sur lie*, and also produced refreshingly *pétillant*. Some fine, light red wine is made from the Pinot Noir.

Italian- and German-speaking Switzerland Ticino, the Italian-speaking canton, produces mainly red *vins de table* from around Lugano and Locarno, the best coming from the Merlot grape. From the German part of Switzerland around Baden come some pleasantly fruity red wines from the Blauburgunder (Pinot Noir) and some everyday whites, mainly from the Müller-Thurgau.

Luxembourg

The wines of Luxembourg are of interest since they are produced along the river Moselle, as it winds its way from France into Germany, where, as the Mosel, it gives its name to some of the world's finest wines. In Luxembourg, as in Alsace, the type of wine is designated by the grape variety. The dominant local grape is the Ebling, which produces light, refreshingly crisp wines, while the Riesling-Sylvaner (Müller-Thurgau, known in Luxembourg as the Rivaner), is heavily planted. Other wines are made from the Pinot Blanc, the softer Auxerrois, the fruity Ruländer or Pinot Gris, the aromatic Traminer and the aristocratic Riesling. Almost all the total production is white, a little of which is made into sparkling wine.

Although Luxembourg wines tend to be overshadowed by those from Alsace and the Mosel, overall quality is high. An internal system of control awards the *appellation* 'Marque Nationale' to wines that have passed a rigorous series of quality controls and tastings. More than half the production comes into this category. Nearly three-quarters of all Luxembourg wine is consumed domestically.

Wine Producing Regions/California 1

The wines of California have made their presence felt on the international wine scene with such extraordinary suddenness that one would be forgiven for imagining that they are a very recent invention. In fact they have a history stretching back over 200 years.

As in many countries, it was the religious orders who first planted vines and made wine. In 1769 the Spanish Franciscans established the first mission in what is now San Diego. During the next 50 years 21 missions were created throughout California, stretching as far north as Sonoma. At each one vineyards were planted and wine produced for the benefit of the travellers who sought shelter for the night. In 1861, a Hungarian nobleman, Agoston Haraszthy, launched an expedition to Europe to bring back cuttings of *Vitis vinifera*. He gathered together over 100,000 different examples. Upon these the vineyards of California are founded.

Many of the famous names of California –

Below Dry Creek Vineyard winery, Healdsburg, Sonoma County, California; founded in 1972 by David Stare, it now produces 30,000 cases a year.

Joseph Schram of Schramsberg, Georges de Latour of Beaulieu and Gustave Niebaum of Inglenook, to name but three – planted their first vines in the latter half of the 19th century and founded wineries which flourish to this day. However, their efforts suffered two serious setbacks; one a natural calamity and the other man-made.

As in Europe, *Vitis vinifera*'s worst enemy, phylloxera, attacked and virtually destroyed vineyards in and around the Napa Valley. Fortunately, it had already been discovered that the native American *Vitis labrusca* root stocks were resistant to the disease. The *Vitis vinifera* was thus grafted onto these roots and the vines were able to recover.

A much more serious setback was the passing of the Eighteenth Amendment to the Constitution prohibiting the sale of alcohol. Between 1919 and 1932 the wine industry came almost to a halt. Vineyards were uprooted or abandoned.

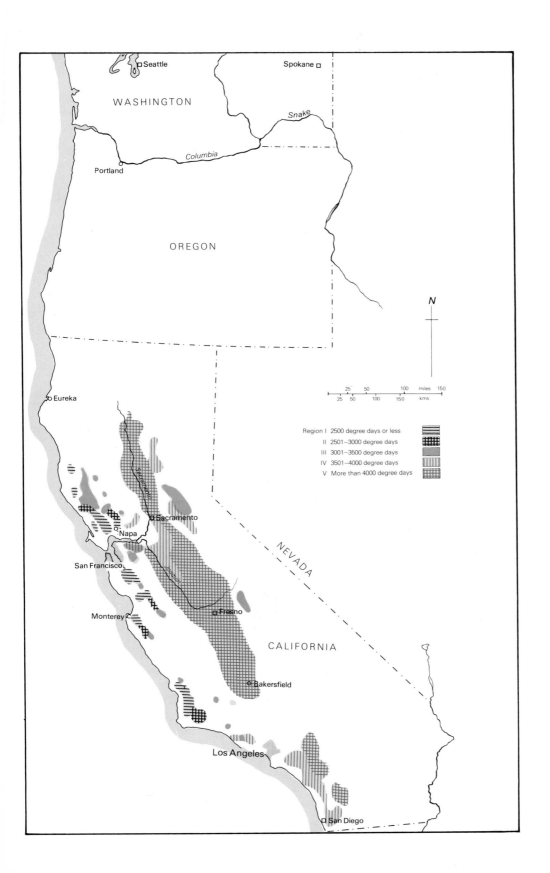

Seattle

Spokane

WASHINGTON

Snake

Columbia

Portland

OREGON

N

25   50   100   miles   150
25   50   100   150   kms

Region I   2500 degree days or less
       II   2501–3000 degree days
       III 3001–3500 degree days
       IV 3501–4000 degree days
       V   More than 4000 degree days

Eureka

Sacramento

Napa

San Francisco

NEVADA

Monterey

Fresno

CALIFORNIA

Bakersfield

Los Angeles

San Diego

Wine Producing Regions/California 2

Above *Quantity vine growing for an ever-expanding American market.*

The American public lost the taste for wine and turned to making their own brews from low-quality grapes, or to patronizing whisky bootleggers. After the repeal of Prohibition, save for the religious orders who had been allowed to continue to make wine for sacramental purposes, few wineries were in a position to take up where they had left off. Stocks of mature wines were tiny and the cocktail craze spread through the country. World War II made life difficult for producer and consumer alike, so it was not until the late 1940s and early 1950s that California wine production was restarted.

Very slowly the American wine drinker began to demand both quantity and quality, and the modern era of production was established. In the early 1960s wineries such as Heitz and Ridge made their first wines and in 1966 Robert Mondavi broke away from the family-owned Charles Krug winery to found

Far right *Barrel cleaning at a Californian winery.*

his now-famous winery in the Napa Valley. California wine had at last come of age and was on its way to making the state one of the most important and certainly the most exciting wine region in the world.

Current production

But what of California in the 1980s? Can the explosion of wineries and interest in wine continue at such a pace? Or will this be the decade of consolidation and retrenchment?

The question of cost has to be taken into consideration. Making high-quality wine anywhere in the world is an expensive business. Modern equipment, French oak barrels, and manpower do not come cheap, particularly in California. The price of grapes tends to increase every year. The capital investment needed to build a winery is thus enormous.

Styles, too, are changing to meet the demands of today's wine drinker. Big is not best any more. A few years ago, if a wine was high in alcohol and had spent many months in the finest French oak, it was thought to be a winner. Now producers are realizing that wine is for drinking, not just for tasting. A lightness and elegance are beginning to show in many of the wines of the 1980s. A better balance between fruit, wood and acid is being achieved. This is not to say that California is trying to produce European-style wines. The different climate will always ensure an individual style, but the finesse which has been missing until now may well be the most important development of the 1980s.

California is a place of change whether in life-styles, habitat or indeed wine-making. The lack of tradition, the youth and enthusiasm of those involved ensure an ever-changing industry; and the 1980s will surely be a crucial and fascinating decade in California's wine history.

Above Repairing barrels.

Wine Producing Regions/California 3

Wine and wine making

The two most important pieces of information on a California wine label are the name of the predominant grape variety, if there is one, and who made it. If the wine is a blend of several varieties it will normally have a brand name, as, for example, Premium White or Valley Red. If it is made with 75% or more from one grape variety it will normally be called by that name. We shall examine the most common grape varieties, starting with the white ones and then moving on to the red.

One of the problems of writing about California wine is that within a few months the scene can change dramatically. A wine maker can leave, a winery acquire new owners, a hitherto unplanted region become a serious vineyard. New wineries appear with mind-boggling rapidity while the sudden influence of European investment is already being felt. The decade of the 1970s was a heady time to be in California wine but the 1980s will show just how far the Golden State can prove itself to the world.

The range of wines, the producers, the grape varieties, grow daily more confusing. The following are currently some of the best Californian wines:

Chardonnay
Chalone, Château St Jean, Stony Hill, Trefethen, Robert Mondavi.
Sauvignon Blanc (Fumé Blanc)
Robert Mondavi, Dry Creek, Sterling Vineyards.
Rieslings and Gewürztraminers
Joseph Phelps, Château St Jean, Firestone Vineyard.
Cabernet Sauvignon
Robert Mondavi, Heitz, Trefethen, Stag's Leap, Ridge Vineyards, Joseph Phelps, Château Montelena, Iron Horse.
Zinfandel
Ridge Vineyards, Château Montelena, Joseph Phelps.
Pinot Noir
Chalone, Firestone Vineyard, Trefethen, Robert Mondavi.
Merlot
Clos du Bois, Stag's Leap, Sterling Vineyards.
Sparkling Wines
Schramsberg, Domaine Chandon.

Inevitably the list is incomplete. The joy of California wine is to experiment with it. To any wine drinker, rich, poor, novice or expert, California offers a plethora of fascinating experience.

The climatic regions

California is made up of a multitude of microclimates. Whereas in Europe great importance is paid to soils, subsoils and their variations within a very small area, in California more attention is given to the climate. The University of California at Davis has divided up the state into five climatic regions. The system is based upon the concept of 'degree days'. These are calculated between April 1 and October 31. One 'degree day' is if the average temperature over a period of 24 hours is one degree over 50°F. Therefore, if the average temperature is for example 70°F, 20 degree days are recorded. 50°F is taken as the starting temperature as below this no plant will grow satisfactorily.

Region 1
0–2500 degree days. The Rhine, Mosel and Champagne regions would fall into this category.
Region 2
2501–3000 degree days. This would be similar to Bordeaux.
Region 3
3001–3500 degree days. This would be similar to northern Italy and the Rhône Valley.
Region 4
3501–4000 degree days. This would be similar to central Spain.
Region 5
In excess of 4001 degree days. This would be similar to North Africa.

Far right Trefethen vineyard, Napa Valley, one of California's most important producers of Chardonnay wines.

The Grapes of California/Red

Alicante Bouschet A grape much loved by home wine makers for its colour and robustness. Now fallen out of fashion for most serious producers, there are still a few examples to be found. Big, heavy and usually high in alcohol on its own, it is also used in the blending of port-style wines.

Barbera Wine makers of Italian origin retain a fondness for this grape. At its best it can make a wine of rich depth and mellow fruitiness, but generally fails to rise to any great heights.

Cabernet Sauvignon The king of red wine grapes and a resounding success in California. The wines produced have been comparable to the great Bordeaux. Any wine maker wanting to make a name for himself will try to produce the finest Cabernet. Deep in colour and flavour, the wines are drinkable earlier than those made in Europe but there is nothing to suggest they will not last.

Cabernet Franc Very rarely found as a wine on its own, it is normally used as a blending grape with Cabernet Sauvignon.

Carignane One of the most widely planted red grapes, it is used mostly as a blending grape. A few examples of it as a simple variety are made but with no marked success.

Charbono A rare grape which is only of interest because Inglenook produce a very decent wine from it. A big, robust – some would say coarse – and tannic wine, it becomes more interesting with age.

Gamay or Napa Gamay The true grape of the Beaujolais, in California the wines seem to lack the freshness and 'gulpability' of their French cousins. Also used to make rosé.

Gamay Beaujolais Confusingly, nothing to do with the Beaujolais grape, but in fact a member of the Pinot Noir family. Somewhat reminiscent of a southern Burgundy, the wines often lack interest but are useful for picnics or barbecues.

Grenache Although used for blending into red wines, as a variety it is more commonly found as a rosé. Almaden make a particularly popular one.

Grignolino Joe Heitz personally waves the banner for this variety. He makes an interesting spicy red wine from it and a rather more successful rosé.

Merlot Some 3000 acres of this grape are planted and several producers are making extremely fine wines from it. It is often used to blend with Cabernet Sauvignon. Certainly a variety with great promise for the future.

Petite Sirah Now established as the same as the Duriff grape of France, it produces dry red wines of robustness, depth and flavour. No great breeding or elegance are discernible, but the wines are honest and drinkable.

Pinot Noir The one grape that has so far defeated even the skills of the California wine makers: examples have been worthy but rather dull. The struggle continues and it is the dream of every winery to produce a great Pinot Noir in commercial quantities.

One or two of the smaller producers have come very close but the field is still wide open. Whether it is the fault of the grape, the climate, the soil or the wine-making is a subject for discussion. Whatever else, it remains a fascinating challenge. Nearly 10,000 acres are planted and it is also used to make sparkling wines.

Ruby Cabernet A cross between Cabernet Sauvignon and Carignane, it is a high-class blending grape, which has proved most successful. Occasionally found on its own, it makes a drinkable low-priced wine of good colour, bouquet and flavour.

Syrah The true grape of the Rhône Valley, very rarely found in California. Joseph Phelps makes a superb example. Spicy on the nose, deep colour, full-bodied, it is a wine to be sought out. It is hoped that the grape will gain in popularity as its excellence becomes more widely appreciated. Not to be confused with the Petite Sirah.

Zinfandel Although often referred to as California's own unique grape, Zinfandel originated in Europe – from which country is a matter of debate, though the odds have recently moved from Hungary to Italy. The latest theory is that it is the same as the Primitivo, but uncertainty still remains.

Zinfandel is produced in a bewildering array of styles. As a light Beaujolais-type wine (this style seems to be dying out), as a medium-bodied claret-style wine, as a big, high alcohol port-style wine (sometimes in the extreme called late harvest), as a rosé wine and as a white wine. It is often as good as the more fashionable reds but half the price.

Wine Producing Regions/California 4

The Napa Valley

The Napa Valley is to California what the Médoc is to Bordeaux. Quite simply, it is the best known and most prestigious wine-making region in California.

Running north-west for about 34 miles, its width varies between 1 and 5 miles. Flanked on either side by mountains, it lies about 50 miles north-east of San Francisco at its most southerly tip. The soil varies in composition but is mostly volcanic in origin.

The climate of the valley also varies and regions 1, 2 and 3 are all registered. The parts farthest away from San Francisco tend to be the hottest, while the southerly parts remain cooler, fanned as they are by the bay breezes. Almost every grape is to be found in the Napa Valley and most do well. In particular, Cabernet Sauvignon and Chardonnay stand out and many of the great Cabernets come from the Napa. Names like Robert Mondavi, Heitz, Mayacamas are among the many famous wineries that make up the 150 or so Napa producers.

Napa wines are invariably good though the area is now too famous to offer many bargains.

Sonoma County

Lying to the west and slightly to the south of the Napa Valley, Sonoma County is made up of three distinct valleys. These are Sonoma, Alexander and Dry Creek. A large array of microclimates means that regions 1, 2 and 3 are registered all over the county. Fog forms an important part of Sonoma's climatic conditions. It rolls off the Bay in the early morning and does not shift until mid-day at the earliest. This maintains a coolness even at the height of summer.

Soils range from clay loam to sandy brown and most are well drained and thus suitable as vineyards. Long felt to be in the shadow of the Napa, Sonoma is now establishing itself as a genuine alternative. Some of the better known wineries include Château St Jean, Jordan and Sebastiani.

Mendocino County

This is the most northern grape-growing area of California and until the late 1960s was not highly regarded for fine wine. During the 1970s a number of premium wineries began to produce wines of quality, even if not perhaps up to Napa or Sonoma standards.

There are three main parts of Mendocino

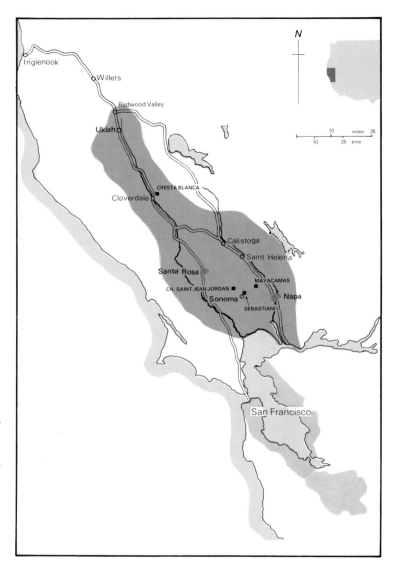

County. The most important, and the largest, is the Ukiah Valley. Ukiah is a charming old town still retaining an atmosphere of the wild west.

The valley is region 3 and such well-known producers as Parducci and Cresta Blanca can be found there.

Another part of Mendocino, also a region 3, is the Redwood Valley. Here the Fetzer Winery dominates the area and produces a wide range of wines of a very acceptable quality. Lastly, there is the least known part called the Anderson Valley. Several wineries have sprung up there. Perhaps the two most interesting are Husch and Edmeades; the climate is region 1.

The Grapes of California/White

Chardonnay Undoubtedly the greatest success of them all. California Chardonnays are nearly always a delight to drink and the best will age well. Like their European cousins, particularly in Burgundy, the best ones are aged in wood to make a rich buttery wine with a lovely golden colour. However, unlike in France, most Chardonnays do not undergo malolactic fermentation, though barrel fermentation, which if anything is on the decrease in Burgundy, is again becoming popular. There are few modern wineries which do not produce Chardonnay. The less expensive ones are usually unwooded, light and fresh, with an apple flavour and green-gold colour. The heavier ones from the small wineries can be big in flavour, complex in style and high in alcohol. The Chardonnay grape is a low-yielder and demands extensive care in the making. California has made its reputation with this grape. There are 20,000 acres planted. It is expensive but usually worth it.

Sauvignon Blanc Also known as Fumé Blanc, this grape variety is used to make a wine of many different styles in California. When blended with Sémillon and aged in oak, it can be a wonderfully rich wine with an elegant and appealingly complex style. On its own it makes a less subtle wine but deliciously fresh and best drunk young. California Sauvignons are quite different from those of the Loire and tend to be made akin to a white Bordeaux. Robert Mondavi, the most famous producer of Fumé Blanc, is now making small quantities of a sweet botrytis Sauvignon. About 10,000 acres of Sauvignon Blanc are planted in California.

Chenin Blanc In 1971 less than 9,000 acres of this grape were planted. Now there are almost 40,000. This is as a result of the great swing towards white wine. Chenin Blanc is a good yielder and can produce a reasonably priced wine with some style and complexity to it. Very often some residual sugar is left in the wine to give more character, and there are few which could be described as dry. Chenin is also used as a blending grape.

Pinot Blanc Although not widely planted, it is responsible for some excellent wines, mainly from the Monterey area. Not a prolific yielder, it is usually fermented dry and when aged in wood can make a wine similar in style to Chardonnay.

White Riesling While this is the correct name, it is widely known in California as Johannisberg Riesling in honour of the famous Schloss Johannisberg of Germany. This traditionally cool-climate grape has adapted in a remarkable way to the warm climate of California. The wines are full, fruity and complex, and quite delicious. They are different from their German counterparts in that they lack the subtlety of a Rheingau, but are mouth-filling and luscious. Dessert-style Rieslings which have been affected by botrytis are among the great sweet wines of the world. Rare as they are, they should be sought out and enjoyed.

Gewürztraminer The traditional spiciness of this grape is less apparent in California versions than, for example, in Alsace. Completely dry Gewürztraminers can be found in California but very often wine makers leave in a touch of residual sugar to give added character to the wine. Some 5000 acres of this early-ripening grape are planted. The wine is best drunk when young and fresh.

French Colombard Something approaching 60,000 acres of this grape are planted in California. It is at its best as a blending grape where its crisp acidity and floral bouquet enhance some of the lesser grapes. On its own it makes a pleasant enough quaffing wine but without any great distinction. It is a high yielder at between 8 to 12 tonnes per acre.

Sémillon Not often seen as a variety on its own, it is widely used to blend with Sauvignon Blanc. In Monterey and Santa Ynez it makes a dry wine of some interest. Sweet versions have so far shown no great distinction.

Emerald Riesling This is one of the better named *vinifera* hybrids produced by U. C. Davis. A cross between White Riesling and Muscadelle, it produces an off-dry wine which is crisp and fruity. Best drunk young and without too much scrutiny. Paul Masson produce a deservedly popular version.

Gray Riesling Known as Chauché Gris in France, it makes a pleasing quaffing wine of no great seriousness. The best examples come from the Livermore Valley.

Wine Producing Regions/California 5

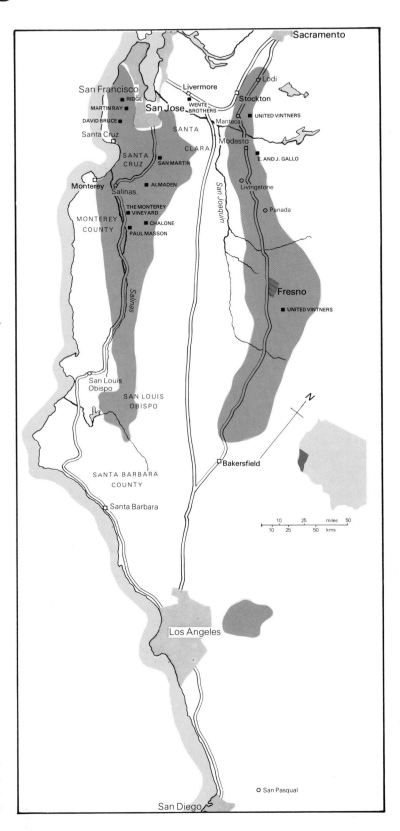

The Central Coast

This is the name of a large area south of San Francisco embracing a number of small regions which are fighting to gain individual recognition. The wineries in these areas generally feel that the term 'Central Coast' denotes the hot central mass of California, not a place from which premium wines come. The region as a whole is very similar climatically to the north coast of California and can, in fact, even be cooler. Some very fine wines come from this area and it is worth a quick examination of the individual regions.

The Livermore Valley, region 3, has been producing grapes for more than 100 years. Its most famous winery, Wente Brothers, was founded in 1883. The white wines deserve particular attention though the reds, too, show signs of promise. The valley's soil is gravelly and well drained and is said to resemble that of the Graves in Bordeaux.

Santa Clara County has been a casualty of urban development. Before World War II there were approximately 60 wineries in this area but they have steadily been forced south by ever encroaching 'civilization'. However, several famous names remain — Almaden and San Martin are two of the largest, while Martin Ray and Mount Eden are smaller but even finer.

The **Santa Cruz Mountains** is a region which is busily trying to establish itself. In terms of area — only about 250 acres and a mere 100,000 cases produced — it might be thought insignificant. However, the quality of the wineries is very special. Ridge Vineyards, one of the finest producers in California is there, as are the David Bruce Winery and Felton-Empire Vineyards, two producers well worth seeking out. The region and its wines maintain a strong identity.

Monterey County may well be the most important part of the Central Coast. It is certainly a most beautiful part of California. The county is the home of the huge Paul Masson winery and of the tiny and remote Chalone Vineyards. Two more opposite producers, in terms of output, could hardly be imagined. Other wineries worth noting are Jekel Vineyards, Mirassou, the Monterey Vineyard and Ventana.

In **San Louis Obispo County**, perhaps the most interesting developments are happening in Edna Valley. The Edna Valley Vineyards lead the way and have produced two successful Chardonnays. Other new wineries are beginning to appear and this is clearly an area to watch. The champagne house of Deutz has bought land here.

Santa Barbara County is the most southerly part of the Central Coast and one of the coolest. It is a region 1, which perhaps explains why Pinot Noir and Riesling seem to do particularly well here. Zaca Mesa and the Firestone Vineyard dominate the area and have produced wines of outstanding quality. All signs are promising for this region, which is already playing a significant part in the development of California viticulture.

The San Joaquin Valley

This is the home of the mass producers. In an area some 300 miles in length, stretching from Sacramento to south of Bakersfield, there are a mere 40 wineries; but from these comes almost 80% of California's wine.

More than half the state's grapes are grown here and the climate ranges from region 3 to about region 5 around Bakersfield.

The most famous producer and probably the largest in the world is the E. & J. Gallo Winery. Here is the great American dream come true: two brothers who, after Prohibition and with limited knowledge about wine, set themselves up as wine makers. They brought to the American consumer wines at irresistibly low prices. In terms of range and quality they have been successful at almost every level. Their production is approaching 50 million cases of wine a year; almost all of it is extremely drinkable and offers excellent value for money.

Other large producers to be found in this part of California include United Vintners, Guild and the Franzia Brothers Winery, this last owned by the Coca-Cola Company of New York.

North of San Diego is the San Pasqual Valley containing three wineries. The most interesting is San Pasqual. Their Chenin Blanc and Fumé Blanc are respectable, while their Gamay is above the average California version.

The southernmost end of California is not the ideal place for grape-growing, as in general the climate is too hot. However, the wineries which have discovered the cooler microclimates are worth noting.

South of Los Angeles

In 1769, a Bordelais by the appropriate name of Jean Louis Vignes planted a vineyard on

what is now the Los Angeles main rail station. For a century this part of California remained the most important grape-growing region and it was not until towards the end of the 19th century that Northern California took over as the dominant wine-making area.

Today pollution and urbanization have all but put an end to wine production in Los Angeles County. The one remaining winery, San Antonio, has been designated as a Cultural Historical Monument.

Farther south, however, there are a few small wineries producing interesting wines. The Callaway Vineyard, completed in 1974, is situated near Temecula. It caused a stir with one of its first releases, a botrytized Chenin Blanc, called Sweet Nancy. Other wines have included a Zinfandel made by carbonic maceration and a port made in the traditional Portuguese way.

Above Massive investment has been made in modern plant for the Californian vineyards: here, a steel vat is undergoing cleaning.

Wine Producing Regions/Rest of United States

Left *Vine growing is extensive in other parts of the United States, besides California, and vineyards in Oregon and Washington now produce wines of appreciable quality.*

The Pacific North-West

California is so far out in front in the race to make fine American wines that other states tend to be forgotten. Washington and Oregon are two that deserve a closer look.

The first *vinifera* grapes were planted in 1950 in a part of eastern Washington called the Yakima Valley. This valley is 120 miles long and runs eastwards along the Yakima River. Three wineries of note are now established in this region with new ones springing up each year.

Château Ste Michelle is the largest and best known. Its first wines were made in 1967 under the guidance of André Tchelistcheff and although not entirely successful showed enough promise to ensure continual production. New wines of all styles are produced, though possibly the white wines have been of a higher quality than the reds. Particularly interesting are the Sémillons and sweet Rieslings. Associated Vintners have the distinction of having an English Master of Wine as their wine maker. David Lake is producing wines of great promise although the quantity remains small. His Chardonnay and Gewürztraminer are well worth seeking out.

Another producer of interest is Preston Wine Cellars. Now the second largest winery

Above High technology: new steel vats in a New York State winery.

in Washington State, it is producing the usual grape varieties. Perhaps not quite up to the standards of the previous two firms, Preston Wines certainly has a future.

Oregon's grape-growing history goes back to the 19th century, though Prohibition put an end to wine production until the 1960s.

Most of the wineries today are situated at the northern end of the Williamette Valley, near Portland. Here the climate is milder than in the rest of the state, and as most of the vineyards are planted on the hillsides the problem of frost is minimized.

Two of the most interesting wineries are the Eyrie Vineyards and the Tualatin Vineyards, both producing most respectable wines. Of the other 30 or so Oregon wineries, it is still too early to make a judgment, though there seems no reason why they should not produce wines to match America's finest.

New York State

The wines of New York State have until recently fallen below what many wine enthusiasts consider acceptable standards of quality. The principal reason is that more than two-thirds of the wines have been made from *Vitis labrusca* vines. Chardonnay and Riesling have now been quite widely planted

and have produced wines of decent quality.

Most of the better producers are situated around the Finger Lakes. A notable exception is Benmarl. Founded in 1971 by Mark Miller, the wines have shown remarkable complexity and character. Both *labrusca* and *vinifera* are planted and are treated with Californian care and skill.

Another New York State producer, at the other end of the scale, is the Taylor Wine Company, which is the largest American winery outside California. Owned by the Coca-Cola Company of Atlanta, it is most noted for its Great Western Champagne. This was a wine that was described in the 19th century as the great champagne of the western world. Great Western is now seen all over the United States.

The Rest of the United States

A number of other states are nowadays engaged with varying success in making wine. Given the depth of skill and enthusiasm which abounds in America, the wine drinker must remain alert to developments from all quarters. California reigns supreme but the challenge is on and comes from parts of America not formerly associated with wine.

Wine Producing Regions/Australia & New Zealand

Australia has been a wine-making country for more than 150 years and is now recognized as the most important producer in the Southern Hemisphere.

In the 19th century much of the wine made was of the fortified variety. Hefty 'ports' and 'sherries' found favour not only with the immigrant population but also with the people of Victorian England who were naturally well disposed towards a product of the Empire. Australia had an export boom.

It was the early settlers, although they were principally farmers, who established the first vineyards. The British settled north of Sydney and planted grapes in the rich soil of the Hunter Valley, while it was left to the Germans to populate the Barossa Valley just outside Adelaide.

Since that time these two valleys have been the backbone of the Australian wine industry. The Hunter Valley is famous for its big earthy red wines made from the Shiraz grape, known also as Syrah or Hermitage. These wines have a distinctive 'barn-yard' bouquet to them and the best benefit enormously from bottle maturation.

Curiously enough, however, it is the classic Hunter white wines which benefit most from bottle-age. These wines are made from the Sémillon grape which locally is also referred to as Hunter Riesling. As in all parts of Australia, the harvest takes place in February/March and Hunter Sémillons can be on the dull side and rather flat when very young. But after five or six years the flavours begin to develop and nowhere in the world is there a wine to match the character and taste of a Hunter Sémillon. The Rothbury Estate is but one Hunter Valley winery specializing in this unique style of wine.

Also planted in the Hunter Valley are Cabernet Sauvignon, Pinot Noir, Chardonnay and Traminer. Tyrrell's Vineyards are one of the most successful makers of Chardonnay and Pinot Noir.

In South Australia many of the larger wineries are to be found in the Barossa Valley. Here, by tradition, a large quantity of fortified wines are produced. However, in keeping with the swing towards lighter wines, most of the wineries now concentrate their efforts on the production of table wines. Shiraz is still the principal grape for the reds, while Rhine Riesling and Clare Riesling make most of the whites. Among the many famous producers of the Barossa Valley are Kaiser Stuhl, Orlando, Seppelt, Yalumba and Penfold's.

Other areas to note include Coonawarra in South Australia, often referred to as the

'Médoc' of Australia owing to the fine Cabernet Sauvignons made there, Milawa in Victoria, where the much respected Brown Bros wines come from, and Western Australia, in the shape of Swan Valley and Margaret River region. Here there are a mass of small wineries opening up every year. Among the successfully established ones are Houghton, Vasse Felix and Sandalford.

Many parts of Australia are now producing wine – there are even vineyards around Alice Springs, one of the hottest parts of the country – including also the island of Tasmania. More Chardonnay and Cabernet Sauvignon are being planted and the whole industry is clearly getting to grips with modern wine-making techniques and the demands of modern wine drinkers.

Australia is set to join California as a producer to rival the best of Europe. It has already introduced the world to the bag-in-the-box phenomenon – some 40% of all Australian wine is sold in this form – and is now ready to show off its high-quality varieties. It is quite possible that Australian wine will make more impact than any other country on the world wine scene in the 1980s.

New Zealand

Even by the standards of the New World, the history of serious wine-making in New Zealand is very short. For although the records show that grapes were planted in 1819 by the Reverend Samuel Marsden at Keri Keri, and wine was first made in 1840 by James Busby (now recognized as the father of the country's wine industry), real wine production was not started until the early 1970s.

In 1974 the vineyard area was increased by 75%, mainly around Blenheim at the north end of South Island and near Gisborne in the western part of North Island. Müller-Thurgau is the most widely planted white grape though there are increasing amounts of Chardonnay, Pinot Gris, Chenin Blanc and Gewürztraminer. Cabernet Sauvignon is also commonly found and makes a pleasant medium-bodied wine. Pinotage is grown with some success, as are Pinot Meunier and Pinot Noir.

There are now over 400 vineyards in New Zealand which produce over 30,000 tonnes of grapes. The best known producers are Montana Wines, McWilliams Wines and Cooks.

The wines of these companies and others are improving all the time, but there is still some way to go. Perhaps the decade of the 1990s will see the New Zealand wine industry come of age.

Below The history of wine-making in New Zealand is very short, but the application of intensive farming methods has brought a rapid increase in production: protective spraying of the vines at the Te Kauwhata Vineyards.

Wine Producing Regions/South America

The continent of South America is one of the world's major wine-producing areas. The wines come from four countries: Argentina, Chile, Brazil and Uruguay (in order of volume), and in terms of bulk the first two rank in the top ten throughout the world. Most South American wine is consumed domestically but as quality continues to improve, more and more is exported.

Argentina

Argentina is at present the fifth largest wine-producing nation in the world. Almost three-quarters of this very considerable quantity is made in the province of Mendoza, where the vines grow in near-desert country on the Andes plain. Most of the rest comes from the province of San Juan, to the north, from grapes grown in similar circumstances. With a maximum of 10 inches of rainfall annually, irrigation is essential, and this is provided by a system of canals complemented by deep water holes. Since Argentina has virtually no laws of *appellation*, the names on the bottles originally bore little relationship to the actual taste of the wine. However, with the planting of French and other European grapes, the varietal name nowadays appears on the label, instead of 'Chablis', 'Champagne' or 'Margaux'. There are now more acres under European vines than under the indigenous Criolla grape. Sémillon, Chardonnay and Riesling are used for white wine, while for red wine the principal grape is the Malbec from Bordeaux, alongside Cabernet Sauvignon, Merlot and Pinot Noir, the Tempranillo from Spain and the Barbera from Italy. The style of Argentinian wine is decidedly more 'modern'; the whites, less markedly oxidized, are becoming fresh and fruity, while the full-bodied reds benefit from the sun without becoming enslaved to it.

Chile

Chile is the tenth biggest wine-producer in the world; and, in contrast to Argentina, its wine is subject to strict government controls. Perhaps the unique characteristic of Chilean wine is that the vines have never been attacked by phylloxera. The high Andes mountains on the border to Argentina, the arid Atacama Desert to the north and the cold Humboldt current along the Pacific coast have combined to keep the insect pest out of the country.

Chile has three main vineyard areas: north,

Above Vineyards near Cafayate, Salta Province, northern Argentina.

central and south. The northern region, from the Atacama Desert to 100 miles north of Valparaiso, produces mostly fortified wines from the Muscat grape. The climate of the Central Valley zone, with cool breezes from the Pacific, has much in common with Northern California, but although the predominant varieties here are from Bordeaux, Burgundy and Germany, the red wine perhaps has more in common with a Rioja than a Médoc, because of the heat. The southern region is notable mainly for table wine from the local Pais grape, although some of the European varieties grown in the Central Valley are being introduced here as well.

Chile, without doubt, produces the finest wines in South America.

Brazil

Wine is made in the southern tip of Brazil, most of it from hybrid grapes that do well in the humid climate. Whereas there is a French influence in Chile, the keynote in Brazil is Italian, with the Barbera producing fruity red wines and the Trebbiano, Moscato and Malvasia dominating the *vinifera* whites. The overall quality, however, is not up to that of Chile or Argentina.

Uruguay

The wines of Uruguay resemble those of Brazil. American hybrids are planted to resist the climate, but experiments are being made with *vinifera* grapes, with some good results from the Cabernet Sauvignon.

South Africa

South Africa has one of the oldest histories of wine-growing in the world. Vines were first planted in the middle of the 17th century in the south-west of Cape Province by the Dutch settlers. By the early part of the 18th century, the famous Constantia – a rich, dessert wine to rival Madeira and Tokay – had already been exported to Europe, and the French Huguenot settlers were expanding the vineyards. The possession of the Cape from 1805 by the British caused a flourishing trade to develop with Great Britain, aided by preferential tariffs. The removal of these tariffs, however, combined with the ravages of phylloxera, led to the collapse of the wine industry at the end of the century. Reconstruction came with the formation, in 1918, of the KWV (Co-operative Wine Growers' Association of South Africa), and in 1931 of the SAWFA (South African Wine Farmers' Association), which began to ensure standards of quality. In 1972 the government introduced control for 'Wines of Origin', designating 14 regional areas and imposing a government seal of identification certifying the origin, the vintage and the grape variety. Control also extended to the terms 'Superior', for which the wine must consist 100% of the named variety, and the 'Estate', which is limited to properties bottling their own wine.

The wines of South Africa come from two major regions: the Coastal Plain, comprising Constantia, Durbanville, Malmesbury, Stellenbosch and Paarl; and, to the east, the Klein Karoo, embracing Robertson, Worcester and Tulbagh. The soil in the plain is sandstone with granite elements, in the Klein Karoo it is more schistous. The climate is very Mediterranean, mild and warm, with twice as much rainfall in the coastal areas than inland.

Grape varieties are mainly European, with local grafting. The major red grape is the Cinsault from the southern Rhône, known here as the Hermitage, which makes an even finer wine under the name of Pinotage, when it is crossed with the Pinot Noir. The Pinot Noir is planted on its own, as is the Shiraz, a variation of the Syrah, the Merlot and the Cabernet Sauvignon. The general style is for full, fruity wines with great warmth and sometimes too much alcohol. The most 'typical' are the Pinotage wines, but some people think the finest comes from the Cabernet Sauvignon-Merlot blends from the Stellenbosch region. For white wine, the most popular grape is the Chenin Blanc, called the Steen, which makes soft, fruity wines and rare botrytized wines like the Nederburg Edelkeur. The Sémillon, Clairette and Ugni Blanc all produce attractive wines rather low in acidity, while the Riesling is very successful in the German style, especially at Nederburg. Also planted is the Palomino, from Andalusia, and – for rich dessert wines – the Muscat d'Alexandrie.

The largest wine-producing area in the country is Stellenbosch, which also makes the finest wines of South Africa. Paarl, second only to Stellenbosch, is known for the well-made wines of the KWV, as well as for the very high quality sherry-style wines, certainly the finest outside Spain, and some very successful ruby, tawny and vintage 'ports'. Where irrigation is necessary, in the Klein Karoo, a large amount of table wine is made.

Below Vines growing on a Cape Dutch homestead near Franschhoek.

3

ADVANCED COURSE

The purpose of the Advanced Course is to put into practice what we have seen in theory. It is all very well to discuss soil, climate, grape varieties, methods of vinification, vintage years and so on; but to describe the actual taste of a wine is something different, and there is no substitute for the direct *verre en main* approach. Indeed, the whole purpose of a wine-tasting course at the Académie du Vin is to let the wines themselves illustrate (or if need be, disprove) the points we wish to make. Although we seldom taste more than eight wines per session, the number of wines in these tastings has been increased to give a wider spread. Because comparison is probably the most important element in wine-tasting, we have attempted to describe the wines themselves, to see how they correspond to their *appellation* or style, and to compare them with wines tasted in the same group. We have also cross-referenced back to the text in Courses 1 and 2, and to other tastings of comparable wines in the Advanced Course.

We have already discussed the actual method of wine-tasting and what points to look for. (The standard work on the subject is Michael Broadbent's *Wine Tasting*, first published in 1968, which has been expanded

and reprinted many times. There are many other excellent books on wine-tasting, listed in the Bibliography. Perhaps the most technical and impressive from France is Professeur Emile Peynaud's *Le goût du vin*, but Broadbent's book remains the essential reading on the subject.) There is no need to repeat this information. Instead we shall now concentrate on the taste of the wines themselves.

The Advanced Course is divided into four sections:

1. Basic wine tasting

We treat wines as ranging from dry to sweet, light to heavy, and our choice is confined to French wines, since the definition of a type of wine as 'dry' or 'medium dry' is in itself controversial and sufficiently subjective when dealing with the wines of a single country, let alone the wines of the world. While some wines are unquestionably dry, sweet, light or heavy, most wines that are made to be drunk with food fit into a middle category. At the same time, the acidity and weight of a wine is perceived differently by different people. A Frenchman from Paris, for example, will find a Muscadet less dry than his counterpart in

Nice; and the latter, in turn, would judge a Châteauneuf-du-Pape to be fruity and pleasant whereas the Parisian tends to regard it as heavy and sleep-inducing. We have chosen wines of all categories, noting variations in style. The three white wine tastings and the three red wine tastings should be studied independently.

2. Different grape varieties

This section focuses on the major grape varieties planted throughout the world, and once again the bias is towards France, since, with the exception of Riesling, the internationally planted varieties tend to be French in origin. The purpose is to show how the same grape performs in different soils, climates and with different styles of wine-making. The characteristic tastes of the grape varieties themselves tend to be strongly marked in young wines. (This is distinct from the overall 'grapy' taste often possessed by young wines.) As a wine ages, the grape loses its dominance as secondary and tertiary aromas and flavours appear, yet the style can still be traced to the variety from which it is made. French wines tend to be judged more from their *appellations* (Meursault, Hermitage), than from their grape varieties (Chardonnay, Syrah), because both are interrelated. Such geographical *appellations* do not exist in the case of grapes planted outside France, so that the wines have to be regarded more as varietal than regional types.

3. The influence of vintage and appellation

In these four tastings, we have two 'vertical' tastings (a single Château or Domaine wine through a series of vintages), and two 'horizontal' tastings (a series of different *appellations* from the same region in the same year). The purpose in the vertical tastings is to isolate the vintage factor, everything being constant except the climatic conditions; and in the horizontal tastings to show up the influence of soil, microclimate, grape selection and vinification through comparable wines in a single year. Once again, we have used only French wines, and have concentrated on Burgundy and Bordeaux, the two most important and homogeneous wine regions. The section concludes with a comparative tasting of fortified wines.

4. The colour of wine

It is easier to describe colour than to describe smell or taste. Wines never, with the exception of Muscat, smell of grapes: when young, they have floral or fruity aromas, which develop into a bouquet of herbs, spices and types of wood – an infinite range of sensations. The taste of a wine follows the same pattern. Wines conform to certain styles (a Médoc is austere, an Alsace fruity, for example), and these depend on many factors, notably where the wine is made and what it is made from. But although the style may be easy to recognize, the taste is hard to describe. Even so, it is instructive to look at different wines from different areas, grapes and vintages, to study the variations in colour and to know why they occur. The series of robes reproduced on pages 180–185 are graded in tone from light to full, young or mature.

We have attempted to reproduce in writing actual tastings at the Académie du Vin. If the tasting notes seem fanciful or long-winded, it is only because we have tried to describe the wines as fully as possible.

Tasting/Very Dry Whites

In this tasting we look at wines that are relatively light in body and relatively high in acidity. Dryness should not, however, be equated with acidity. All wines have acidity, even the very sweetest, such as Château d'Yquem. What we are considering here is the total absence of sweetness. If the acidity is pronounced, it should be a crisp, mouth-watering acidity, in harmony with the wine's fruit and character. A wine that has too much acidity either comes from unripe grapes or from poor vinification.

The majority of very dry white wines are young as well as light. This is because wines appear to lose acidity with age. In fact, acidity remains constant, the wine either gaining in body and fruit, or losing its youthful freshness, both factors combining to make the wine appear less tart. Some of the wines for this tasting are made to be drunk very young, some may be drunk or kept, according to taste, while others are included simply because they *are* very young.

	APPEARANCE	BOUQUET	PALATE	COMMENTS

Gros Plant du Pays Nantais 1981 Léon Boullault — Loire-Atlantique/*Gros Plant*

APPEARANCE	BOUQUET	PALATE	COMMENTS
Very pale clear yellow, almost white.	Dry, distinctive tangy bouquet, rather seaweedy-iodine. Clean and fresh.	Straightforward, very dry, even green, austere yet agreeable. Perfect with shellfish.	A relatively minor wine, but perfectly in character: precise, uncomplicated. Difficult to imagine a wine more dry.

Muscadet de Sèvre et Maine 1981 *sur lie* Léon Boullault — Loire-Atlantique/*Melon de Bourgogne, known as Muscadet*

APPEARANCE	BOUQUET	PALATE	COMMENTS
Pale, white gold, with green tinge.	Fruity, floral, slightly musky, racy.	Excellent clean, fruity attack, good acidity, pleasant aftertaste of green apples. Fine, well balanced.	More fruit and complexity than the Gros Plant. Bone dry, but less austere. Lovely wine from a good grower.

Apremont NV Vin de Savoie Boniface et Fils — Savoie/*Aligoté, Roussette and Jacquère*

APPEARANCE	BOUQUET	PALATE	COMMENTS
Very pale, hardly a touch of yellow.	Pretty, floral bouquet, slightly smoky, angelica.	Quite round in the mouth, floral, opens up very well helped by a little CO_2.	Very attractive wine, less dry than the first two. Pleasant *goût de terroir*. Drink young.

Coteaux Champenois (Blanc de Blancs) NV R. & L. Legras — Champagne/*Chardonnay*

APPEARANCE	BOUQUET	PALATE	COMMENTS
Clear, pale yellow, very fresh looking.	Very fine, racy bouquet, complex, typically flinty Chardonnay from a chalky soil plus yeasty overtones.	Less attractive, slightly rough taste. Fruity, but finishes tart with high acidity. Difficult to drink a lot.	Probably some *vin de presse* and high malic acid gives a rough finish. Should have more finesse.

Pouilly-Fumé 1981 J. C. Dagueneau — Loire/Centre/*Sauvignon*

APPEARANCE	BOUQUET	PALATE	COMMENTS
Pale, yellow gold. Fuller than the first four, richer looking and more weight.	Fruity, spicy bouquet, mint, blackcurrants, redcurrants, finishes a little vegetal.	Clean, aggressive Sauvignon taste, more discreet than on the nose, some finesse, dry finish.	Not as elegant as expected, although with no faults. A Sancerre would have been fruitier.

Ch. Reynon 1982 Bordeaux — Bordeaux/Entre-Deux-Mers/*Sémillon and Sauvignon*

APPEARANCE	BOUQUET	PALATE	COMMENTS
Pale, crisp clean yellow, with a very attractive 'whiteness' about it.	Grapy, elegant, not too assertive, pure.	Some body, crisp slightly salty tanginess. Lovely fruity finish, still a little hard.	Very well made wine, balancing fruit, distinction and class. A classic example of the 'new style' Bordeaux white wines.

APPEARANCE	BOUQUET	PALATE	COMMENTS

Ch. Rougemont 1981   Graves
Bordeaux/Graves/Sémillon and Sauvignon

Pale yellow, clean and fresh.	Rather elusive bouquet, clean, faintly herbaceous.	Good attack, herbaceous, floral; jasmine, fresh almonds, very fine, complex, finishes dry but not acid.	More complex and interesting than the Pouilly-Fumé (100% Sauvignon). Will age well. Excellent example of a minor Graves.

Crozes-Hermitage 1981   Paul Jaboulet Aîné
Northern Rhône/Roussanne and Marsanne

Lovely clean, very pale yellow.	Delicate, attractive floral bouquet, honeysuckle.	Quite full in the mouth, fruity, honeysuckle. Finishes very dry, even rather austere.	Very well made, the absence of a malolactic fermentation leaves it *very* dry after its delicate floral bouquet.

Bourgogne-Aligoté 1979   J.-F. Coche-Dury, Meursault
Burgundy/Côte de Beaune/Aligoté

Pale straw-yellow with slight green tints. Quite full looking.	Quite complex, fruity, hazelnutty bouquet, very attractive.	Classy, slightly lemony attack, excellent acidity and good body, fruity flavour. Finishes slightly tart.	A bigger Aligoté than some (due to the Meursault *terroir* and possibly Meursault casks), excellent example.

Vouvray 1981 'sec'   Le Haut Lieu, Huet
Loire/Touraine/Chenin Blanc

Very striking, clean pale yellow. Really lovely to look at.	Explosive floral bouquet: roses, jasmine, honeysuckle, lemon. Complex and lingering.	Young, appley, slightly tart attack, more honeyed in the middle and excellent follow-through. Very young.	Perfect example of a young Vouvray (100% Chenin Blanc) from a good year. Will age perfectly, allowing the acidity to soften and the fruit to develop.

Riesling 1981   'Schlossberg'   Domaine Weinbach
Alsace/Riesling

Brilliant, pale yellow.	Very sprightly primary fruit aroma: lemon, grapefruit.	Good attack with clean fruity acidity. Explosive grapiness. Fine and elegant.	A *grand vin* that is nowhere near at its best. Like the Vouvray, it will become more dramatic, fuller and less noticeably dry as it ages.

Mâcon-Villages 1981   Coupe Pérraton   Georges Duboeuf
Burgundy/Mâconnais/ Chardonnay

Lovely clean pale yellow with a touch of gold. Quite a full wine.	Herbaceous Chardonnay, almost exotic-fruit aromas.	Exciting taste, fruity, but lean and full of 'zip'. Lots of style.	Fine example of Mâcon Blanc, clean, elegant, a perfect minor wine. At its best after one year, but will last.

Chablis 1981   1er Cru Fourchaume   Cave La Chablisienne
Burgundy/Chablis/ Chardonnay

Clean, fresh colour, pale yellow with greenish tints.	Pretty, subtle bouquet, slightly toasty, angelica, crisp, quite light.	Well structured, fruity, flinty flavour. Lively, good length and clean finish.	Elegant wine, a 'modern' Chablis that has not seen any wood. Very well made and will improve.

Puligny-Montrachet 1980   Domaine Leflaive
Burgundy/Côte de Beaune/Chardonnay

Clean, lively pale-yellow gold.	Lovely floral bouquet, eglantine. A touch of wood, great finesse.	Well balanced, still young but already very attractive. Finishes well, but rather abruptly.	A well-made Puligny-Villages from a light year. Will drink well for 2–3 years, but will always lack a little 'stuffing'.

Tasting/Dry Whites

This tasting category covers the vast majority of white wines made in France. They have no residual sugar after the fermentation is finished, and are therefore dry. We have chosen fuller bodied, more complex wines for this tasting both to point out the different styles of fine dry white wine in France, and also to show the influence of vintage years, vinification and ageing.

If we have been more critical in the commentaries in this tasting than in the previous one, it is because these wines have a greater potential character than very light dry white wines. Most of these dry whites are drinkable young, right after bottling, but it is not then that they are at their best. The extra levels of alcohol, fruit sugar, acidity and extract need time to develop their inherent style and character. When developed, they are the perfect accompaniment to food, often transcending the meal.

APPEARANCE	BOUQUET	PALATE	COMMENTS
Arbois 1980 Rolet Père et Fils			Jura/Arbois/*Savagnin-Chardonnay*
Clean straw-yellow, but not rich-looking like a Sauternes	Nutty, slightly oxidized bouquet, special sherry-like aromas.	Aromatic, nutty flavour, fills the mouth, lots of structure, almost tannic, finishes with a taste of fresh walnuts, bone-dry.	Classic example from the Jura, with the particularly oxidized character, but not quite a *vin jaune*. Already 'aged' and will last well.
Ch. de Fieuzal 1981 Graves			Bordeaux/Graves/*Sauvignon and Sémillon*
Very pale straw yellow, looks quite rich.	Aromatic, spicy on the nose, wild flowers, acacia, slightly herbaceous.	Some dryness in attack, owing to wood ageing. Flavours still all in the front of the mouth. Dry finish. Needs a year to open out.	A fine white Graves from a *cru classé* château. More complex than Ch. Rougemont (page 143), but not quite in the class of the finest white Graves, like Domaine de Chevalier or La Ville Haut Brion.
'R' de Ch. Rieussec 1981 Bordeaux Supérieur			Bordeaux/Sauternes/ *Sémillon, Sauvignon and Muscadelle*
Pale yellow, fresh looking, but with more weight and glycerine than the colour alone shows.	Faintly honeyed, floral bouquet, hint of linden (scent of a lime tree). Very pretty.	Very pretty flavour, softer than Ch. de Fieuzal, but good acidity, slight saltiness, and just starting to be ready. The softness of the Sémillon with early picked acidity.	A successful example of a dry wine made in Sauternes, the best known being the much richer 'Y' from Ch. d'Yquem. Will blossom with age and change character.
Pouilly-Fuissé 1981 Domaine de l'Arillière			Burgundy/Mâconnais/*Chardonnay*
Lovely pale yellow-gold, quite full, richer than the Chablis Fourchaume 1981 (page 143).	Buttery, slightly nutty aromas. Still a little SO$_2$.	Fleshy and full in the mouth. Slight hardness in the finish from the SO$_2$, and needs 2 years to show at its best.	This is the second wine from Château Fuissé, made from the younger vines. Even so, a Pouilly-Fuissé is bigger, and needs longer to come round than a Mâcon Blanc.
Hermitage 1980 J.-L. Grippat			Northern Rhône/*Marsanne and Roussanne*
Lovely clean pale gold, whiter than the Pouilly-Fuissé, but quite *gras*.	Full, unctuous bouquet, floral, round, sensual, complex, peaches, good combination of acidity and richness.	Lighter on the palate, excellent fruit, slightly musty-vervain overtones. Well balanced body and finesse, good finish, perfect now.	A lovely wine from a lightish year. Less aromatic than the 1979 from Guigal but much finer than the Crozes 1981 (page 143).
Pinot Auxerrois 1979 'Hengst' Josmeyer			Alsace/*Pinot Blanc and Auxerrois*
Lovely medium pale greeny gold.	Aromatic, slight Sauvignon bouquet, good lemony acidity to balance the fruit.	Fruity, aromatic, fairly full bodied, could be fruitier and more elegant.	Classic Alsace from a good vineyard. A little too heavy for an aperitif, and lacks the style of the Riesling grape.

APPEARANCE	BOUQUET	PALATE	COMMENTS

Châteauneuf-du-Pape 1980   Château de Beaucastel

Southern Rhône/ *Roussanne and Grenache Blanc*

Medium pale yellow with slight greeny tinges, quite a lot of weight.	Intense aromas of crystallized fruits, burnt white sugar or caramel.	Full on the palate, suave, smooth, finishes clearly with good acidity after the weightiness of the alcohol. A 'sunny' wine.	Quite a rarity (only 1% of the *appellation*). This is mostly drunk young, but develops interesting flavours if kept.

Vouvray Sec 1978   Clos Baudoin   Prince Poniatowski

Loire/Touraine/ *Chenin Blanc*

Very fine yellow-gold, quite *gras* and with some age.	Distinguished honeyed bouquet, followed by rather tart back-up, interestingly 'musky'.	Good balance between lemony Chenin Blanc acidity and fruit. Still young, even rather aggressive. Needs food to be at its best.	Fine dry Vouvray (no residual sugar) from a very good year. Lost some of the 'zing' of a young wine.

Chablis 1979   Grand Cru 'Les Clos'   René Dauvissat

Burgundy/Chablis/*Chardonnay*

Pale yellow gold, firm clean colour.	Quite intense nutty, almonds bouquet, becoming complex.	More evolved on the palate, serious wine, steely edge, acidity in finish from wood ageing. Typical, perhaps a little hollow.	A well made Grand Cru Chablis from one of the best growers. The slight disappointment and lack of grandeur come from a year of overproduction.

Puligny-Montrachet 1979   1er Cru Clavoillon   Domaine Leflaive

Burgundy/ Côte de Beaune/*Chardonnay*

Very pale yellow, slight greenish tints, pale for the year, elegant aspect.	Light, elegant bouquet, very little wood, floral (eglantine). Still rather shut in.	Light and lively on the palate, flowery, fresh almonds, a little reticent but has an elegant finish.	Potentially a much better wine than the Puligny-Montrachet 1980 (page 143), but needs another year.

Corton-Charlemagne 1979   Bonneau de Martray

Burgundy/Côte de Beaune/ *Chardonnay*

Fullish yellow, slight golden edge, already a very big wine.	Rich almond-essence, nutty bouquet. Not very open yet, but will be very intense. Very promising, great class.	Tough, sinewy, complex flavour mixed with new wood. High natural acidity, great fruit and length waiting to penetrate a firm exterior.	Great Corton-Charlemagne, can rival a Montrachet in body and depth. This very fine copy-book wine needs at least 3 years.

Meursault 1978   Clos de la Barre   Comte Lafon

Burgundy/Côte de Beaune/ *Chardonnay*

Pale straw yellow, lovely colour, young for a 1978. Quite *gras*.	Rich, full bouquet with honey and peaches mixing with new oak.	Rich, suave on palate with great depth of fruit, firm abrupt finish left by wood ageing. Great style, complexity and length. Needs 3 years.	One of the finest examples of the Meursault style: rich, full but clean and complex. Vinification in small oak and wood ageing enhance the basic character.

Chassagne-Montrachet 1978   1er Cru 'Morgeot'   Delagrange-Bachelet

Burgundy/ Côte de Beaune/*Chardonnay*

Quite mature greeny-gold colour. Big wine, looks more *gras* than the Meursault.	Intense nutty, buttery bouquet, still youthful, complex, suave, good back-up of acidity.	Big rich flavour, but elegant texture and fine edge of acidity. Serious wine, complete contrast to the Puligny, which is elegant but light. Can be drunk, but should be kept.	Very different to the Meursault, equally fine. M. Delagrange re-acidified his wines in 1976 and 1978 (legally) to keep a firm backbone and let them mature to their best.

Tasting/Medium Sweet and Sweet Whites

This tasting concerns wines that finish sweet, or at least off-dry, and wines that are so headily aromatic that they cannot be fitted into the dry white wine category. Nor do these highly perfumed, full-bodied wines go particularly well with food.

The degree of sweetness of the *demi-sec* and *moelleux* wines varies with the type of wine and the vintage. Wines that are sweet by definition, like Sauternes, will be sweeter and richer in a year with a lot of sun, since there is a higher level of natural sugar in the grapes to be converted into alcohol and residual sugar. Wines that are sweet by the choice of the wine maker, such as those from Vouvray, Anjou and Alsace, will only appear in years when there is enough over-ripeness in the grapes to produce the desired concentration and richness. The over-ripening of the grapes is the key factor, and given the right climatic conditions, most noble grape varieties will achieve a high concentration of sugar. In specialized climates, this will be achieved through *pourriture noble* or botrytis. Attempts to make a well-balanced sweet wine in years when the grapes do not ripen sufficiently, or when there is no botrytis, are not generally very successful.

Fine sweet wines, however rich, should not be too cloying. They should *look* sweet, just as very dry wines *look* dry. Unlike medium-bodied dry wines, they are best drunk on their own.

	APPEARANCE	BOUQUET	PALATE	COMMENTS
	Condrieu 1981 E. Guigal			Northern Rhône/*Viognier*
	Clean pale medium yellow with a touch of greeny-gold. Very unctuous looking.	Explosive aromas of dried apricots, vanilla, almonds, even lychees. Almost overpoweringly aromatic, but not cloying.	Richly expansive on the palate, big wine, elegant, sensual, irresistible, floral, almondy flavour, lingering dry finish.	Extraordinary balance of richness, suaveness, floweriness and exotic fruit, a voluptuous wine that finishes clean and dry. Should be drunk on its own.
	Tokay d'Alsace 1979 Domaine Weinbach			Alsace/*Tokay (Pinot Gris)*
	Lovely clean yellow, younger than expected, rich.	Strikingly floral bouquet of rose-water, hot-house flowers. *Grande classe.* Aromatic, lemony finish.	Great elegance on the palate, lingering supple finish. Lovely contrast between slightly lemony bouquet and full suave flavour. Very long.	A *réserve* wine from a very fine domaine and a good year. Wonderfully aromatic, good now but can be kept. Rich but not cloying, almost as good as the Condrieu.
	Gewürztraminer 1981 Vendanges Tardives Domaine Weinbach			Alsace/*Gewürztraminer*
	Pure yellow-gold, youthful, very *gras*.	Huge bouquet. You can almost feel the weight of sugar in the grapes. Aromatic, spicy, musky, rich, voluptuous. Definitely the result of botrytis.	Explosive feeling in the mouth, rich, perfumed, smooth. No apparent acidity, not quite all together. Needs a year for it to become really superb.	A very exciting wine from the same domaine. Rich, but not fully sweet. Great texture, aroma and impact.
	Gewürztraminer 1976 Vendange Tardive Sélection Personelle Jean Hugel Hugel et Fils			Alsace/ *Gewürztraminer*
	Palish gold with slight green lights. Young looking.	Wonderful pure, concentrated bouquet, at first honeyed then citric, distinguished and intense.	Great elegance and class, panache and personality. The flavour of dried raisins and superb back-up of rich fruit, at once lively and velvety.	A classic wine from the Hugel family who are famous for their Vendanges Tardives. Interesting contrast to the 1979, the 1976 being a little livelier and less rich.

	APPEARANCE	BOUQUET	PALATE	COMMENTS

Vouvray 1976 demi-sec 'Le Mont' Huet — Loire/Touraine/*Chenin Blanc*

Middle yellow, starting to turn to gold. | Rich, honeyed, with the elegant floweriness of the Chenin Blanc. | Full, rich, with an almost caramelly aftertaste. Big wine, will improve. | 1976 was the sunniest year of the 1970s, and this *demi-sec* is richer than one would expect.

Bonnezeaux 1969 Château de Fesle — Loire/Anjou/*Chenin Blanc*

Full yellow gold with green tints, lovely vibrant colour. | Magnificent, explosive floral bouquet, still young and almost a little 'Riesling'. | Rich, sweet, honeyed taste with clean touch of acidity. Very fine. | A little more concentrated than the Vouvray in terms of taste, but not in sweetness.

Vouvray 1966 Moelleux 'Le Mont' Huet — Loire/Touraine/*Chenin Blanc*

Lovely colour, pure straw-yellow-gold. | Very rich, flowery, almost ageless honey-suckle bouquet. | Great finesse, lightish for a *moelleux*, but pure Touraine style, lovely harmonious finish. | Lighter than the 1976, since 1966 was not so rich a year, even though this is a *moelleux*. Perfectly balanced wine, at its best. Wonderful on its own.

Ch. Hauras 1976 Cérons — Bordeaux/Cérons/*Sémillon and Sauvignon*

Splendid full gold. | Full, majestic Sémillon bouquet, *rôti* rather than botrytis, good structure, dried apricots. | Well balanced, rich, good follow-through. Impressive wine. | A 'minor' *appellation* in the spectrum of Bordeaux *liquoreux*. Great success.

Ch. Coutet 1971 Barsac — Bordeaux/Barsac/*Sémillon, Sauvignon and Muscadelle*

Stunning full lemony yellow. Younger than expected, lovely. | Honeyed, faintly straw-like, just beginning to take on some maturity. | Very rich, luscious flavour, with the crisp lemony edge. Richer than expected, very fine. | Excellent wine from a somewhat overlooked vintage that is proving very fine. Enough richness and acidity to keep it going for years.

Ch. Suduiraut 1976 Sauternes — Bordeaux/Sauternes/*Sémillon and Sauvignon*

Light amber gold, fabulous colour, deeper and more advanced than Ch. Coutet. | Almost overpower-ingly rich bouquet, dried, concentrated fruits, intense, rich, biscuity. | Very, very rich. All the fat, fruit and glycerine of a great Sauternes. Just the right touch of acidity to keep one drinking it. | More explosive than the Coutet, more massive and impressive, not delicate, but flamboyantly sweet.

Ch. Coutet 1976 Barsac — Bordeaux/Barsac/*Sémillon, Sauvignon and Muscadelle*

Medium yellow-gold, young and fresh looking. Quite *gras*. Classic. | Bouquet of flowers, apricots, peaches, quite rich but restrained by a lemony edge. | Relatively rich, honeyed taste, balanced by an appealingly crisp acidity. Very well made wine. Lovely. | Almost perfect example of the Barsac style, completely harmonious although understated compared to Sauternes.

Ch. Suduirant 1967 Sauternes — Bordeaux/Sauternes/*Sémillon and Sauvignon*

Lovely rich straw-yellow, but not yet straw-gold. Looks very unctuous. | Heady, rich, opulent, almost perfect Sauternes bouquet. | Massively rich and sweet, straightforward, hardly any acidity, a huge concentrated wine. | Very small yield from very ripe/botrytized grapes. Here, the alcohol is holding the wine rather than the acidity. Still very young.

Tasting/Rosés

In this tasting we compare the different styles of rosé made in France. There are very few wines that are specifically rosé, that is to say that the *appellation* is for a vin rosé alone. Examples in the tasting are Tavel, Rosé de Marsannay and Rosé des Riceys. Otherwise, the production of rosés is up to the *vigneron*. While *appellation contrôlée* wines do not admit the mixing of red and white wine, they do accept the addition of white grapes to red, generally to a maximum of 20%. Basically, a rosé is a light red wine, the pretty pink colour coming from a much shorter contact of the skins with the must than for true red wines. The style of vinification and ageing will determine the taste of the wine as much as will the region from which it comes.

One conclusion from this tasting is that a rosé should be fresh and appealing, and that, with very rare exceptions, such as the Arbois and the Palette, they lose their point if they are not. Another aspect is that rosés have much less bouquet than either a white or a red wine, and that where the bouquet is pronounced, it is generally from a wine made with a single grape variety (Pinot Noir, Cabernet Franc), than from a selection of grapes.

	APPEARANCE	BOUQUET	PALATE	COMMENTS
Bourgueil Rosé 1981 Domaine des Raguenières				Loire/Touraine/*Cabernet Franc*
	Very pale, touch of violet, lovely, spring-like.	Light fruit aromas, raspberries, violets. Delicate.	Dry, light, not much follow-through, all finesse and lightness. Faint *goût de terroir*, a perfect summer rosé.	Made by the *saignée* process of vinification, hence its pale colour. Very delicate, fragrant, charming, exactly what a Loire rosé should be.
Sancerre Rosé 1981 Vincent Delaporte, Chavignol				Loire/Centre/*Pinot Noir*
	Pale rosé, but more colour than the Bourgueil, salmon pink.	Fruity, more aggressive and more structure than the Bourgueil, but still light.	Good fruity attack, dry, mouth-watering acidity at the finish. Best with food.	Lovely coloured rosé from the Pinot Noir vinified by maceration, with the natural acidity of a Sancerre *terroir*.
Vin Gris de Toul 1980 Michel Vosgien, Buligny			North-east/Lorraine/ *Pinot Noir, Pinot Meunier and Gamay*	
	Very pale, hardly a rosé, really gris.	Reticent, faintly fruity.	Clean, fresh, light and finishes rather tart. Very much a local wine, and best drunk on the spot with the Lorraine cuisine.	The very slight colour comes from the juice running direct from the press after *foulage*, hence a gris rather than a rosé. Up to 15% of white grapes may be added before pressing.
Rosé de Marsannay 1980 Domaine Clair Daü				Burgundy/Côte de Nuits/*Pinot Noir*
	Pretty, orangy rosé, losing a little freshness.	Fleshy, high toned bouquet, floral, hint of roses.	Soft, good fruit and follow-through, hardly any acidity, particularly if compared to the Sancerre, also from the Pinot Noir.	One of the most famous rosés of France. Colour obtained by maceration for 48 hours, run off into barrels after fermentation.
Rosé des Riceys 1980 Morel Père et Fils				Aube/Champagne/*Pinot Noir*
	Deep rosé, rich, quite *gras*, losing a little freshness.	Aromas of crab-apple, quince.	Dry flavour of quince with the texture of a red wine. Interesting more than enjoyable.	A *saignée* rosé, and one where the grapes have probably been pressed too much.
Côtes de Provence Rosé 1981 Domaine des Féraud				Provence/*Grenache and Cinsault*
	Full dry pinkness, deeper than the Tavel, quite *gras*.	Sweet strawberry/spicy bouquet, lovely.	Soft, fruity, good flavour, excellent balance, just about everything a rosé ought to be.	Maceration for 36 hours and low temperatures obtain more colour than is usual in a rosé, thus more flavour. A very stylish wine, interesting to compare to the Bandol.

APPEARANCE	BOUQUET	PALATE	COMMENTS

Arbois Rosé 1980 Rolet Père et Fils Jura/Arbois/*Poulsard*

Faded tawny, more red than rosé.	Faintly strawberry bouquet, mature.	Fruity, woody, quite intense, even tannic: very typical, rosé only in colour, otherwise behaves like a red wine.	This rosé is made like a red wine, maceration for 3 weeks in vat.

Alsace Rosé 1978 Pierre Seltz Alsace/*Pinot Noir*

Deep rosé, midway between rosé and red, same colour as the Rully 1979 (page 150).	Very strawberry, Pinot bouquet, classic, sweet.	Quite full, alcoholic, lost a little youthful freshness (should try the 1981), but a good example.	The Pinot grapes are *égrappé*, a 24-hour maceration follows *à froid*, and after 2–3 days fermentation, the must is taken off the skins, and the fermentation continues in barrels.

Rosé de Porto-Vecchio 1981 Domaine de Torraccia Corsica/*Niellucio, Grenache and Sciacarello*

Really lovely colour: pale pink with a touch of orange.	Aroma of dried herbs on a fruit base.	Clean, fruity, quite high in alcohol, but refreshing and lively. Good acidity, very well made, an excellent rosé.	The grapes are picked early before they become too ripe and oxidize quickly. Short maceration to obtain the lovely colour, often the main point in a rosé.

Bandol 1981 Domaine Tempier Provence/Bandol/*Grenache, Cinsault and Mourvèdre*

Pale orangy rosé, not really pink.	Soft, subdued bouquet.	Excellent structure and definition after a rather dull bouquet. Full but harmonious, and has a definite personality. One of the finest rosés from Provence.	Made from 5 or 6 grape varieties, principally Grenache for body, Cinsault for finesse and Mourvèdre for colour and structure.

Tavel Rosé 1980 Ch. de Trinquevedel South Rhône/Tavel/*Grenache and Cinsault*

Lovely pale pink, light for a Tavel, but quite rich looking.	Fresh, austere fruit aromas.	Fleshy, spicy, good fruit, distinctive. Quite high in alcohol, but balanced by good vinification.	Tavel is probably the most famous rosé made in France. The style varies according to the wine maker, fullish wine aged in wood, and lighter wines drunk fresh and young.

Palette Rosé 1979 Ch. Simone Provence/Palette/
Mourvèdre, Grenache, Cinsault and many minor varieties

Medium-full, soft looking orange-red. Very *gras*.	Woody, cedar-like bouquet, serious.	Lots of wood, *vieux vin* impressions. Tannic, aged, almost more like a Bordeaux, and would certainly be taken for a red wine on the taste.	Long wood ageing increases the tannin already brought by the Mourvèdre, making this wine difficult to appreciate as a rosé. Very small production.

Cabernet d'Anjou 1979 demi-sec Domaine de Fesle Loire/Anjou/
Cabernet Franc and Cabernet Sauvignon

Very pretty pale pink. Quite rich.	Soft, fruity aromas.	Soft, sweet, attractive, lovely with fruit or gâteaux.	This type of wine has to have 1° of residual sugar minimum, and is therefore *demi-sec*.

Tasting/Light Reds

In this tasting we look at wines that are at their best drunk young. Light red wines, like very dry white wines (pages 142–3), may be kept, but their main attraction is their freshness and fruit. What we are looking for is a lively fruit, fresh acidity and little or no tannin. We have excluded the basic everyday table wines, since these are blended for immediate consumption anyway, and whether light, medium or heavy, are not meant to be kept.

We have also underplayed the excellent wines now coming from the Provence and Languedoc-Roussillon vineyards, wines that are generally drunk young, but are not really very light.

The key to wines in this tasting is their drinkability: they have no great ageing potential in terms either of origin, grape variety or vintage, sometimes all three, but they all have a definite and recognizable style.

	APPEARANCE	BOUQUET	PALATE	COMMENTS
Cheverny 1982 Jean Gueritte	Lovely carmine red with violet tinge. Vibrant.	Crushed summer fruits.	Still quite tart and rough, but lovely, straight-forward, fruity *goût de terroir*.	Loire/Centre/*Gamay* Not as flattering as a Beaujolais, but a good example of Gamay grown in the middle Loire.
Côte de Brouilly 1981 Pierre Ferraud	Strikingly pretty red with violet edge, looks young and fresh.	Wild flowers, violets, crushed fruit.	Clean, fruity, refreshing, perhaps too much alcohol.	Burgundy/Beaujolais/*Gamay* A Beaujolais *cru*, with more body than a Villages. Very attractive wine to drink within two years. Semi-maceration vinification.
Saint Pourçain 1981 Gérard Pétillat	Soft, full, deep cherry colour.	Same sort of bouquet as the two above, less high-toned, more rustic.	Medium weight, slightly tart finish, but good balance and good with food, especially local dishes.	Loire/Lower Centre/*Pinot Noir and Gamay* From just above the Massif Central, the Gamay comes across more acid. Very good everyday wine; can be kept.
Arbois 1979 Rolet Père et Fils	Pale, faded brick-red, almost rosé.	Rather rustic, strawberry bouquet, light.	Lovely fruit, faded roses, agreeable, feminine.	Jura/Arbois/*Trousseau, Poulsard and Pinot Noir* Not quite as 'special' a taste as the white (page 144). Interesting. At its best after 2–4 years.
Bourgogne Passetoutgrains 1979 René Thévenin	Medium red, attractive.	Pleasant, fruity.	Firm, fruity, bigger than the Côte de Brouilly, finishes rather thin.	Burgundy/Côte de Beaune/*Pinot Noir and Gamay* A pleasant wine from Saint Romain. The preponderance of Gamay leaves the taste light. Drink young.
Rully 1979 Domaine de Prieuré Armand Monassier	Pale, orange-red, only fractionally fuller than the Arbois, but quite *gras*.	Pretty strawberry-Pinot bouquet. A little soft.	Pleasant at the start, easy to drink, a little too much alcohol for the fruit.	Burgundy/Côte Chalonnaise/*Pinot Noir* Probably heavily chaptalized in a year of big production. Attractive if drunk young and slightly cool.
Savigny-lès-Beaune 1979 Simon Bize	Medium red, soft, pale edge, quite good for a 1979.	Lovely bouquet of strawberries, wild cherries, maturing interestingly.	Lissom, sense of ripe fruit, lovely middle taste, finishes firm.	Burgundy/Côte de Beaune/*Pinot Noir* A lightish wine from a grower noted for elegant wines. Can be drunk now, to catch the lovely Pinot aromas, but can be kept 3–4 years.

APPEARANCE	BOUQUET	PALATE	COMMENTS

Côtes de Provence 1981   Domaine des Féraud

Provence/
Cabernet Sauvignon, Grenache and Syrah

| Very attractive violet-carmine. Quite *gras*, good-looking. | Lovely fruity aromas, crushed blackberries, spicy. | Explosive fruit in the mouth, good *terroir* and depth in flavour. Pleasantly rough in the finish. Extremely good now but can be kept. | Very well made 'modern' wine from Provence. Semi-maceration gives the young fruit, while the Cabernet gives the backbone and gets away from the Provence style. |

Côtes-du-Rhône-Villages 1981   Domaine Sainte-Anne

Côtes-du-Rhône/South/
Grenache, Cinsault and Syrah

| Strikingly young purple-violet, very fresh. | Very fruity, blackcurrants, peony. | Immediate, fruity attack, but harder than expected, lacks suppleness. Big mouthful of wine. | Same semi-maceration as the Provence has produced a tougher wine, fitting for a Côtes-du-Rhône-Villages. Can be kept 2 years or drunk now. |

Crozes-Hermitage 1979   Paul Jaboulet Aîné

Côtes-du-Rhône/North/*Syrah*

| Big, full colour, lost the purpleness of youth. | Fruity, spicy bouquet: blackcurrants, mint. | Lovely first impression of soft fruit and spice, a bit of tannin on the finish. Good. | Could have been drunk very young, with all the explosive primary fruits masking the tannin. Softening out now. Probably at its best and won't improve past 1984. |

Chinon 1981   Charles Joguet

Loire/Touraine/*Cabernet Franc*

| Pretty, soft carmine-red with violet edge. | Very attractive fruit, violets. | Clean fruit, raspberries, good acidity, typical Loire character and balance. | Lovely wine, could last, but at its best a year or two old for the fruit. |

Côtes de Bergerac 1981   Ch. de Géraud

South-West/Bergerac/
Merlot, Cabernet Sauvignon, Cabernet Franc and Malbec

| Attractive cherry-red, young violet tinge. | Strikingly attractive bouquet, quite like the Chinon. | Quite light, but good balance and lovely follow-through. A very nice wine. | Could last until 1984, but it's so stylish now, why wait? |

Ch. Rougemont 1981 Graves

Bordeaux/Graves/
Merlot, Cabernet Sauvignon and Cabernet Franc

| Strikingly pretty young red. | Full of primary fruit aromas, a little bigger than the Bergerac. | Attractive, fruity attack. More character and definition than a simple Bordeaux, long aftertaste, slightly herbaceous. | Modern style wine made by Pierre Coste, packed with fruit which hides the tannin, and makes it delicious now. Could be kept 3–4 years. There are more and more young Bordeaux being made in this style. |

Ch. Prieuré-Lichine 1980   Margaux 4ème Cru Classé

Bordeaux/
Cabernet Sauvignon, Cabernet Franc, Merlot and Petit Verdot

| Medium ruby, rather pale edge. | Very agreeable nose, striking, fruity, feminine. | Supple blackcurrant fruit, good balance, attractively elegant, no tannin. | A light well balanced wine from a 'light' vintage. Very good now and for 2–3 years. (Page 153 for the 1978.) |

Tasting/Medium Reds

This tasting should cover most French red AOC wines. The lighter wines are seldom less than 11° alcohol, and even the fullest red wines stay under 14°. The average is probably around 12°. However, we are not looking merely for weight, but also for depth, complexity and balance, wines with potential.

We have chosen wines from the main regions of France, following the pattern of the light red wine tasting. Thus it includes some of the same wines, either from better vintages, older vines, or finer parts of the *appellation*. The same principle is followed in the next tasting on full-bodied red wines.

There is no straight answer as to when a wine should be drunk any more than there is as to what it should be drunk with. Each type of wine, even every individual wine, arrives at a point when it is past its best. The younger wines in this tasting can be drunk now; the older wines could have been drunk a few years ago. But they do not have to be drunk young, as do the lighter reds. The interesting factor here is the ageing potential.

APPEARANCE	BOUQUET	PALATE	COMMENTS
Morgon 1981 Clos de l'Evêque Pierre Ferraud			Burgundy/Beaujolais/*Gamay*
Full, vibrant violet-ringed ruby	Firm, fruity, even slightly leathery, animal.	Big, mouth-filling taste of fruit. Almost tannic, good structure, good now and can be kept 2 years.	This single vineyard wine, with a smaller than average yield, is a very good Morgon, one of the few Beaujolais *crus* that last.
Chinon 1981 Dioterie Cuvée Vieilles Vignes Charles Joguet			Loire/Touraine/*Cabernet Franc*
Wonderful deep carmine-violet, complete right to the rim.	Crushed violet, black-currant leaves, lively young, lovely fruit, pure *terroir*.	Deep fruit on palate, clean, blackcurrants, raspberries. Great depth but not at all heavy. Rather firm finish, but *so* much fruit.	Fabulous wine, can be drunk now with enormous pleasure, but will improve tremendously and take on more facets.
Crozes-Hermitage 1979 Thalabert Paul Jaboulet Aîné			Côtes-du-Rhône/North/*Syrah*
Huge, intense, youthful colour. Leaves traces of colour and glycerine on the sides of the glass.	Primary, spicy aromas, blackcurrants, vanilla, cinnamon. Exciting.	Complex, blackcurrant flavours, finishes tannic but with good middle fruit. Has lost the 'explosive' fruit of a young wine, and become more serious.	Compared to the simple Crozes-Hermitage 1979 (page 151), the Thalabert is more serious, although not as long lived as the Hermitage 1961 (page 155). Will be lovely and very interesting in 2–3 years.
Bandol 1975 Domaine Tempier			Provence/*Mourvèdre, Grenache and Cinsault*
Very big deep velvety red, young for a 1975.	Rich 'Russian leather' bouquet, complex, rather animal.	Long, concentrated fruit, good depth, excellent structure, sweet finish. A long way still to go.	One of the best wines from Provence. The length of flavour and depth of fruit is brought by the Mourvèdre grape. An old Bandol often resembles a Médoc.
Morey Saint-Denis 1980 Domaine Dujac			Burgundy/Côte de Nuits/*Pinot Noir*
Medium ruby, slightly pale rim, good colour for the year.	Pretty, spicy, cherry aromas. Lovely Pinot Noir nose.	Good fruit, still firm, acidic finish, good *terroir*, will be very elegant in 2–3 years.	Good example of a very well made Morey Saint-Denis in an 'average' year in Burgundy.
Aloxe-Corton 1978 Tollot-Beaut			Burgundy/Côte de Beaune/*Pinot Noir*
Good solid, deep ruby, still very young.	Animal-velvety bouquet. Typical Corton style.	Excellent attack, faint sweetness balanced by young hard edge. Lovely fruit and depth. Too young.	Very fine wine from probably the best year in the 1970s for Burgundy. Lovely balance, pure Burgundy, great promise. Drink 1988–2000.

APPEARANCE	BOUQUET	PALATE	COMMENTS

Corton-Bressandes 1969   Dubreuil-Fontaine   Burgundy/Côte de Beaune/*Pinot Noir*

| Medium brick-red, firm in the middle, pale at the edge. Mature. | Sweet, fruity *fondu* strawberry bouquet, slightly foxy, gamy. | Clean firm Pinot fruit, still lively, though mature. Good but not great. Can be kept, but won't improve. | Many 1969s, particularly Cortons, were more robust. Quite elegant, this probably suffered from a light vinification. |

Cahors 1978   Ch. de Haute-Serre   South-west/Cahors/*Malbec, Merlot and Tannat*

| Full, velvety, plum-red. Very good colour. | Fairly intense, berry-like nose, more interesting than flattering. | Smooth, mouth-filling fruit, rather rustic finish. Can be drunk now or kept. Very good with local cuisine. | In the last century, Cahors used to be one of the longest-lived wines of France. This is one of the better recent examples. |

Ch. Haut-Bailly 1979   Graves Grand Cru Classé   Bordeaux/Graves/
Cabernet Sauvignon, Cabernet Franc, Merlot and ungrafted vignes françaises over 80 years old

| Full, vibrant ruby. Very fine colour. | Strikingly stylish, full of fruit and overtones of oak. | Firm, racy, full of flavour only just losing its *primeur* image. | 1979 was very good in Bordeaux, where the over-production mattered less than in Burgundy. |

Ch. Prieuré-Lichine 1978   Margaux 4ème Cru Classé   Bordeaux/Médoc/
Cabernet Sauvignon, Cabernet Franc, Merlot and Petit Verdot

| Very good deep ruby, no real age, complete. | Slightly smoky, woody nose with blackcurrants. | Very good fruit and texture: softness of the Merlot and the Margaux style, concentration of the Cabernet. | A well balanced, good but not exceptional 1978. (See page 151 for the much lighter 1980.) Not ready now, but not far off. |

Ch. Laroze 1978   Saint-Emilion Grand Cru Classé   Bordeaux/Saint-Emilion/
Merlot, Cabernet Franc and Cabernet Sauvignon

| Deep, full rich colour, starting to acquire a tawny rim. | Sweet, almost sticky, concentrated Merlot fruit. Quite elegant. | Full and rich on the palate, with some tannin but coming round well. Quite good length and character. | 1978 was not as good in Saint-Emilion as in the Médoc, the reverse being generally true in 1979. |

Ch. Grand-Puy-Lacoste 1976   Pauillac 5ème Cru Classé   Bordeaux/Médoc/
Cabernet Sauvignon and Merlot

| Clean, deep colour, just starting to mature. | Excellent, intense Pauillac nose: lead capsules, crushed fruit. | Full bodied, rather concentrated attack, lots of extract, not much finesse, not quite ready. Drink 1983–86. | The very hot year 1976 produced, in general, deep coloured wines with lots of meat but a little short on flavour. |

Ch. Latour 1973   Pauillac 1er Cru Classé   Bordeaux/Médoc/
Cabernet Sauvignon, Cabernet Franc, Merlot and Petit Verdot

| Full, lovely garnet ruby. No real ageing. | Wild violet, cedar aromas, clean, classic and polished. Not as intense as Latour usually is. | Delicious fruity-cedar taste. Tannin completely dissolved, can be drunk or kept a few years. Lovely balance. | Over-production in 1973 resulted in lightish but very attractive wines. Most of them will be past their best at 10 years; not this one. |

Ch. Ducru-Beaucaillou 1971   Saint-Julien 2ème Cru Classé   Bordeaux/Médoc/
Cabernet Sauvignon, Cabernet Franc, Merlot and Petit Verdot

| Firm medium-red. Mature. | Fine red berry fruit bouquet, violets. Harmonious. | Firm taste with soft, mature (an almost feminine Ducru) flavour and fruit. | The 1971s were lighter (in the Médoc especially) than the 1970s (page 173). This is a lovely example. |

Tasting/Full-bodied Reds

Light red wines can, and should, be drunk young; medium-bodied red wines can, but should not, be drunk young; full-bodied red wines cannot be drunk young. This said, we are not looking at wines that are merely high in alcohol, but those with great depth, a lot of extract and tannin, and hence great ageing potential.

We have limited the wines to the three great red wine regions of France: Burgundy, Bordeaux and the Rhône Valley. Other areas produce fine, long-lived wines: Cahors, Madiran, Bourgueil, Bandol, but they are not of the same calibre. The potential here is in the grapes – planted in most other fine wine-growing regions in the world – and the soil, compounded by a favourable (great) vintage and skilful (great) wine-making.

APPEARANCE	BOUQUET	PALATE	COMMENTS
Ch. Grand-Puy-Lacoste 1978 Pauillac 5ème Cru Classé			Bordeaux/Médoc/
			Cabernet Sauvignon and Merlot
Intense deep ruby, very dark with fine ruby glints.	Massive, concentrated, still very shut in.	Big structure, masses of hidden fruit, very ripe grapes, still unyielding. Keep at least 10 years.	Classic old-fashioned long-term Pauillac made at a time when many châteaux are producing less tannic wines.
Ch. La Mission-Haut-Brion 1975 Graves Grand Cru Classé			Bordeaux/Graves/
			Cabernet Sauvignon, Cabernet Franc and Merlot
Very, very deep colour, intense, dark. Very rich.	Huge, aromatic, concentrated, intense, still very young.	Big, solid mouth-filling, still very hard, but masses of blackcurrant-spicy fruit in the background. Complex, very long. Will be superb in 10 years and last for 30 years and more.	A very successful wine from a fine year, but one where the Médocs are rather more austere than the Graves. Fabulous amount of fruit packed in, marvellous ageing potential. Impossible to consider drinking it young.
Ch. Latour 1970 Pauillac 1er Cru Classé			Bordeaux/Médoc/
			Cabernet Sauvignon, Cabernet Franc, Merlot and Petit Verdot
Phenomenal colour for a 1970, intense dark red with youthful bluish tinge. Extraordinary.	Concentrated aromas, cedar, ripe berries, wood. Still a little shut in, but with great promise and power.	Magnificent structure and style. A huge wine in perfect harmony with its parts, so not heavy. Still tannic, but not rough. Incredible fruit. Drink 1990–2010.	Very youthful for a 1970, perhaps since this bottle came direct from the château cellars (in 1982). Pauillac (and Latour) at its best.
Ch. Trotanoy 1964 Pomerol Grand Cru			Bordeaux/Pomerol/
			Merlot and Cabernet Franc
Big, rich, deep, burnt red, complete, only slight tawny rim. Very solid for an 18-year-old wine.	Rich, high-toned, lots of wood dissolved into almost waxy aromas.	Rich, sweet concentrated fruit, mature, vibrant, rounded out. A big sturdy wine of great finesse. Drink now–1995.	Splendidly concentrated but elegant wine, hardly showing any age. Pomerol and Saint-Emilion were better in 1964 than the Médocs. Hot year, small production, lots of extract. Needed at least 15 years to show at its best, rare for a Pomerol.
Volnay 1964 1er Cru Les Champans H. de Montille Burgundy/Côte de Beaune/*Pinot Noir*			
Deep solid red, hardly touched by age. Very fine.	Concentrated bouquet of mature, sweet, berry-like fruit, blackcurrants, mulberries.	Lovely sweet attack, concentrated fruit backed up by lots of extract. Firm, but tannin dissolved. Very fine. Drink now.	A hot, concentrated vintage but less so than 1976. Many wines had too much alcohol, and not enough fruit. This Volnay is perfectly balanced, and so has lasted almost 20 years.

APPEARANCE	BOUQUET	PALATE	COMMENTS

Richebourg 1978   Domaine de la Romanée-Conti   Burgundy/Côte de Nuits/*Pinot Noir*

Dark intense garnet. Very big colour for a Burgundy, but not heavy-looking.	Dense, black-cherry nose, still closed in, but with great elegance and depth.	Wonderful concentrated, velvety flavours. Superb balance and definition, long concentrated finish. Keep until 1988 and for as long as possible after that.	A huge mouthful of wine, with perfect balance. Very few Burgundies have this power and potential. 1978, although its best year in the decade, was less powerful than 1976, but had perfect balance.

Corton Clos du Roi 1976   Chandon de Briailles   Burgundy/Côte de Beaune/*Pinot Noir*

Deep ruby, slight paling at edge.	Concentrated, dense fruit, quite closed in.	Dense, even rather austere and Médoc style. Tannic, little of the Pinot appears as yet. Should be very fine when it softens up, say 1988.	A freak year in Burgundy; the heatwave in 1976 shrunk the grapes and thickened the skins to give the wines unexpected, and often unwanted, extra tannin.

Vosne-Romanée 1972   1er Cru Les Beaux Monts   Leroy Burgundy/Côte de Nuits/*Pinot Noir*

Very deep colour, red with a hint of brown.	Rich, sumptuous bouquet, slightly herbaceous, which is the style of the 1972s. Firm.	Wonderfully well made wine, solid, rich but lively, complex mature fruit. Velvety, still tannic at the end. 'An iron hand in a velvet glove.'	Very fine. The 1972, always rather acidic but with an excellent structure, was generally thought less of than the much more flamboyant 1971. This sort of wine is reversing that judgment.

Côte-Rôtie 1978   'La Mouline'   E. Guigal   Côtes-du-Rhône/North/*Syrah and Viognier*

Huge colour, black-red, almost opaque. Wonderful.	Immense aromas of blackberries, rich ripe fruit. Astoundingly impressive and persistent.	Massive wine, but velvety and elegant. Perfect texture, flavour, great length, incredible richness and complexity. At its best around 1990.	The 1976 'La Mouline' was reckoned by many of us to be the best wine made that year in France.

Châteauneuf-du-Pape 1978   Ch. de Beaucastel   Côtes-du-Rhône/South/
Grenache, Syrah, Cinsault, Mourvèdre, Picpoul and Counoise

Very deep colour, almost black, but not so intense as 'La Mouline'.	Still very shut in, masses of fruit, animal, leathery overtones. Great promise.	Rich, complex, spicy, very big rough wine, almost port-like in intensity, concentrated fruit. Drink 1986–2000.	One of the Châteauneuf-du-Pape domaines making wine to last, when the vintage is good.

Vacqueyras 1967   Paul Jaboulet Aîné   Côtes-du-Rhône/South/*Grenache, Syrah and Cinsault*

Deep aged red, losing a little colour at the edge.	Burnt, smoky bouquet (almost cigar), camphor odours. Fine.	Sweet, with concentrated taste. Rich fruit, now slightly past its best and drying out.	Originally a relatively minor wine from a very successful vintage in the south.

Hermitage 1961   'La Chapelle'   Paul Jaboulet Aîné   Côtes-du-Rhône/North/*Syrah*

Wonderful dark colour, clear, mature after 20 years but not ageing.	Sumptuous bouquet of blackcurrants and leather, very complex and rewarding.	Rich but refreshing taste, plummy, conserved cherries, big lingering aftertaste, goes on and on. At its best, but will last.	Hermitage is one of the finest, and longest lasting wines of France. The tiny *récolte* produced a prodigious, perfect wine, with a concentration that required and repaid ageing.

Tasting/Sparkling Wines

This tasting shows the different styles of sparkling wine made in France. The best known sparkling wine is, of course, Champagne, and the *méthode champenoise* is accepted as being the finest (and for many wine makers and wine drinkers, the only) way to induce bubbles into still wine. It is, however, the most time-consuming and by far the most expensive way to achieve this. A good deal depends on how much the consumer is prepared to pay for his *vin mousseux*. There are some very fine sparkling wines, mostly *méthode champenoise*, from countries other than France, notably Spain, Italy, Germany and the east and west coasts of America.

APPEARANCE	BOUQUET	PALATE	COMMENTS
Espigou Brut Vin Mousseux Sicarex-Méditerranée			South of France/ *Muscat, Ugni Blanc*
Pale, clean, fine bubbles.	Slight Muscat aroma, no real bouquet.	Pleasant, sharp, refreshing. No real flavour, bubbles do not last in the mouth.	Clean and fresh, pleasant on a hot day or as a mixer. The *cuve close* method does not make interesting sparkling wine.
Gaillac Brut Jean Cros		South-west/Gaillac/*Sauvignon, Sémillon and Mauzac-Blanc*	
Lovely pale clean colour, fine *mousse*, good.	Pretty floral bouquet, lightly aromatic.	Very dry, almost brutal, then softer finish. Clean, interesting, lasting *pétillance*.	Well made, less aggressive than most champagne.
Clairette de Die Brut Cave Coopérative		Côtes-du-Rhône/South/*Muscat and Clairette*	
Clean, pale yellow.	Very muscaty, just like eating Muscat grapes.	Sweet, fruity attack, muscat, but less so than many Astis, finishes soft, pleasant, quite dry.	Well defined style of wine, and in character with the grapes. Very popular in France.
Vouvray Brut Pétillant Huet			Loire/Touraine/*Chenin Blanc*
Medium full yellow. Not much *mousse*.	Honeyed bouquet. Pure Chenin Blanc, lovely and has kept the Vouvray nose.	Soft, only slightly sparkling, summery and elegant.	Lovely wine, could have had more *pétillance*. The *méthode champenoise* Saumurs and Vouvrays have more bubbles but are more aggressive.
Crémant d'Alsace Blanc de Blancs Pierre Seltz			Alsace/ *Riesling, Pinot Blanc, Pinot Noir and Auxerrois*
Medium yellow. Rather few bubbles.	Quite aggressive, lacks finesse	Rather heavy for a sparkling wine, not much elegance. Should be better.	The best Crémants d'Alsace are made from the Riesling with a little Pinot Blanc. They are very popular, the production having passed 1 million bottles a year.
Crémant de Bourgogne Cave Coopérative de Lugny		Burgundy/Mâconnais/Chardonnay/ *Aligoté, Pinot Blanc and Pinot Noir*	
Excellent appearance, clean light yellow. Lots of tiny bubbles.	Lovely flowery Chardonnay bouquet, very fine, well made.	Clean, fruity attack, good acidity. Very little *dosage*, crisp, clean finish.	A perfect example of a non-champagne, excellent Chardonnay-style aperitif.

	APPEARANCE	BOUQUET	PALATE	COMMENTS

Champagne Bonnaire Blanc de Blancs Brut Cramant   Champagne/*Chardonnay*

APPEARANCE	BOUQUET	PALATE	COMMENTS
Pale, slight yellow, very fine bubbles and very effervescent.	Young Chardonnay aromas: green apples, fresh and mouth-watering.	Clean, fresh, light, elegant, not much weight, but some style and definition. Perfect aperitif.	A mono-*cru* champagne from a good proprietor in Cramant, one of the 100% *crus* in the Côte de Blancs. Would gain more character with a year's bottle age.

Champagne Jean Vesselle Blanc de Noirs Brut   Bouzy   Champagne/*Pinot Noir*

APPEARANCE	BOUQUET	PALATE	COMMENTS
Medium full yellow, quite different to the Bonnaire, quite good *mousse*.	Biscuity, rich bouquet, but clean and direct.	Powerful, fairly aggressive, big flavour. Clear finish, uncompromising meaty wine, not really to modern taste for lighter wines.	Another mono-*cru*, again from a vineyard classed 100%, but from Bouzy. The complete opposite in style to the Cramant from Bonnaire. These two styles make up the basic elements of a blended champagne.

Champagne Lanson Black Label   Reims   Champagne/*Pinot Noir, Chardonnay and Pinot Meunier*

APPEARANCE	BOUQUET	PALATE	COMMENTS
Light, pale yellow, lots of bubbles.	Fresh bouquet, wine quite young and aggressive.	Clean, good fruit and persistent sparkle. Finishes rather acidic.	A classic non-vintage champagne from one of the well-known *Grandes Marques*. Well made, but with less definition of style than either of the mono-*crus*.

Champagne Besserat de Bellefon Brut Intégral   Reims   Champagne/*Chardonnay and Pinot Noir*

APPEARANCE	BOUQUET	PALATE	COMMENTS
Pale yellow, slightly turning to gold, fine *mousse*.	Toasty, biscuity, almost nutty bouquet, more Chardonnay than Pinot.	Clean, well made, very dry. Excellent finish.	A mature Brut 'intégral' (with no *dosage* at all), very well made, but still appears slight if it follows a big wine.

Champagne Bollinger Brut 1976   Ay   Champagne/*Pinot Noir and Chardonnay*

APPEARANCE	BOUQUET	PALATE	COMMENTS
Lovely medium yellow, full but not heavy. Very fine bead, bubbles rising persistently to the surface.	Rich, winey aromas. Mature.	Very complete, biscuity flavour. Good *mousse*, smooth and rich on palate but with a complex dry finish. A serious champagne, completely satisfying.	The very hot year of 1976 made a champagne that was abnormally rich, a great contrast to the firmer, more austere 1975. This is an old-fashioned style of champagne where the flavour dominates the sparkle.

Champagne Bollinger Brut 1973 (RD)   Ay   Champagne/*Pinot Noir and Chardonnay*

APPEARANCE	BOUQUET	PALATE	COMMENTS
Full, slightly more golden than the 1976. Fine, persistent bubbles.	Mature, almost straw-like bouquet, touch of honeysuckle.	Complex, old wine flavour, firm edge, good *mousse*. Actually finishes drier than the 1976. A very interesting champagne, almost a work of art.	From the 1973 vintage, this wine was disgorged on 16 June 1982, after more than 8 years on its lees. Great depth of flavour and character. Possibly too mature for some people.

Champagne Gosset Brut Rosé   Ay   Champagne/*Pinot Noir, Chardonnay and Pinot Meunier*

APPEARANCE	BOUQUET	PALATE	COMMENTS
Lovely salmon pink, excellent *mousse*, very attractive colour.	Supple, fruity Pinot aromas, strawberries.	Quite fruity, almost rich flavour, well balanced and not at all acid.	A very well made, probably high *dosage* pink champagne. Lovely colour, perfect at any time.

Tasting/Grape Varieties/Riesling

In an attempt to show how the classic French varieties behave in differing soils and climates, we have set up eight tastings. French wines have been used as the criterion in all these tastings with the exception of the Rieslings, where we have used wines from Germany. We have tried to be as broad as possible with the selection of wines, and have used those in which the characteristics of each variety are plainly to be seen.

The *cépages* have already been discussed earlier (pages 70–85), and they have all appeared in earlier tastings. The wines in these tastings are cross-referenced where applicable.

It can forcefully be argued that the Riesling grape makes the finest white wine in the world. It is a low-yielding grape and is very slow-ripening in cool climates, yet it is this ability to ripen over a long sunny autumn and into winter that produces the concentration of sugar and flavour that makes these wines so extraordinary.

In Europe, the Riesling thrives only on slopes fully exposed to the sun, and only works well if planted in the right conditions. If the exposition is wrong, the soil unsuitable or the vintage poor, the resulting wine will be hard and acid. The basic Riesling style is dry, lively, with delicate, floral aromas and a smooth, perfumed, clean taste. It is relatively low in alcohol and high in acidity, but it has a youthful lemony acidity that balances beautifully the fruit of the wine on the palate.

The Riesling grape is planted all over the world, more so than any other fine grape variety. This tasting concentrates on the German Rieslings, for it is they that set the criterion for these wines. With the varying degrees of origin and sweetness, the style of the grape comes through every time: the high quality, positive attack, the great freshness, delicacy and length of flavour.

APPEARANCE	BOUQUET	PALATE	COMMENTS
Kaseler Nieschen Riesling Kabinett QMP 1981 Deinhard			Rüwer/Germany
Quite pale, clean, spring-like.	Fresh, crisp, lemony.	Lovely fruit, clean crisp finish. A relatively simple wine, but well made and pure Riesling.	A typical German style Riesling: low in alcohol and high in natural tartaric acid. Will probably be better with 6 months more age, say autumn 1983.
Wehlener Sonnenuhr Riesling Spätlese 1981 QMP Deinhard			Mosel/Germany
Lovely primrose-yellow, slightly fuller than above.	Light, 'zingy' lemon fruit, very stylish.	Clean, fresh, fruity, rather more rich than above, but still has the lemony after-taste. Very long. Lovely wine and will improve.	A wine from the same vintage, but picked after a longer ripening period. Fuller, richer, more quality but not sweet. Wonderful freshness, varied character and length.
Riesling 1981 Domaine Weinbach			Alsace/France
Medium pale, but more colour than, say, a Muscadet or Sylvaner.	Strikingly lemony-fruity, similar but less intense than the 'Schlossberg' from the same Domaine (page 143).	Excellent fruit, lots of style and very Riesling in its direct classy taste, a certain fullness and good acidity. Can be kept.	A bigger wine than the dry German style, more body, less pretty, equally aromatic, better with food than on its own. This natural weight comes from the sunnier climate.
Riesling Renano Colli Orientali dei Friuli 1980 DOC Az. Viticola Valle			Friuli/Italy
Medium yellow, soft looking.	Attractive soft fruitiness.	Touch of CO_2, fairly peachy flavour, quite full with pleasant Riesling 'tang' overlaying the fruit. Should be drunk younger.	Very much softer and less structure than an Alsatian Riesling, and less bouquet and less acidity than in Germany.

APPEARANCE	BOUQUET	PALATE	COMMENTS
Johannisberg Riesling 1980 Joseph Phelps Vineyards			Napa Valley/California USA
Pale yellow, clean and fresh.	Aromatic, lemony-tart bouquet, unmistakably Riesling.	Clean fruity attack, refreshing, more weight than expected, slight peachy flavour and lemony finish. Really explosive fruit; drink now.	An early harvest Riesling with 11° alcohol and 1.25% residual sugar. More German than French in style, but Germany would have this ripeness only in good years.
Rhine Riesling 1979 Petaluma			Piccadilly/South Australia
Full yellow with green tints. *Gras* very fine.	Very aromatic lemon-honey nose, still youthful and quite intense.	Fruity, spicy, some fullness in the middle, but excellent acidity and good lift in the finish. Can be drunk or kept.	A lovely wine, fuller than the Alsatian style, but very good acidity to back up the ripeness from the warm climate.
Riesling 1978 'Clos Ste Hune' Trimbach			Alsace/France
Light yellow, clean and still slightly green.	Citric Riesling bouquet, complex, stylish but still closed in.	Firm, excellent fruit but still char in and relatively acidic. Better with food, but many years before its peak.	Riesling of great intensity and finesse. A very serious wine, in contrast to the pretty early-drinking styles of lesser *cuvées*.
Riesling 1976 Vendange Tardive Sélection Personelle Jean Hugel Hugel et Fils Alsace/France			
Medium yellow, greenish tinge, very young looking for a 1976. *Gras.*	Lovely concentration of aromas: fruit, flowers.	Delicious, explosive floral attack. Very Riesling. Full rather than sweet, with good acidity. Will last for years.	A wonderful example of a late-picked French Riesling. Compare to the Gewürztraminer of the same year (page 146).
Johannisberg Riesling 1980 Late Harvest Joseph Phelps Vineyard			Napa Valley/California USA
Lovely yellow-gold, very rich looking.	Honeyed, powerfully aromatic nose. Plainly very sweet.	Really luscious, rich taste, with good acidity in the finish. A classic 'dessert' style wine, best drunk on its own.	Quite in the German style, low (9.6°) in alcohol, high in residual sugar (8%) but also high in acidity. A very fine example, where the grape, as the Riesling often does, dominates the character of the region.
Oestricher Lenchen Riesling Auslese 1976 QMP Deinhard			Rheingau/Germany
Yellow-gold, a little more depth than the Hugel Riesling 1976. Very *gras.*	Complex honey and flowers bouquet, not unlike a Vouvray.	Good follow-through, impression of mature fruit and good acidity. More of a 'restrained sweetness' than a fully sweet wine. Will continue to improve.	1976 was the last great vintage in Germany. This wine was made from very ripe grapes with some botrytis.
Oestricher Lenchen Riesling Auslese-Eiswein 1979 QMP Deinhard Rheingau/Germany			
Full, yellow-gold, very rich and concentrated.	Unctuous, honeyed bouquet, peaches, apricots.	Very full and intense, as much so as Ch. d'Yquem, luscious, long on concentrated essence of a wine, still with good acidity and not cloying.	Incredible wine, for its concentration, richness and balance. Eiswein, made only from the Riesling, is a tribute to the dedication of German wine growers and wine makers.

159

Tasting/Grape Varieties/Chardonnay

The Chardonnay grape makes the world's finest dry white wine. This is not to decry the qualities of the other fine varieties, but if the emphasis is on *dry* white wine, the Chardonnay has no equal. In character it is not so definitive as, say, the Riesling, which tastes quite plainly Riesling wherever it is grown and however it is vinified, and therefore it is less easy to cast as a type.

There are classic Chardonnay styles from France: Blanc de Blancs from Champagne, Chablis, Meursault, the Montrachet family, Pouilly-Fuissé, Mâcon Blanc – yet these wines are so different that at first sight they might not even be made from the same grape. But, in fact, what other grape could they come from? Certainly not the Riesling, the Chenin Blanc, the Sauvignon or the Sémillon. It is the idea of *terroir* that leads one to recognize certain styles of Chardonnay: Chablis is different from Meursault, Coteaux Champenois very different from Pouilly-Fuissé. The character of these basic *appel-lations* comes from their soil and climate, enhanced by the generally accepted methods of wine-making. Thus, a tank-fermented Meursault that has not seen oak will differ from what might be expected, as will a Mâcon Blanc that has been barrel-fermented and aged in wood. Even outside France, where the principles of *appellations* are less strict with regard to where grape varieties may be planted, the style still evolves from the soil, climate, vinification and ageing.

Common to all these wines is the taste of the Chardonnay itself: fresh yellow in colour, ranging from pale to golden, sometimes with green tints; fruity on the nose, sometimes appley, flowery, buttery, nutty, oaky; much the same on the palate, well-balanced, never sweet and seldom tart. Chardonnay is the perfect wine to drink with a meal.

This tasting shows the great adaptability of the Chardonnay to different regions and styles of wine-making.

	APPEARANCE	BOUQUET	PALATE	COMMENTS
Chardonnay du Haut Poitou 1982 VDQS Cave Coopérative du Haut Poitou Poitou/France				
	Light, pale yellow, only a little fuller than a Muscadet.	Crisp, clear, slightly tart fruit.	Crisp and fresh, almost as dry as a Bourgogne Aligoté, or a dry Vouvray. Attractive and refreshing.	While the Chardonnay characteristics are discernible, there is less fruitiness than in, say, a Mâcon.
Chardonnay di Mezzocorona da Tavola 1981 Cantine Soc. Mezzocorona Trentino/Italy				
	Palish yellow with slight greenish tinge, Mâcon type.	Appley aromas, even a slight butteriness. Good definition.	Light, fruity, good flavour and some good acidity. Fine as an aperitif, excellent with food.	Very good example of a northern Italian Chardonnay: light, lacking the flesh of Pouilly-Fuissé, but Mâconnais in style.
Chardonnay di Lavis da Tavola NV Cantine Givelli Trentino/Italy				
	Pale yellow, about the same as the Haut Poitou.	Light, discreet, some finesse.	Clean, light, in the style of a minor Chablis, quite elegant but not much depth.	Interesting contrast to the Mezzocorona from the same region; probably not so much ripeness in the grapes.
Coteaux Champenois Chardonnay Ruinart Père et Fils Champagne/France				
	Clean, crisp pale yellow, a little more depth than the three above.	Crisp, fruity, high acidity.	Firm, good attack, quite good fruit but very high acidity and finishes green.	Very much a cold country Chardonnay, steely but lacks ripeness, and could have more of the Champagne *terroir*.
Chablis 1979 Grand Cru 'Les Clos' Louis Michel Chablis/Burgundy France				
	Clear straw yellow, pretty.	Less bouquet than expected, some fruit, slightly flinty, quite elegant.	Firm and dry. Not too much fruit, clean flinty finish. Quite typical Chablis, but disappointing for a Grand Cru.	The Chardonnay bouquet and taste is less obvious in Chablis than in the Côte de Beaune or the Mâconnais.

APPEARANCE	BOUQUET	PALATE	COMMENTS

Beaune 1979 Clos des Mouches   Joseph Drouhin — Côte de Beaune/Burgundy France

Lovely colour, pale yellow, lemony tints, quite *gras*.	Very fine Chardonnay bouquet; fruity, fresh, slightly nutty, overlaid by new oak.	Still very oaky, lots of fruit and great finesse. Needs time for the oak to blend in. *Grand vin*.	The complexity and character are achieved as much by the vinification as by the geographical position of the vineyard.

Chardonnay 1981   Iron Horse — Sonoma Valley/California USA

Very pale yellow, but not at all thin-looking.	Lovely crisp fruit, some oak, faint appley aromas.	Clean, well balanced fruit with mouth-watering acidity. Oak nicely blended in. Crisp and elegant. Will improve.	Quite a restrained example of northern California Chardonnay, with an avoidance of too much alcohol and too much oak.

Chardonnay 1981   Edna Valley Vineyard — San Luis Opispo/California USA

Medium yellow, much fuller and richer than Iron Horse.	Rich, biscuity, butterscotch aromas, lots of sap.	Rich, quite complex, oaky, viscous, a big fleshy fruity wine with the weight of a Bâtard-Montrachet.	Quite different to Iron Horse, yet another classic style of Chardonnay.

Chardonnay 1980   Château St Jean — Sonoma County/California USA

Medium pale yellow-green. Very attractive.	Suave, slightly balsamic aromas, quite complex.	Smooth, fruity, slightly buttery, touch of citric acid on finish, good balance. Very good with food.	Less massive than the Edna Valley, this is a very good middleweight Chardonnay. The lemon acidity hides the alcohol (13.5°).

Chardonnay 1980   Robert Mondavi Winery — Napa Valley/California USA

Yellow-gold, lovely buttercup colour.	Oaky, buttery, viscous, rich Chardonnay bouquet.	Big wine, well structured with fruit, acids, alcohol and oak well blended in. Has to age to become more than the sum of its parts.	Not so stylish and appealing as the Château St Jean, but more ambitious. A rather riper version of the Beaune Clos des Mouches.

Chardonnay 1978   Trefethen Vineyards — Napa Valley/California USA

Medium yellow, slight greenish tinge, quite *gras*.	Lovely soft floral bouquet, with a touch of vanilla-oak.	Smooth, suave fruit, lemony, vanilla touches. Very elegant and stylish. At its best. Very fine.	A lovely wine in the style of a Puligny-Montrachet. A complete wine, very harmonious.

Chardonnay 1980   Brown Brothers — Milawa/Victoria Australia

Clean, buttercup yellow, quite full.	Buttery, oaky, vanilla bouquet. Very much in the California style.	Smooth, good rich Chardonnay fruit, good balance, finishes a little bland despite the oaky acidity.	Classic, modern, warm-country Chardonnay. More oak acidity than fruit acidity. Well made, middle-weight wine.

Chardonnay 1978   Cowra Vineyards Petaluma — Piccadilly/South Australia

Full, yellow-gold, much deeper than 'Mondavi' Chardonnay 1980, the richest colour of the series.	Rich, charred-oak bouquet, lots of fruit and body.	Very full, fleshy wine with good acidity and oaky overtones. As full as a Bâtard-Montrachet or a Corton-Charlemagne. Great length of flavour. Impressive.	Most resembles the Edna Valley in style: rich, buttery, oaky but complex enough to stop it being bland. A 'hand-made' wine of great power and style, inherently Chardonnay.

Tasting/Grape Varieties/Chenin Blanc

The Chenin Blanc, also known in France as the Pineau de la Loire (no relation to the Pinot family of Burgundy, Alsace and Champagne), is a most versatile grape variety. In France it produces all the great wines in Touraine and Anjou, wines on a par with the finest whites that the country can produce. Montlouis, Vouvray, Saumur, Savennières, Bonnezeaux and Coteaux du Layon all share the honeyed fruit and lemony acidity that rivals the Riesling grape, and in the years when the grapes are attacked by botrytis, the results are wines in the class of the finest Sauternes. The Chenin Blanc, like the Riesling, has the quality of making fruity, crisply acidic wines from an early harvest or a light year, semi-sweet wines from a later picking, and luscious dessert wines from grapes sometimes picked well into November. It is also one of the classic grapes for the *méthode champenoise* sparkling wines, as is proved by the well-established sparkling wine production around Saumur.

Outside France, however, the Chenin loses some of its acidity, and produces softer wines with an easy charm. If the fully sweet Chenins from California do tend to be a little cloying, the early harvest wines are quite delicious.

This tasting shows the Chenin Blanc in all its facets from the Loire Valley, with two wines from California.

APPEARANCE	BOUQUET	PALATE	COMMENTS
Chenin Blanc 1981 Kenwood Winery			Sonoma Valley/California USA
Light pale yellow, lovely.	Fresh, floral, very attractive.	A touch of CO_2, fruity, hint of sweetness, clean finish, refreshing.	Very pretty and versatile wine, like a Vouvray 1982.
Chenin Blanc 1981 Alexander Valley Dry Creek Vineyard			Sonoma Valley/California USA
Lovely bright, pale yellow, much the same as Kenwood.	Crisp, clean fruit, not that rich.	Extremely clean, clear fruit, touch of sugar in the finish. Lovely wine.	Cold fermentation to produce 12° alcohol and leave 0.5% residual sugar.
Jasnières 1978			Coteaux du Loire/Loire Valley/France
Straw-yellow, quite full.	Nutty, honeyed, butterscotchy, more like a California Chardonnay than a French Chenin Blanc.	Semi-sweet attack with a firm finish. Quite a lot of weight and acidity. Complex, interesting.	In poor years, Jasnières is so acidic as to be undrinkable. In 1978 the grapes were late picked fully ripe.
Savennières-Coulée de Serrant 1976 Madame Joly			Anjou/Loire Valley/France
Pale straw-gold, brighter than the Jasnières, very *gras*.	Slight honeyed bouquet, lemony edge and a touch of SO_2.	Clean (not so much SO_2), flowery, very Loire-Anjou style. Firm, even acidic finish, especially for a 1976. Will last 10–20 years, and needs time to soften up.	A very rare wine, showing the firmness and high-natural acidity of the Chenin Blanc in the Loire Valley. A great contrast to the first two, which are made to be drunk young.
Montlouis 1976 Demi-sec Claude Levasseur			Touraine/Loire Valley/France
Clean, fresh medium yellow with a touch of green, very young for a 1976.	Honeyed bouquet, lovely lemony back-up, no trace of age.	Much sweeter than the Coulée de Serrant, although it is only a *demi-sec*, but much less dense. A wine of great charm to drink any time.	Until 1938 Montlouis was sold as Vouvray, which it resembles closely, with perhaps a little more finesse but less body.
Coteaux du Layon 1953 Château de Beaulieu			Anjou/Loire Valley/France
Old gold, amber colour with an underlying green-ness. Could pass for a fine Armagnac.	Deep rich honeyed fruit, impression of dissolved gold essence.	Fully mature, sweet, concentrated 'Oxford marmalade' fruit, and finishes delicate and very long. Quite perfect at 30 years, but with many years ahead of it.	Sweet, plainly a botrytis wine, but not cloying. The varietal identity is evident from the Loire character: complex honeyed sweetness, light acidity, much more delicate than a Sauternes.

Tasting/Grape Varieties/Sauvignon Blanc

The Sauvignon Blanc cannot claim the same complexity and depth as the Chardonnay or the Riesling, or (in France) the Chenin Blanc, but it is still one of the world's major white wine grape varieties. Its dominant characteristics are: an explosive bouquet of gooseberry or redcurrant fruit, often with grassy or leafy overtones, an immediate fruit on the palate and a slightly tart finish. The Sauvignon is at its most typical, or most obviously Sauvignon, in the centre of the Loire Valley, where it is solely responsible for the wines of Sancerre, Pouilly-Fumé, Quincy, Reuilly and Ménétou-Salon, as well as the popular Sauvignon de Touraine. These wines share the fresh assertive fruitiness of the grape, with varying amounts of *goût de terroir*. Along with the Sauvignon de Haut Poitou and the Sauvignon de Saint-Bris (near Chablis), they are perfect wines for everyday drinking, go well with food, are generally straightforward and at their best drunk young.

When transplanted to the south-west of France,

however, and the region of Bordeaux in particular, the young assertive style is softened. In the Graves *appellation*, where it is planted on poor, gravelly soil and blended principally with the Sémillon, the Sauvignon produces a wine of great finesse, firmness and longevity. The Sauvignon also plays a minor but essential rôle in the Sauternes, Barsac and other sweet white wines.

An aspect that the Sauvignon Blanc shares with its cousin the Cabernet Sauvignon is that it thrives in warm climates. It is now being planted across the south of France, in the north of Spain, in Italy and in the USA, South America and Australia. It has done particularly well in California, where the style seems to be divided between the Loire Valley 'Blanc Fumés' and the Graves, which is due more to the decision of the wine maker than the grape itself.

This tasting, along with the notes on the three Sauvignon-based wines on pages 142–3, shows some of the classic examples of the grape variety.

APPEARANCE	BOUQUET	PALATE	COMMENTS
Sauvignon 1982 Cheverny Jean Gueritte			Loire/France
Clean, very pale yellow, young and fresh.	Fruity, slightly tart redcurrant bouquet, very lively.	Fresh, lively, slightly acidic fruit. Good varietal definition and some character.	Typical Sauvignon central-Loire style. Perfect French country wine.
Sancerre 1982 Jean Vacheron			Sancerre/Loire France
Clean pale yellow, fuller-bodied than the Cheverny.	Explosive Sauvignon Blanc aromas, redcurrants, gooseberries, and lots of fruit.	Good balance between fruit (obvious), alcohol (high), acidity (low), and Sancerre character.	This is classic Sancerre, one of the classic Sauvignon styles. Drink young.
Château La Louvière 1979 Graves André Lurton			Graves/Bordeaux France
Very clean, crisp pale yellow.	Less fruit than the Sancerre, slightly aggressive, needs time.	Well knit, firm, very reticent compared to the Sancerre. Good fruit, a little hidden behind the austere façade. Better in 2 years' time.	This wine from the best part of the Graves *appellation* has none of the obvious Sauvignon characteristics, except dryness. The Graves character is dominant.
Sauvignon 1981 Sterling Vineyards			Napa Valley/California USA
Pale, clean yellow, paler than expected.	Crisp acidity, some oak, lovely clean subtle bouquet.	More Graves than Sancerre in style, not flamboyantly Sauvignon, but good definition and fine long finish. Drink now or keep.	Very well made. Just the right amount of new oak.
Fumé Blanc 1980 Robert Mondavi Winery			Napa Valley/California USA
Medium yellow, much fuller than the rest, quite rich and glyceriny.	Full musky (almost catty) bouquet, red-currants, some oak.	Full, rich in attack, but finishes dry. About the same weight as a Chardonnay (14.4°), kept up by a typically crisp Sauvignon finish.	The classic Mondavi style, over 6 months in French oak and very ripe grapes produce a big wine in complete contrast to the Sterling.

GRAND VIN DE GRAVES

1979
CHÂTEAU
LA LOUVIÈRE

ANDRÉ LURTON

Tasting/Grape Varieties/Pinot Noir

The Pinot Noir is the only grape from which red Burgundy may be made, and it is inextricably connected with wines from this region. Although it is also the major grape in Champagne, and is found in other areas of France, as is the Chardonnay, it is not so adaptable as the white grape variety. While the Chardonnay has many styles, the Pinot Noir has a narrower definition. The colour, with few exceptions, is never too heavy or too dark; young, it should have an aroma of crushed fruit, principally of strawberries or wild cherries, while in ageing it evolves towards a bouquet of faded fruit or even animal. The taste should be clean and refreshing, however voluptuous the wine, for, despite the popular image of Burgundy as a rich, full wine, the best wines from the Pinot are elegant, with a lingering fruit. Furthermore, unlike the Cabernet family, the Merlot or the Syrah, it does not blend well with other grapes, its finesse and breed being lost in the process. The Pinot Noir fares best in a cool growing climate and, more than any other grape variety, it tends to reflect the soil and the climate in which it is grown.

In France the Pinot is grown in many different places: Champagne, the Loire, Burgundy, Jura and Alsace. It produces a distinctively different wine from each region, even from each microclimate; but outside France, it is the Burgundy style that is sought. Not possessing the same growing conditions, the wines will be very different. Perhaps because wines with a true Pinot Noir bouquet and flavour are rare, both from France and elsewhere, a comparative tasting is apt to be less balanced than, for example, a tasting of Cabernet Sauvignons. In this tasting we tried to select Pinots that have kept their varietal character, while giving an indication of their regional origin.

APPEARANCE	BOUQUET	PALATE	COMMENTS
Pinot Valais NV			Valais/Switzerland
Medium brick-red, soft, quite mature.	Full of fruit, quite powerful but lacks finesse.	Good fruit, good Pinot style and flavour, perhaps a little high in alcohol.	Well made, fruity, straightforward, lacks complexity and depth, but quite satisfactory.
Pinot Noir NV Merdinger-Bühl			Baden-Württemberg/Germany
Pale, young colour, very pretty.	Not much bouquet, but clean and fresh.	Straightforward, lovely clean fruit, light, well balanced.	Very light in alcohol (10.5°), agreeable and refreshing, lets the Pinot fruit come through.
Pinot Nero Alto Adige 1980 DOC Casa Vinicola W. Walch			Alto Adige/Italy
Pale, deep rosé, more tawny than red.	Not much Pinot on the nose, but some fruit, more reminiscent of a Morgon or a Fleurie.	Soft, fully typical Pinot, quite like the Valais or the Arbois in style; ripe but good acidity.	Pleasant well made wine from South Tyrol. Lacks the authority of the Burgundy-style Pinots.
Arbois Pinot Noir 1979 Rolet Père et Fils			Jura/France
Light, young looking, fuller colour than the Arbois 1979 from the blended grapes.	Fruity, discreet, fruit of wild cherries. Mature.	Good fruit, well balanced, but more acidity than the previous wines. At its best.	More typical of the style of region than the variety. A 1981, a more concentrated year than 1979, had more Pinot bouquet and flavour, and more depth.
Sancerre 1979 Jean Vacheron			Sancerre/France
Lovely, striking colour, deeper than the preceding wines, deeper than expected.	Fruity, floral aromas, 'pure' Pinot character. Fine quality.	Good follow-through with a certain astringence from wood-ageing that adds to the quality. Very carefully made.	Probably as good as a Sancerre Rouge can be. The finesse of the Pinot grape is plain, but it does not overwhelm the *terroir*.
Bouzy Rouge 1979 Jean Vesselle			Champagne/France
Pale, clean light red. Pretty, but a little thin.	Light, delicate fruit, fine but light.	Delicate, rather shy fruit, lacks body. Too simple for a representative Coteaux Champenois Rouge Grand Cru.	Obviously a wine from the north, natural but rather light. 1978 was a better year for Bouzy Rouge owing to lower yields.

APPEARANCE	BOUQUET	PALATE	COMMENTS
Volnay-Santenots 1979 Comte Lafon			Burgundy/France
Youthful deep crimson with blue-violet edge. Excellent colour and body for a 1979.	Vibrant aroma of briar, blackcurrants, wild cherries, oak. Complex and smooth.	Wonderful fruit, still lots of tannin, almost sturdy for a Volnay, clean, great depth and length of flavour. Very pure and very fine.	Pinot Noir at its best, low-yielding and vinified with skill and dedication. The sort of benchmark wine that gives Burgundy its reputation.
Viña Magdala 1976 (mainly Pinot Noir) Torrés			Villafranco del Penedés/Spain
Medium red, well balanced, pale edge.	Lovely strawberry aroma of the Pinot, ripe fruit, touch of vanilla from the oak casks.	Soft, mature wine, good acidity to balance the soft fruit. Very attractive wine, not at all heavy.	Very well made wine, softer than the Pinots from France, and lighter than those from California.
Pinotage 1976 (Pinot Noir and Cinsault) Meerendal Estate			Durbanville/South Africa
Deep ruby red, young-looking for the vintage.	Concentrated, even slightly cooked currant-raisin bouquet.	Similar taste to bouquet. Concentrated, lacks finesse, but has punch and flavour.	A contrast to the Torrés wine: plainly a hot-country wine, and the finesse of the Pinot is lost by blending with the Cinsault.
Hawkes Bay Pinot Noir 1981 Cook's Wine Company			Auckland/New Zealand
Medium, cherry-red, pale edge, very pretty.	Fruity, slightly 'rustic' bouquet more Mercurey in style than, say, Beaune.	Clean, well made, good fruit and acidity. Slightly metallic edge. Still a little young.	Good example of a young Pinot Noir with some oak-ageing. The fairly cool climate flavours this light fruity style of wine.
Pinot Noir 1978 (half-bottle) Knudson – Erath			Oregon/USA
Medium cherry-red, still quite young looking.	High tone, pure Pinot bouquet, seems quite high in acid.	Attractive clean, fruity attack, with slight crabapple acidity.	Interesting wine, lacks sweetness but has fine Pinot Noir quality.
Pinot Noir 1978 Carneros Creek			Napa Valley/California USA
Very attractive colour, garnet-red, lovely balance.	Lovely Pinot bouquet, pure fruit, almost feminine.	Delicious flavour, all the fruit and finesse of the Pinot, very direct clean taste. Excellent balance and follow-through.	Fine wine, from a cool part of the Napa Valley. Lovely balance of extract and fruit, French in style, letting the fruit come out, and relatively low in alcohol.
Pinot Noir 1979 Chalone Vineyards			Monterey-County/USA California
Medium-full brick red, slightly paling at edge.	Spicy, youthfully acidic bouquet, giving way to rich flavour and intense fruit.	Still aggressive and young, combines richness of fruit and alcohol with firmness of tannic and acidity. Well structured wine, and very fine Pinot style.	Chalone is known for its very Côte d'Or style of Pinot Noir and Chardonnay. Less immediate than the Carneros Creek, more complexity.
Pinot Noir 1979 Robert Mondavi			Napa Valley/California USA
Medium full, showing signs of maturity, very rich-looking.	Soft, sweet-fruit bouquet, richer than the other wines from America.	Lovely sweet-strawberry Pinot flavour. Great length of flavour supported by lots of alcohol but remains well balanced.	A very big wine, perhaps aiming at the style of a Richebourg. A wine of this weight has to be very well made to preserve the characteristics of the Pinot Noir. This one is.

Tasting/Grape Varieties/Cabernet Sauvignon

When considering the character of different grape varieties, the basic style is usually found to be inseparable from that of a particular type of wine made in France. Thus, Chardonnay equals white Burgundy, Gamay equals Beaujolais, Syrah equals Hermitage, and so on. On these lines, Cabernet Sauvignon equals Médoc. Although Médoc is very, very rarely 100% Cabernet Sauvignon, and is never intended to be so, it is to the wines of this region, and to Pauillac and Saint-Julien in particular, that the Cabernet is most often compared. Wherever planted, however, the characteristics are the same: a very full, intense red colour (almost inky black when young), a pungent aroma of blackcurrants, peppers, with a touch of cinnamon or cedar, great depth of flavour, austere, chewy, often rough and always tannic when young, but with a clear fruit throughout. Except when very young, when it is forbiddingly tannic, the Cabernet Sauvignon is firm and refreshing; red wines do not normally cloy on the palate, but none of them are as delightfully clean as the Cabernet, as we shall see below.

The Cabernet Sauvignon is a most consistent grape variety and is planted (at least where red grapes can ripen) throughout the world. In France, where its northern limit is the Loire Valley, it is grown throughout the south-west, and has found its way into vineyards across southern France that are anxious to improve their quality. In Italy, the raspberry-scented Cabernet Franc is more popular, yet the Cabernet Sauvignon is producing a handful of exceptional wines. Throughout eastern Europe, South Africa, Australia and the Americas, the Cabernet Sauvignon is looked on as the classic red grape, even if other varieties are indigenous or more successful.

When unblended, the Cabernet Sauvignon style is four-square and uncompromising; with the addition of suitable varieties like the Merlot or the Cabernet Franc (according to the soil and climate), the inherent finesse is only enhanced, while as a blender grape in itself, it adds structure, fruit and elegance. The Cabernet Sauvignon grape is a thoroughbred, as these wines, and others from previous tastings, should prove.

APPEARANCE	BOUQUET	PALATE	COMMENTS
Château Saint Jean 1980 Vin du Pays Varois M. & Mme Hirsch			Provence/France
Deep, rich crimson, quite full.	Herbaceous bouquet, 'warm', rather Californian in style but not so intense.	Blackcurrant, mint, typical primary Cabernet fruit. Still quite tannic, but not much back-up of fruit.	A good example of 100% Cabernet planted in Provence.
Cabernet Sauvignon 1979 Rothbury Estate			Hunter Valley/New South Wales Australia
Crimson, brick-red, vibrant youthful colours.	Rather reticent berry-like aromas, elegant, good depth of fruit.	Soft fruit and firm finish. Youthful tannin. Well made, classic Cabernet in the Médoc style. Keep.	An elegant wine, with a slight musty austerity behind the fruit that is quite French.
Cabernet Sauvignon 1978 Nobilo Vintners			Auckland/New Zealand
Full, deep ruby, just starting to mature.	Fragrant blackcurrant aroma with a touch of oak.	Very well balanced wine, clean fruity attack and elegant fruit and oak finish. Will be very stylish in 2–3 years.	Excellent wine, in the Saint-Julien style. The cooler growing climate allows the Cabernet to ripen without becoming too concentrated and intense.
Cabernet Sauvignon 1978 'Penedés' Jean León			Pla de Penedés/Spain
Very young, plummy, purple-red.	Pure Cabernet bouquet, leafy, briary fruit, with definite oak.	Lean, pure fruit, still tannic, almost teeth-coating but lovely fruit waiting to come out. A fine, sinewy wine.	Very firm after the Nobilo, not so rich as the Italians. Distinctive, rather uncompromising Cabernet of high quality.
Venegazzù 1978 Montello e Colli Asolani Vino da Tavola Comte Loredan-Gasparini Veneto/ Italy			
Full, deep ruby red, a very complete colour.	Soft, rich plum-briar fruit. Firm.	Lovely smooth fruit, with a tannic edge. Distinctive regional character, excellent balance. Can be kept.	A very successful wine from the hills above Venice. Has the soft plummy touch of Merlot.

APPEARANCE	BOUQUET	PALATE	COMMENTS

Sassicaia 1978 Vina da Tavolo   Tenuta San Guido, Bolghini   Tuscany/Italy

| Very deep dark red, almost opaque, with purple edge. Impressive. | Masses of fruit, well closed in, vanilla-oak overtones. Intense great quality. | Copy-book follow-through from the bouquet, spicy, plummy, oaky, great fruit, depth and complexity. Much too young. Superb vinification. | A perfect example of the Cabernet Sauvignon. Overshadows the very good Venegazzù. A wine in the Ch. Pichon-Lalande or Ridge Vineyards style. |

Cabernet Sauvignon 1978   York Creek Vineyard Ridge Vineyards   Santa Clara City/California USA

| Very deep rich red with the colour sticking to the side of the glass. | Complex *sauvage* fruit, concentrated but not heavy. | Intense fruit flavours, plummy middle palate and firm fruit-tannin and alcohol backbone. Very long, very much alive. | The rather high degree of alcohol (13.9°) give this wine a richness that contrasts with the slight austerity of the Sassicaia or the Ch. Léoville-Las Cases. |

Cabernet Sauvignon 1978   Jordan Winery   Alexander Valley/California USA

| Concentrated, full ruby red; excellent colour. | Lovely bouquet, black-currants, smoky herbaceousness. | Lovely follow-through, rounded fruit, soft fruit, elegant, very appealing and very fine. Definitely French in style. | A Cabernet in the finest Haut-Médoc style. A great success, but less grandeur than the Sassicaia or the Léoville. |

Cabernet Sauvignon 1978   Taltarni Vineyards   Victoria/Australia

| Huge colour, almost opaque blackcurrant-red. | Full spicy, minty bouquet. Masses of fruit, with eucalyptus overtones. | Massive, rich, black-curranty and spicy, lovely sweet fruit, tannin, but not too obtrusive. Very well made. | A classic Cabernet from a vineyard with lots of sun. High extract from the natural concentration in the grapes. |

Ch. Léoville-Las Cases 1978 2ème Grand Cru Classé Saint-Julien-Médoc   Médoc/Bordeaux France

| Deep, concentrated, plummy, youthful and intense. | Spicy, ripe fruit, bouquet of young blackcurrant leaves, clean new wood. | Pure, clean Médoc taste: fruit, alcohol and oak in perfect harmony. Great class, a perfect wine. | Here the austerity of the Cabernet Sauvignon is softened by the Merlot and the Cabernet Franc, while the Petit Verdot adds to the colour. |

Cabernet Sauvignon 1974   Montebello Vineyard/Ridge Vineyards   Santa Clara City/California USA

| Deep, full crimson. Still very young. | Spicy, briary bouquet, mature, slightly woody. | Clean, well knit fruit, but still has some tannin to lose. Leaner and more French in style than the 1978 York Creek. | Relatively light in alcohol (12.7°) for a Cabernet from California. This wine has less of the plumminess of the grape and more of the sinewy fruit of a Médoc. |

Ch. Léoville-Las Cases 1970 2ème Grand Cru Classé Saint-Julien-Médoc   Médoc/ Bordeaux France

| Deep, rich burnt mahogany. Very fine. | Rich, concentrated pure berry-like fruit from ripe grapes. Intense, complex. | Wonderfully rich fruit, backed up by tannin and followed up by fruit. Great depth with no excesses or exaggeration. | A totally confident statement of the Cabernet Sauvignon in the Médoc. |

Tasting/Grape Varieties/Merlot

The principal characteristic of wines made from the Merlot grape is their soft fruit. In contrast to the Cabernet Sauvignon, with which it is often blended, it is less austere and intense, more rich and fruity. It also has less tannin, although the Cabernet Sauvignon on its own often has too much, and needs the softness of the Merlot to balance this. Except in great years (1961, 1982), or from vineyards with plenty of sun (Australia, California), the Merlot will not have the deep concentration of colour of the Cabernet Sauvignon, but rather a soft, welcoming ruby tone. Being an early budder, it is often subject to spring frosts, and during a cool, wet harvest is very prone to rot. However, it ripens early, and in good years acquires a richness in sugar that gives to the wine a plummy sweetness of fruit and great intensity of flavour.

The Merlot is best known in France in the region of Bordeaux, especially in Pomerol and Saint-Emilion. Here it is the dominant grape variety, and one has only to consider the reputation of wines such as Châteaux Pétrus and Trotanoy to see the potential of the grape. In the Médoc and Graves regions, the Merlot is secondary to the Cabernet, but Sauvignon is a vital part of the makeup of these wines. It is planted throughout south-western France, and there have been experimental plantings along the Mediterranean coast. In Northern Italy it makes lovely, soft, fruity wines, while the hotter the climate, the more robust it becomes. It is extremely successful in California and Oregon, where the Cabernet Sauvignon can be a little massive and unyielding.

Merlot wines are attractive and easy to drink, but that is not all: if they are not over-produced they can be taken as seriously as the great Pomerols.

APPEARANCE	BOUQUET	PALATE	COMMENTS
Merlot Colli Berici 1979 DOC Viticoltone Fabbian			Veneto/Italy
Ruby red, quite *gras* and soft looking.	Pleasant soft fruit, not very distinctive.	Fruity, quite full, not much length in the finish.	A pleasant wine, rather like a lean Saint-Emilion. The soft fruit is typically Merlot, but there is not much else.
Château La Fleur-Pétrus 1980 Pomerol Grand Cru			Pomerol/Bordeaux France
Brick-red, lively young colour.	Soft fruit, slightly Pinot Noir in style, new oak.	Clean soft fruit with oaky back-up. A light wine, not a great year for Merlot.	The lightness of the year makes this wine seem less typically Merlot.
Château Magdelaine 1979 1er Grand Cru Classé Saint-Emilion			Saint-Emilion/Bordeaux France
Fine, full ruby, good body.	Lots of fruit and new oak, still very young.	Very attractive 'up-front' fruit and the new oak gives a fleeting impression of a young Burgundy. Lovely, supple wine that will last well and become much more complex.	Magdelaine is the 1er Grand Cru Classé in Saint-Emilion with the highest proportion of Merlot (80%). A bigger wine with more personality than La Fleur-Pétrus, still dominated by oak.
Merlot 1979 Stag's Leap Wine Cellars			Napa Valley/California USA
Very full, rich, soft deep ruby.	Soft, rich fruit, spice, blackcurrant. Exciting.	Wonderful spicy fruity flavour. Lovely silky texture. Could be drunk but should be kept.	Beautifully made, with all the softness of the Merlot and the spiciness of the Napa Valley.
Merlot 1978 Sokol-Blosser Winery			Washington/USA
Fairly full ruby red, quite rich looking.	Sweet crushed fruit bouquet, quite concentrated.	Fruity, quite lively and viscous with a touch of vanilla, still young with a slightly tart fruit finish.	Much more of a northern wine than the Stag's Leap, with vibrant fruit but less plumminess.
Merlot 1976 Sterling Vineyard			Napa Valley/California USA
Very deep colour, intense ruby, no ageing at all.	Spicy, concentrated fruit, solid, still shut in.	Very full, still very tannic, but full of clean fruit and not at all bitter. A hot vintage, giving lots of colour and extract.	Complete contrast to the silky open style of Stag's Leap, this wine is a good Merlot made to stand up to serious Cabernets.

Tasting/Grape Varieties/Syrah

The Syrah grape flourishes in a sunny climate: in France it is at its best in the Rhône Valley, particularly the northern part, and is now heavily planted throughout Provence. It is very successful in Australia, where it is known as the Shiraz or the Hermitage (to underline the French parentage), in South Africa and in California, where it should not be confused with the Petite Sirah. Wines made from the Syrah have a deep purple colour, an intense aroma of blackcurrants and spices, are rich and robust on the palate with a rough fruit that often needs several years to smoothen out and show the complexity behind the power. Professor Saintsbury called Hermitage 'the manliest of wines', which seems a fitting description. There can be no doubt that Hermitage and Côte-Rôtie,

where vines planted on the steeply terraced slopes above the Rhône river produce wines of incomparably concentrated bouquet and flavour, show the Syrah at its peak.

The Syrah is the sole grape responsible for Hermitage, Cornas, St Joseph, and Crozes-Hermitage, is generally so for Côte-Rôtie (which may add up to 20% of the Viognier white grape), and plays a significant rôle in the wines of Châteauneuf-du-Pape, of southern Côtes-du-Rhône and of Provence, where its firm spicy fruit balances the rich fullness of the Grenache. Despite its reputation as a big wine, it is seldom heavy, and it has a natural acidity that, except in very hot climates, prevents it from becoming over-ripe. The true Syrah style is consistent and quite easy to recognize, as this and previous tastings show.

APPEARANCE	BOUQUET	PALATE	COMMENTS
Syrah 1981 Vin du Pays de l'Ardèche			Ardèche/France
Medium-full carmine red. Attractive.	Soft, crushed-fruit aromas, mainly black-currants.	Good straightforward, rich fruit, nice touch of acidity, natural tannin.	Very attractive table wine grown to the west of the Rhône Valley.
Syrah 1978 Joseph Phelps Vineyard			Napa Valley/USA California
Medium-full, lighter than the French Syrahs.	Spicy high-toned fruit.	Good spicy fruit, but less blackberry and more acidity than expected.	Lacks the robustness and class of the Hermitage style.
Cornas 1978 Auguste Clape			Rhône Valley – North/France
Very deep colour, blackberry-red.	Plummy, spicy fruit, intense but less *nuancé* than the two Guigal wines.	Excellent first impression of pure Syrah fruit: black-currant and blackberries, finishes young and tannic. Very fine example of the Cornas *appellation*.	Cornas lacks the suavity of Côte-Rôtie and the richness of Hermitage, yet as a straightforward example of Syrah, pure, but slightly rustic, it cannot be bettered.
Hermitage 1978 E. Guigal			Rhône Valley – North/France
Intense dark red, almost concentrated.	Voluptuous bouquet of concentrated Syrah fruit, blackberries, blackcurrants, spice.	Huge wine, extraordinary concentration of richness and smoothness with great depth of character.	Hermitage in a great year. Combination of *cépage noble* plus *terroir noble*, and dedicated wine-making.
Côte-Rôtie 1978 'La Landonne' E. Guigal			Rhône Valley – North/France
Absolutely black, with rich ruby glints.	Powerful, almost violent concentration of fruit. Much the same impression as a young vintage port.	Extremely concentrated, masses of fruit and extract, added depth through 30 months ageing in wood. Incredible style and panache for such an immature wine; will make an extraordinary bottle.	Fascinating contrast to the Côte-Rôtie 'La Mouline' 1978 (page 155), which contained 15% of the Viognier. 'La Landonne' is to 'La Mouline' as Chambertin is to Musigny or Latour to Lafite.
Shiraz 1978 Taltarni Vineyard			Victoria/Australia
Very big colour, rich purple, opaque, even thicker than two above.	Spicy berry-like bouquet, sweet fruit, massive.	Very big wine, lots of fruit but masses of teeth-coating extract and tannin. Finishes too concentrated and rather hard.	The Shiraz (Hermitage) grape has produced here a wine tasting like a cross between a Syrah from France and a Zinfandel from California.

169

Horizontal Tasting/Red Burgundy 1972

The purpose of this tasting is similar to the horizontal tasting of 1970 Bordeaux on pages 172–3, namely to show the difference between the *appellations* in the Côte de Beaune and the Côte de Nuits. With one single grape variety, the Pinot Noir, differences in style and character are caused by the geographical siting of the vineyards, soil, subsoil and microclimate. Since the Burgundy vineyards are so fragmented, the differences in wine-making often either exaggerate or blur the intrinsic character of the various *appellations*. For this tasting, therefore, we decided to choose the majority of wines from one highly respected *négociant-éleveur*, Leroy. The wines were purchased from individual *propriétaires* and bottled unblended. They tend to reflect Madame Bize-Leroy's personal preference for well-structured long-lived wines as much as they do the style of the various *villages*,

and we feel that this sort of homogeneity serves to underline the differences between them.

1972 is a controversial vintage, but it is the only mature vintage of quality, alongside 1971, from the 1970s. The year was generally dry but cold, until September, which was very sunny. The vintage was late, with the grapes healthy but high in acidity. The style of wine was more suited to the Côte de Nuits, where the wines are tougher by nature, than to the Côte de Beaune, and was in complete contrast to the full, voluptuous 1971s. As the two vintages matured, the lack of acidity under the rather excessive richness of the 1971s became apparent, while the charmless 1972s opened up considerably. Whereas 1971 is still considered the more impressive vintage, many growers prefer the closer-knit 1972s. They are mostly fully mature, but will keep for some years.

	APPEARANCE	BOUQUET	PALATE	COMMENTS
Côte de Beaune-Villages Leroy				
	Fine deep red, solid, very good for a minor *appellation*.	Still young, even animal-like, full of fruit.	Full, clean, solid wine, very attractive and well made, perfect at the moment.	Very good example of an often over-rated *appellation*; a very typical 1972.
Auxey-Duresses Leroy				
	Medium colour, light and pleasant, tawny edge.	Fully mature, ripe fruit, quite light.	Pleasant, tannic, typical Côte de Beaune style, a touch acid but ends well.	Attractive wine from an *appellation* north-west of Meursault. Does not have the structure and breed of the Volnays or Pommards under which names it was sold before the AOC system.
Monthélie Leroy				
	Medium full, deeper than the Auxey-Duresses.	Elegant fruit, quite firm and good class.	Lovely, rounded fruit flavour, almost balsamic, not very intense but beautifully balanced. At its best.	Monthélie lies slightly above and to the west of Volnay, north of Meursault. These wines have much of Volnay's style, but tend to be more rustic.
Savigny-lès-Beaune Leroy				
	Clear medium-pale red, rather more mature than most.	Complex bouquet, hint of chocolate and vanilla, interesting fruit.	Lovely, elegant at first, but finishes with some tannin, a little green. A classy wine, but not as well balanced as the Monthélie. Better with food.	Savigny-lès-Beaune, at the other end of the Côte from Santenay, is its opposite in style, being lighter and more graceful. This wine still needs time in bottle.
Beaune-Montée Rouge 1er Cru Leroy				
	Fuller than the Savigny, more interesting in appearance, soft ruby red.	Quite rich, soft red-fruit bouquet.	Full, attractive almost sweet flavour and still some tannin. Very good straightforward wine, at its best, but will keep.	Beaune seldom has the power of Corton, the structure of Pommard or the finesse of Volnay, but it is wonderfully harmonious.

APPEARANCE	BOUQUET	PALATE	COMMENTS

Pommard Clos des Epeneaux   Comte Armand

APPEARANCE	BOUQUET	PALATE	COMMENTS
Very deep colour, still youthful and intense. By far the richest colour of the Côte de Beaunes.	Rich bouquet of velvety-like fruit, slightly concentrated.	Very big mouthful, most impressive balance of fruit and natural tannins, lovely long complex flavour. Can be kept.	A wine made from very old vines, resulting in a small production of intense, tannic wine but with masses of fruit. Not many modern Pommards have this solidity.

Côte de Nuits-Villages   Leroy

APPEARANCE	BOUQUET	PALATE	COMMENTS
Good full-medium red, well built, quite mature.	Mature bouquet, fruit, still some wood.	Good fruit, firm and tannic.	An altogether rougher wine than the Côte de Beaune-Villages, perhaps less immediate fruit.

Fixin-Hervelets 1er Cru   Leroy

APPEARANCE	BOUQUET	PALATE	COMMENTS
Very big colour, full, rich, most encouraging.	Wonderful bouquet, fruit, wild flowers, great depth.	Excellent robust wine, slightly sinewy, but complete and a total success. Can be drunk now and will keep well.	The epitome of Fixin, the most northerly of the fine wines in the Côte de Nuits; a big wine well worth looking for.

Vosne-Romanée   Leroy

APPEARANCE	BOUQUET	PALATE	COMMENTS
Medium colour, quite good, but looks light after the Fixin.	Lovely, lightish feminine bouquet, lissom with a touch of vanilla.	Well-balanced, lightish wine of great breed. Less hard than many 1972s. Would be perfect with chicken. Drink now. Compare to Vosne-Romanée Les Beaux Monts 1972, page 155.	Complete contrast to the Fixin, being lighter but with much more finesse. A very good example of the class of the Vosne wines, especially as it is only a *villages* and not a Premier Cru.

Chambolle-Musigny   Leroy

APPEARANCE	BOUQUET	PALATE	COMMENTS
Very good colour, clean mature red.	Lovely velvety bouquet, smooth, elegant.	Excellent balance, perhaps more fruit than the Vosne, but finishes with less length. Drink now, a good wine from the commune.	Well made wine from the 'Volnay of the Côte de Nuits'. Soft fragrant fruit with a firm backbone.

Gevrey-Chambertin Lavaux-Saint-Jacques 1er Cru   Leroy

APPEARANCE	BOUQUET	PALATE	COMMENTS
Same colour as the Chambolle, perhaps more brick-red.	Fine, pure bouquet of fruit and a touch of liquorice.	Elegant, good fine fruit but still rather green, needs 3–5 years.	Very much a *vin de propriétaire*, distinctive, and very much 1972. A vigorous wine.

Gevrey-Chambertin Clos Saint Jacques 1er Cru   Domaine Armand Rousseau

APPEARANCE	BOUQUET	PALATE	COMMENTS
Good medium mature ruby, more concentrated than the Lavaux.	Long lingering bouquet, still a hint of blackcurrants, great complexity.	Great depth of flavour, perfect balance of mature Pinot fruit with great class and staying power. A very fine wine.	A very good Premier Cru, reckoned by Charles Rousseau to be almost as fine as Chambertin. A very stylish wine, to serve to the detractors of the 1972 vintage.

Bonnes-Mares 1972   Louis Jadot

APPEARANCE	BOUQUET	PALATE	COMMENTS
Solid brick-red, tawny edge, looks fully mature.	Concentrated bouquet, fruity, rich, long and quite subtle.	Firm clean fruit on palate, quite robust. Typical acidic edge of the 1972s. Good balance of elegance and power. Can be drunk.	Quite a big wine, but less impressive than the Clos Saint Jacques. Shows the harder Bonne-Mares – Morey-Saint-Denis style.

Horizontal Tasting/Red Bordeaux 1970

The purpose of this tasting is to illustrate the differences in style between the major *appellations* in Bordeaux, showing the influence of soil and climate, and especially grape varietal mix and personal vinification. We selected the 1970 vintage, since this is, with 1975 and 1978, one of the three best vintages in the decade, perhaps even the best, and it is the only one becoming ready to drink. The individual wines are among the finest and most distinctive in their respective *appellations*, in order to underline the differences in style.

1970 was an excellent vintage, rare in combining quantity with quality. A late spring was followed by a healthy flowering in mid-June, a very hot July, a cooler August, and then from early September almost unbroken sunshine until the end of the vintage. The grapes were very healthy and there were lots of them. There was no frost early in the year, no hail later on to destroy a part of the crop, and all the *cépages* ripened perfectly. With a successful, well-balanced vintage like 1970, there is a common style to the wines: fine, deep colour; clean, concentrated fruit on the nose and palate, and a firm tannic backbone. Wines that do not correspond to this basic description are not typical 1970s.

The 1970s showed very well in cask and received universal acclaim. After bottling, they went through a dumb stage for about five years. The minor wines are now at their best. The wines in our tasting will generally be at their peak 1984–90.

APPEARANCE	BOUQUET	PALATE	COMMENTS
Ch. Camensac 5ème Cru Classé Haut-Médoc			*Cabernet Sauvignon 60%, Merlot 20%, Cabernet Franc 20%*
Full, rich, concentrated red, slight caramel tinge.	Expansive, quite powerful, sweet 'Russian Leather', mature.	Concentrated, waxy, old fruit Médoc taste. Well developed, good acidity. Solid, meaty.	A very well made wine, without the definition and style of the *crus classés* that are situated nearer the Gironde. At its best.
Ch. de Pez Grand Cru Bourgeois Saint-Estèphe			*Cabernet Sauvignon 70%, Cabernet Franc 15%, Merlot 10%, Petit Verdot 5%*
Very deep ruby, young colour, no sign of browning, consistent.	Concentrated, rather 'muscly' berry-like bouquet, lots of fruit, very fine.	Firm attack, reticent and tough at first, but opened up wonderfully to an earthy sweetness. Excellent, just mature now, will last.	A quite exceptional example of a Bourgeois Médoc. More of a success than the Cos d'Estournel, more harmonious.
Ch. Cos d'Estournel 2ème Cru Classé Saint-Estèphe			*Cabernet Sauvignon 50%, Merlot 40%, Cabernet Franc 10%*
Very intense colour, slightly fuller than the Pez, but rather older-looking.	Firm bouquet of ripe fruit with cedar overtones. Slight dryness at the end.	Very well knit with intense concentration of fruit, slightly spicy, very good middle taste, finishes rather hard.	Impressive wine, rather *ancien style*, and the softer fruit of the Merlot does not show up against the tannin from the Cabernet and the style of vinification.
Ch. Palmer 3ème Cru Classé Margaux			*Cabernet Sauvignon 45%, Cabernet Franc 10%, Merlot 35%, Petit Verdot 10%*
Very big deep rich colour, very little brown, most impressive.	Rich, mature fruit, great depth, plummy, elegant.	Very full, velvety, lovely texture, intense flavour all the way through. Still not at its best.	A superb wine, certainly the best in the commune in 1970. Wonderful balance of rich fruit from the Merlot.
Ch. Ducru-Beaucaillou 2ème Cru Classé Saint-Julien			*Cabernet Sauvignon 65%, Merlot 25%, Cabernet Franc 5%, Petit Verdot 5%*
Very intense deep red, a bit less rich-looking than the Palmer, but firm and clear.	Fine concentrated classic bouquet, woody, starting to mature, great promise.	Intense, rich concentrated fruit flavours, with firm tannic edge. Great depth and complexity, beginning to open up. Very fine.	Another superb wine. More austere than the Palmer, less voluptuous. A classic, will last until 2000.

APPEARANCE	BOUQUET	PALATE	COMMENTS

Ch. Grand-Puy-Lacoste 5ème Cru Classé Pauillac — *Cabernet Sauvignon 75%, Merlot 25%*

APPEARANCE	BOUQUET	PALATE	COMMENTS
Immense colour, almost black, magnificently deep and young-looking.	Rich, ample, intense bouquet. A touch of spice, tobacco, cinnamon. Full of interest, persistent.	Extremely rich with firm tannic edge. Great depth of flavour, clear, almost fresh. Very great promise, will last 20 years.	Classic Pauillac, intense briary fruit with a serious tannic backbone. This is an almost perfect wine, as were the Ducru and the Palmer, both quite different in style from each other.

Ch. La Lagune 3ème Cru Classé Haut Médoc — *Cabernet Sauvignon 55%, Cabernet Franc 20%, Merlot 20%, Petit Verdot 5%*

APPEARANCE	BOUQUET	PALATE	COMMENTS
Very deep, dense red with a touch of brown. Solid and rich-looking.	Slightly stalky, cedar, smoked wood, vanilla, good rich fruit.	Concentrated, almost burnt flavour, good middle fruit, finishes tannic. Still, big wine.	Classic, almost old-fashioned style of wine, before the era of new wood. Almost mature, and will hold up well.

Domaine de Chevalier Grand Cru Classé Graves — *Cabernet Sauvignon 65%, Merlot 30%, Cabernet Franc 5%*

APPEARANCE	BOUQUET	PALATE	COMMENTS
Full ruby red, not so intense as some of the Médocs. Quite young.	Lovely aromatic bouquet, soft fruit, roses, impressive and entrancing.	Delicious, rather dry flavour, reticent at first, followed by great elegance and long finish.	Classic Graves. An incredibly elegant wine, still too young. Beautiful, owing as much to its owner as to its Graves soil.

Ch. La Mission Haut Brion Grand Cru Classé Graves — *Cabernet Sauvignon 65%, Merlot 30%, Cabernet Franc 5%*

APPEARANCE	BOUQUET	PALATE	COMMENTS
Very rich, deep blackcurrant colour. Intense, impressive.	Intense, spicy aromas, almost minty, rich concentration of fruit.	Rich, plummy, spicy, blackcurrant fruit. Still dense and needs 2–3 years. Very much in the La Mission style. Powerful and long-lasting.	Totally different to Domaine de Chevalier, although equally Graves with the refreshing finish. All the colour and concentration of the best 1970s.

Ch. L'Evangile Grand Cru Pomerol — *Merlot 66%, Cabernet Franc 34%*

APPEARANCE	BOUQUET	PALATE	COMMENTS
Very big, deep, dark red, almost opaque, young, no real ageing.	Firm, hint of wild violets, still rather shut in.	Very firm, meaty, chewy wine. Lots of extract, not too much charm. Needs time.	A very big, tough wine, harder than expected (and younger) from a Pomerol. Vinification and the high proportion of Cabernet Franc could explain this.

Ch. Figeac 1er Grand Cru Classé Saint-Emilion — *Cabernet Sauvignon 35%, Cabernet Franc 35%, Merlot 30%*

APPEARANCE	BOUQUET	PALATE	COMMENTS
Very deep colour, deep rich warm red. Firm and rich-looking.	Lovely rich fruity bouquet with spicy, eucalyptus overtones. Very exciting.	Rich, sweet fruit. High-toned. 'Russian Leather' element, violets. Still very young, very big wine. Just softening up.	Quite excellent, a complete success, very well defined, and years from its best. Has the fruit that L'Evangile lacks.

Ch. Ausone 1er Grand cru Classé Saint-Emilion — *Merlot 50%, Cabernet Franc 50%*

APPEARANCE	BOUQUET	PALATE	COMMENTS
Full, mature, burnt brick-red. Slight tawny edge.	Woody, redolent of vanilla. Quite concentrated, mature fruit.	Firm flavour of fruit and wood, but a little dried-out and should be drunk.	Different style to Figeac (grown on the 'Graves' soil), Ausone is from the Côtes, where the light soil lies on rock.

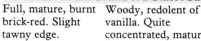

Vertical Tasting/Red Burgundy

The purpose of this tasting is to show the difference between ten vintages in Burgundy in the 1960s and 1970s. We have chosen a single vineyard Volnay, the Clos de la Bousse d'Or, where the wine has been made by the same person (Gérard Potel) in each vintage, so as to best isolate the vintage factor. Volnay is considered to produce the archetypical Côte de Beaune.

Clos de la Bousse d'Or, Volnay

The Domaine possesses 13 hectares of vines, with vineyards in Pommard and Santenay as well as Volnay. The vineyard of the Clos de la Bousse d'Or (which reverted in 1967 to its original name from that of Clos de la Pousse d'Or) is a *monopole*. With the estates of the Marquis d'Angerville and Mme Hubert de Montille, the Domaine is the finest estate in Volnay, and Gérard Potel is one of the most skilful wine makers in the Côte d'Or.

Except in cold years, when the stalks will give an astringent taste to the wine instead of a tannin support, M. Potel does not *égrappe* before fermentation. Fermentation takes place in glass-lined enamel vats. *Pigeage* is still done with the feet, and the cap is broken up and pressed down several times a day, with the must being pumped over. Fermentation usually lasts 12–14 days. The wine spends an average of 14 months in cask, of which 50% are renewed each year. In the 1960s, M. Potel did not filter his wines before bottling, but the lack of star-brightness was not understood on the export markets, and now the wines receive a very light filtering. He chaptalizes as little as possible, and when the natural sugar permits (1971, 1982), he does not chaptalize at all. The yield is average to low, owing to the rare practice of *ébourgeonage* in the spring, preceded by a very severe pruning. The vines have an average age of 20 years.

	APPEARANCE	BOUQUET	PALATE	COMMENTS
1979	Very pretty youthful ruby. Quite *gras*.	Lovely Pinot fruit, vanilla overtones.	Very attractive, harmonious, still young, but lissom and more drinkable than the 1978 though less substantial.	Late, but good flowering, a moderate summer and fine weather during the vintage (29 Sept.) produced a large crop of early-maturing wine, but with enough body to last a decade.
1978	Big solid ruby, deeper than the 1979, youthful edge lost.	Rich, velvety, complex, great depth and potential.	Firm on the palate after the voluptuous bouquet, excellent balance, all the finesse of a fine Volnay. 1985–95.	Cold spring, late, reduced flowering, very poor summer, but constant, perfectly dry sunny weather from the end of August produced a 'miracle' vintage. Small crop of firm, beautifully balanced wines, the best in the 1970s.
1977	Fullish red, good for the year, but tawny edge showing early age.	Pleasantly fruity, ripe, almost jammy.	Mature, light, rather metallic finish, would be better with food. Drink now.	Long wet summer, low natural sugar, high acidity and general lack of colour.
1976	Incredibly young, firm, dark red, right up to the rim. Very *gras*.	Briary bouquet, concentrated fruit, impression of distilled cherries, *marc*.	Very tannic, uncharacteristic of this Domaine, more extract than fruit at the moment, but worth waiting for. 1988–2000.	Average crop of tannic, deep-coloured wines, that needed careful wine-making to keep the finesse of the Pinot. Even more extract than the 1964s, which they otherwise resemble.
1973	Medium pale red, fading away.	Light strawberry fruit, attractive, but fading.	Well balanced, still some fruit, but past its best; very attractive in the late 1970s.	A year of record production, many *déclassements*, and some very pretty wines for drinking young.

VOLNAY Iᵉʳ CRU
CLOS de la BOUSSE D'OR
Monopole
19.6
LA POUSSE D'OR

APPEARANCE	BOUQUET	PALATE	COMMENTS
1972			
Full brick-red, tawny edge, definitely mature.	Rich, animal, quite intense.	Sweet, mature Pinot flavour; ready to drink, a little charmless in the finish, untypical of Volnay, but very good.	Fairly late flowering, then cold but dry until early September. Latish vintage (4 Oct.) with good colour and high acidity, rather austere wines, a complete contrast to 1971. Perhaps better in the Côte de Nuits, and a better year than many.
1971			
Brick-red, mature tawny, but brighter than the 1972. Very rich-looking.	Sweet candied fruit bouquet, voluptuous but not fat.	Rich, smooth, rich in fruit, slight mildewy impression in the middle (*goût de grêle*), finishes very well with a lively acidity. Very good example, and will last a few more years.	A patchy flowering was followed by good weather throughout the summer broken by hailstorms in mid-August. This further reduced the crop, giving the grapes greater concentration of sugar, but also a characteristic *goût de grêle* from the effects of hail. Early vintage (16 Sept.) of over-ripe grapes resulted in rich, powerful wines.
1969			
Medium-red, tawny, pale edge; paler than expected.	Concentrated, curiously rather shut in.	Firm and tough, big wine, not very Volnay. Midway between the 1971, with some way to go, and the much older 1964. Not showing at its best. 1983–90.	Late flowering, fine July and August, rainy September, but very fine weather for the late (6 Oct.) vintage. Produced a smallish crop of very tannic wines. A very good, rather old-fashioned vintage.
1966			
Lovely clean tawny red with yellow rim. Beautiful colour.	Sweet, concentrated mature fruit. Great finesse.	Sweet, lissom, harmonious, lovely length and balance, pure Volnay. Perfect at 16 years old.	Cold spring, warm June, poor July and August and lovely weather for the vintage (29 Sept.) produced racy, distinguished wines, not very assertive at first, but beautifully balanced.
1964			
Fullish tawny red, deeper and richer than the 1966.	Mature, almost petroleum bouquet with chocolate overtones.	Well balanced, firm, a sturdy, mature wine, without the sweetness of the 1966. Very fine, perfect with food. (See Volnay de Montille, page 154.)	Very cold spring, but excellent weather in June and a good flowering. A very hot summer (like 1976) reduced the crop, and the vintage (24 Sept.) produced solid, full-bodied wines of great character and potential.

Note: Vintages, where quoted, denote the date the Domaine began picking.

Vertical Tasting/Red Bordeaux

The aim of this tasting is to show the differences in the character of the vintage and their state of maturity at a particular time. The chosen decade of the 1970s, apart from being recent, exhibited the best selection of vintages this century. Improvements in viticulture and vinification, played just as significant a rôle in this as did the weather. Château Giscours is one of the finer châteaux in the Médoc, and the selection is a true representation of the different years.

Château Giscours, 3ème Grand Cru Classé Margaux

The property is owned by Pierre Tari, President de l'Union des Grand Crus Classés du Médoc, whose father, Nicolas Tari, bought it in 1952. The vineyards cover an area of 75 hectares, 68 of which are planted at present with a balance of 65% Cabernet Sauvignon, 20% Merlot, 10% Cabernet Franc and 5% Petit Verdot. The soil is composed of a thin layer of arable topsoil above a thick layer of gravel on a sandy base. The gravel provides for adequate drainage – important because excess water is damaging to the vine roots. The vinification combines modern and traditional techniques: The *éraflage* is followed by a light *foulage*, the must is fermented in enamelled vats, and the temperature is carefully controlled to make sure it does not exceed 30°C. The duration of the *cuvaison* varies from 10–20 days, depending on the year. At the *assemblage*, up to 15% *vin de presse* is added. The wines spend 17 to 28 months in barrels, one-quarter of which are replaced each year.

	APPEARANCE	BOUQUET	PALATE	COMMENTS
1979	Very full deep ruby, vibrant, youthful.	Full, almost voluptuous aromas, masses of fruit.	Firm, evidently tannic still, but full of fruit, charm and class. Lovely big wine. Lots of promise. 1985–95.	Ideal weather conditions in June led to a big flowering; the vintage started at the beginning of October with a large crop of small, healthy grapes. The ratio of skins to juice was high, and the wines generally have a deep colour and good body.
1978	Deep ruby, a shade darker than the 1979, but less youthful.	Still closed, but beginning to develop a solid berry-like fruit.	Big, robust, great length and style, complex, long finish, slow maturing. 1988–2000.	Uneven flowering and cool weather until late August, then brilliantly sunny weather until after the vintage. Sound, healthy grapes, good sugar levels, small to average crop. The wines have very good colour, fruit and tannin balance, a classic vintage.
1977	Good brick-red, obviously paler than the 1978.	Attractive fruit, a little asperity.	Good flavour and balance, some acidity, but the fruit still dominant. 1983–84.	Spring frosts attacked the Merlot, and all varieties flowered late. Disappointing summer, but fine dry early October vintage.
1976	Ripe, mature colour, soft brick-red with browning at the rim.	Floral and elegant, already mature.	Attractive, delicious taste, still fresh and lively, but lacks depth. Good for the vintage. 1983–86.	After a very hot dry summer, picking started exceptionally early in September. A bigger crop than 1977 or 1975. Very good colour, but the wines lack a little structure, some being rather dull, hollow and lacking in acidity.

APPEARANCE	BOUQUET	PALATE	COMMENTS
1975			
Solid ruby, a shade less full than the 1979 and 1978.	Complex Cabernet aromas, still closed, firm, great promise.	Firm, complete, dense, strongly Cabernet in style, still very hard. 1986–2000.	Successful flowering; hot, dry summer with a little rain before the September harvest. Small crop due to dry conditions. The wines are of very high quality, deep colour, plenty of body and should be kept.
1974			
Very fine ruby, surprisingly young.	Good fruit, forward and appealing.	Well made, good fruit, quite long, finishes well. Has none of the meanness of the vintage. A fine Médoc, now at its best.	Good conditions until mid-September, when cold wet weather started and continued throughout the harvest. Large crop of rather hard wines of no great class.
1973			
Medium brick-red, mature.	Soft, ripe fruit nose, open.	Attractive and supple, soft fruit. Well made, good for the vintage, but must be drunk now.	A good flowering, and a fine summer gave the year the look of 'the vintage of the century', then heavy storms hit Bordeaux and the rain continued for the first 10 days of the harvest. Enormous crop of pleasant but rather light wines.
1972			
Full mature reddish brown, a shade darker than the 1973.	Firm, still some fruit.	Well made, good balance and length for the year, slightly astringent finish. Should have been drunk.	Cold spring, and a poor flowering were followed by a cool, rainy summer. Very late harvest, beginning mid-October. The wines produced are uneven and generally without much interest.
1971			
Deep colour, but fully mature with a tawny edge.	Complex, aromatic, cedar wood, spice. Lovely.	Ripe, mouth-filling but not rich. Excellent balance and finesse showing the breed of a Grand Cru Classé. 1983–85.	Poor flowering resulted in a small crop. Moderate weather during the summer, fine for the vintage. The quality is less regular than the 1970s and the wines are lighter, but it is a fine vintage.
1970			
Very good, full colour, with brown tints.	Complex, secondary aromas, not fully open but with great depth.	Full, silky flavour and texture, very promising, already elegant but not fully apparent. Very long, slight peppery aftertaste. Drink 1985–2000.	An outstanding vintage, combining a huge crop and high quality. Cool spring, late flowering, fine summer, a cool, rainy spell before, fine warm weather during, the vintage, which began in early October.

Tasting/Fortified and Dessert Wines

Fortified wines are generally drunk on their own, either as an aperitif or after meals. There is no reason, however, why they should not be drunk at certain times during a meal: sherry or madeira with the soup, port with the cheese, for instance, but these customs vary from country to country. This tasting is therefore a comparison of some of the basic styles of fortified wine, to which we have added two very rare wines from the Jura: a *vin jaune* and a *vin de paille*. Although they are not, strictly speaking, fortified, they are made in such a way that they fit more easily into this group than any other.

Coming from so many different regions, these wines are not easily compared. The natural wine is fortified at different stages during vinification, some being bone dry, some being naturally sweet and others having sweetness added. Sherry and madeira are basically white wines that become darker (maderize) with age, while port and Banyuls are red wines that lose colour with age. Unless they are sweetened during the ageing process, they all have a tendency to become progressively drier, until the alcohol dominates the fruit. This, however, takes many, many years.

APPEARANCE	BOUQUET	PALATE	COMMENTS
Sherry Fino			'La Ina'/Domecq
Pale, straw-yellow, bright, almost Mâcon Blanc colour, clean and fresh.	Dry, almost salty. Perfect sherry *flor* nose, tangy, subtle. Dry but not austere.	Pure in attack, good length and intensity of flavour, clean, tangy, refreshing finish.	Classic dry fino, young, finesse and body in harmony.
Vin Jaune d'Arbois 1975 Bottled 1982			Rolet Père et Fils/Arbois
Full yellow-straw colour, with greenish tints, almost oily looking.	Concentrated, *flor* bouquet, nutty, high in acidity, very distinctive.	Long, concentrated flavours but rather hard to taste, being high in acidity and uncompromising. Has none of the rich charms of a fortified wine.	A vintage wine. Tastes like an old fino sherry with more concentration and less alcohol. Very intense as a result of the time in the cask.
Vin de Paille d'Arbois 1979			Rolet Père et Fils/Arbois
Golden-amber, lovely vibrant colour, very rich.	Concentrated sweet apricotty fruit, rich and unctuous.	Sweet, concentrated almost as 'essence' rather than a wine. As rich as a German TBA or Eiswein.	Perfect as an aperitif or as a dessert wine, after dinner. Very aromatic and great richness from the concentration of sugar in the dried grapes.
Vin Doux Naturel Muscat de Beaumes-de-Venise			Domaine de Durban/Leydier et Fils
Straw-yellow, a little fuller than the La Ina. Incredibly rich, viscous on the glass.	Very aromatic, apricots, almonds, marzipan. Sun-filled bouquet, sweet and luscious.	Rich, unctuous, very full. Dried apricots. Good acidity at the start, but finishes a bit cloying. Not too much alcohol.	Non-vintage, mostly 1981. Lacks the finesse and floweriness of some Muscats. Very rich, but could be more lively for an aperitif.
Vin de Liqueur Pineau des Charentes			Domaine Haute-Roche/Mme Raymond Ragnaud
Straw-yellow-gold, a bit deeper than the Muscat, but less rich-looking.	Floral, fruit-fermentation aromas. Quite viscous, and pronounced presence of alcohol.	Young, fruity taste, wild (mirabelle) plums. Rather straw-like impression of alcohol in the finish.	From the 1982 vintage. The alcohol has not had time to blend in with the must. Clean, well made and not too sweet.
Sherry Amontillado			'Dry Don'/Sandeman
Medium amber, clean and bright.	Sweeter, more burnt than the La Ina. A little caramelly, sticky.	Richer body and more weight than the La Ina, same slightly burnt flavour as on the nose, clean finish and good acidity to balance the sweetness.	Good commercial blend, rather than an aged wine. Sweetened and darkened with caramel to achieve the desired colour and finish.

APPEARANCE	BOUQUET	PALATE	COMMENTS
Vin Doux Naturel Banyuls Vieux 1978			Propriété St Louis/Mme Bertan-Maillot
Pale brick-red, fading to tawny edge. Quite rich-looking.	Sweet, concentrated fruit, impression more of wine than spirit.	Sweet, quite light but lingering flavour. Rather more over-ripened by the sun than strengthened with alcohol.	Lighter than expected from a 4-year-old Banyuls. Less concentrated and port-like, more of an after-dinner wine.
Port Ruby			Fine Ruby/Sandeman
Fine medium ruby, lightish and no purple tinge left. Brick-red, but not yet fading to tawny.	Good raisin-grape concentration, and considerable alcohol.	Spirituous and spicy. Attractive sweet attack, peppery, quite light for a ruby.	Good concentrated blend, pleasant without being impressive.
Port Vintage			1980/Taylor
Deep, intense carmine-purple, almost opaque, purple edge, very rich.	Deep, rich, berry-like bouquet, like a rich Zinfandel. Slight bitterness in the finish. At this stage, a hint of cherry brandy.	Rich, mouth-filling, sweet, spicy, less rough than expected. Lovely concentrated middle, and solid finish.	Cask sample, 'the Château Latour of the port world'. Will be very fine in 20 years. Classic.
Port Vintage			1960 (bottled 1962)/Dow
Deep, aged brick-red, like a 1966 claret. Maturing at edge to tawny, lovely gradation of colour.	Rich, complex, but fruity and soft. Still some spiciness but complete and beautifully blended in.	Lovely attack, soft, slightly burnt taste, concentrated and full in the middle, hint of violets. Sugar already being absorbed. Lovely reposing finish.	Fine example of a fully mature vintage port from a good, slightly soft vintage.
Port Tawny			20 year old (bottled 1981)/Taylor
Classic, orange-tawny colour of a red wine 20 years in cask. Lovely warm glow; slight greeny-yellow edge reminiscent of an old cognac.	Dry, nutty bouquet, particularly walnuts. Spicy, spirity, slightly musty-dried fruit impression. Beautiful lingering aromas.	Sweet, overall long and lingering impression of fruit and spices. Fine balance and length. Very well made.	Perfect contrast to the vintage port. Perhaps a little finer, and more digestible.
Sherry Oloroso			'Royal Corregidor'/Sandeman
Lovely caramel-amber, paling to greeny-yellow rim. Rich, jewel-like burnt middle. Great depth.	Fine, burnt sugar-molasses bouquet. Clean and clear. Very lively despite the sweetness.	Rich, molasses in the attack, lingering sweet-ness on the tip of the tongue, touch of acidity at the end to balance the richness. Completely mature.	A 20-year-old rich Oloroso. Very complex, almost as rich as a Ch. d'Yquem. Very fine and rare flavour.
Madeira Verdelho			c. 1846/Blandy
Yellow-gold-amber, paler than Oloroso (a white wine that has *gained* colour with age, unlike the 20-year-old Taylor tawny port).	Wonderful tangy, ethereal bouquet, burnt almonds. Almost as spirited as a fine cognac.	Tangy and spirity taste, incredible intensity of flavour, with no richness or fatness left to hold it up. Beautiful rosewood fruit from the original wine.	A wonderful experience. Perfect.

Tasting/Robes/Whites

Muscadet de Sèvre et Maine 1981. *Light Loire White*
Very pale, almost colourless, fresh and mouth-watering.
A Muscadet may be a little more yellow in a very sunny
year like 1976, but should always be pale.

Pouilly Fumé 1981. *Light Loire White*
Slightly fuller than the Muscadet, Pouilly-Fumé or
Sancerre from the Sauvignon grape should have the
colour of a dry, crisp white wine. Once the colour loses
its freshness, after 3–4 years, the wine will have too.

Riesling 1981. *Young White from Alsace*
Much the same tone as the Pouilly Fumé, but a little
firmer with a touch of green. The colour is as expected
from a young wine, and will fill out as the wine
matures, the acidity keeping it relatively fresh.

Meursault 1978. *Classic White Côte de Beaune*
A softer, more buttery colour, deeper and richer than
the Riesling. The colour is still youthful, as is to be
expected from a well-made 1978 Meursault, and a good
level of acidity from ageing in barrel will keep it fresh.

Chardonnay 1978. Trefethen. *Chardonnay from the Napa Valley*
Very similar to the Meursault – a Chardonnay from the same vintage – but slightly softer. This is considered quite fresh for a Chardonnay from California.

Arbois 1980. *Mature Jura White*
Medium yellow, and mature looking, even though it is a younger wine than the two Chardonnays. Part of the colour comes from the Savagnin grape, and part from the time spent in wood.

Vouvray 1966. Demi-sec. *Mature Semi-Sweet Loire White*
A remarkably fresh colour for a 16-year-old wine, due to the acidity of the Chenin Blanc, but a very complete honey-yellow. Will hold for many years.

Ch. Suduiraut 1967. *Maturing top quality Sauternes*
Full, rich golden yellow of a *very* sweet wine after its years. From this point the colour will mature quite quickly (10 years) to an amber-gold.

Tasting/Robes/Rosés

Bourgueil Rosé 1981. *Very light Touraine Rosé*
Very pale, clean rosé, analogous to the Muscadet (page 142). Very little skin contact produces these delightful colours. The wine must be drunk as young as it looks.

Bandol Rosé 1981. *Rosé de Bandol*
The pale colour is due to short skin-contact, and the soft oranginess from wood ageing. The wine, already quite mature, will hold well.

Domaine des Férauds 1981. *Rosé de Provence*
The other style of Provence or Rhône rosé. A longer maceration gives more colour, but the wine is kept in stainless steel and bottled young to keep the fresh fruit. Should be treated like a very light red wine.

Arbois Rosé. *Rosé d'Arbois*
This is a *vin rosé* vinified like a red wine as above, but rosé due to the low level of pigment in the Poulsard grape. The brown edge puts it apart from the others.

Reds/Volnay

Volnay 1979. *Young Côte de Beaune*
Shows the fresh young colour of a Pinot at 3 years from a large vintage. A lovely, fruit-looking wine, the slightly watery rim denoting a relatively quick maturing future.

Volnay 1978. *Immature Côte de Beaune*
From a much smaller crop, the colour is more intense, richer-looking and less *primeur* than 1979. The ox-blood hue denotes that it is not a *very* young wine; but it is not yet showing any age.

Volnay 1976. *Very immature Côte de Beaune*
From a year when the skins were exceptionally dark and thick, and the colour accordingly concentrated. Looks younger than the 1978 and will not be drinkable for years. The Pinot Noir is rarely this intense.

Volnay 1971. *Mature Côte de Beaune*
A perfectly mature red Burgundy with lots of life left. The full red of the 1978 has taken on a mahogany richness. It will lose colour from now on.

Tasting/Robes/Reds

Brouilly 1981. *Classic young Beaujolais*
Full, violetty, youthful red. The Gamay should always have this look: not too heavy, not too light, very appealing. In two years the colour will have lost its youth, as will the wine.

Chinon 1981. (Chinon Charles Joguet Diotorie. Vieilles Vignes) *Fine Touraine Red*
A very fine colour from old Cabernet Franc vines, a rich carmine with a young purple edge. These wines can be, and usually are, drunk young for *goût de terroir*.

Crozes-Hermitage 1979. *Young Côtes-du-Rhône Red*
Very deep, blackberry red, as you would expect from the Syrah. Just losing the opaque purple of a too-young wine. Could be drunk now for its massive fruit, or kept.

Zinfandel, Ridge Vineyards, Paso Robles Estate 1978. *Intense Zinfandel from California*
Even more intense than the Crozes-Hermitage, rich blackcurrant with no sign of age. The plumminess and tannin can be sensed from the colour.

Ch. Laroze 1978. *Young Saint-Emilion*
Full, rich mahogany, with a slightly soft edge. The
level of maturity can be seen from the pale rim,
although the wine is still very young looking.

Ch. Giscours 1979. *Immature young Médoc*
Very deep, vibrant colour from very successful Haut-
Médoc. Perfect extraction of colour, with the deepness
of the Cabernet Sauvignon. No sign of maturing.

Ch. Giscours 1971. *Mature Red Médoc*
A fully mature Bordeaux from a good but not great
year. The colour a brick-red, with a tawny rim, and the
watery edge suggests that the wine is at its peak.

Vacqueyras 1967. *Mature Red Côtes-du-Rhône*
A deeper, robust colour, warmer than the Giscours, but
at much the same stage of evolution, being fully
mature, with a potential to last, but not improve.

4
SPECIAL STUDIES

Wine and Food

Serving Wine

Fortified and Distilled Wines

Oak

Wine and Health

Tasting Cards

Tasting Terms

Vintage Table

Wine & Food 1

The four primary flavours

The interplay between food and wine, offering a wealth of potential combinations, is a complex matter. Although there are only four basic flavours – salty, acidic, sweet and bitter – the taste buds do not perceive these four elements simultaneously, nor do the flavour components linger equally long in the mouth. Sweet flavours, for instance, are perceived almost instantaneously but hardly last for more than ten seconds in the mouth. Acidity and saltiness are also quickly savoured but their impression lasts longer on the tongue. Bitterness, on the other hand, takes a time to build up, but once fully developed, it persists for much longer than the other three.

Laboratory research has shown that these primary flavours act on one another in the following ways:

Saltiness reinforces bitterness.

Acidity conceals bitterness, though only temporarily, and enhances the perception of sweetness.

Sweetness reduces the impression of saltiness, bitterness and acidity.

Bitterness reduces acidity.

Great vintages are of course created to be drunk during meals, and so food and wine ought always to complement each other perfectly.

The right sequence

The sequence in which food dishes should be served is governed by a number of specific rules. Here are some:

Never begin with spicy dishes; flavours should grow progressively.

Always serve salty dishes before sweet ones.

Never garnish with too many starchy foods.

Do not serve too many dishes in heavy sauces.

Wines too should obey certain principles:

Start with the youngest and go on to the oldest (which does not mean those that are 'tired').

Proceed from the lightest to the most full-bodied; from the coolest to the most *chambré*; from the weakest in alcohol to the most potent; and from dry to sweet.

Drink whites before reds.

If you do not vary the wine, at least vary the year.

Matching wines with food is a tricky business and it is not always possible to follow each of these rules to the letter; nevertheless it is important to ensure that a new wine never

Above Lobster and trout dishes with a bottle of Sancerre.

overshadows the one that has just been drunk.

Tradition usually demands that like matches like: a delicate dish goes with a delicate wine, while a full-flavoured course requires a full-bodied, robust wine. More adventurous combinations may succeed in bringing out unexpected and delightful contrasts, although regional specialities will probably clash with non-local wines. Finally, a dish cooked in wine should be enjoyed with the same wine or a slightly superior one.

One-wine menus

A whole meal with just one type of wine may be easier to organize, but beware of pitfalls!

Red wines leave a fair amount of room for manoeuvre; with rosé, however, the sequence of dishes is less easy to plan, and should be restricted to simple, flavourful Mediterranean cooking.

An all-white menu will revolve around fish, white meats and goat's cheese.

A classic meal with champagne offers the opportunity to select between ordinary and top-of-the-range grades, and wines with different proportions of white and black grapes. Red Bouzy should be drunk with cheese, but naturally *fromage des Riceys* is best enjoyed with Rosé des Riceys.

Even a meal accompanied only by fortified wines or ports can be an unqualified success, but it does require oenological and culinary skill and imagination.

Wine & Food 2

Aperitifs

Dry white wines are traditionally used as aperitifs, but there are a number of alternatives. These do not, however, include spirits, which spoil the palate for the wines to come.

Aperitifs can be drunk by themselves or accompanied by peanuts, savoury biscuits, caviar or salmon fingers, cocktail sausages, cheese straws, anchovies and so on. Such snacks will not affect the taste of the wine, but beware of olives and pickles. Dry whites, sparkling whites and dry champagne (Blanc de Blanc) make excellent aperitifs, as do certain rosés, while the dry-before-sweet rule might occasionally be broken by serving sherries and other fortified wines before the meal. Sweet wines and *vins doux naturels* are, of course, generally associated with desserts, but as we shall see, the combination of sugared desserts and sweet wines is not necessarily a happy one; besides, by the end of the meal one's guests may well be quite satisfied and will balk at the thought of a rich, heavy wine.

The choice of menu will affect the choice of aperitif, and a melon offered as a starter should be preceded by a fortified wine which the guests can use to pour over the cool, refreshing fruit. A meal that starts with *foie gras* might well commence with one of the great sherries instead of a mature vintage white or red.

Hors d'oeuvre, cold meats

Wine should never be served with soup, of course, and *sauce vinaigrette* should also be avoided since vinegar is the sworn enemy of wine. Lemon dressings are likewise undesirable, and so the problem can be solved simply by using white wine instead, as, for instance, in a potato salad.

Egg-based starters should be avoided, unless the eggs are actually prepared in wine. Cold meats, however, go well with a rosé, a light red or possibly an Alsace white. Here again though, caution is needed, since cooked ham gives wine (especially red) a metallic side-taste.

Rillettes and some pâtés have a softness and richness that is excellently enhanced by a Coteaux du Layon, the sweetness of which is offset by acidity to lend it plenty of vitality.

One final word of warning – snails and

Right Jambon persillé with *Mâcon-Viré*.

wine do not go together! The garlic used in the preparation of snails will ruin the taste of any wine.

As a general rule, fish and seafood should never be served with good red vintages, though there are certain exceptions.

Shellfish

Oysters are generally eaten with dry whites, but because seawater salt adds unpleasantly to the wine's acidity some connoisseurs have turned to light reds instead. Tannins are incompatible with the proteins present in shellfish and an over-exuberant fruity wine will certainly clash with the strong odour of seafood.

If you still insist on a classical white wine accompaniment, choose wines that are both dry and well-rounded (Chablis) or slightly more gentle (Côte de Beaune).

Crustaceans

Most crustaceans – lobster, crayfish, scallops, etc. – are too costly to be treated lightly in the kitchen and therefore deserve to be accompanied by the great whites of Bordeaux, Burgundy or the Rhône.

Fish

Most fish goes well with white wine, and the more complex the preparation the more subtle the wine should be. Fish served cold with mayonnaise is best eaten with ordinary whites that are young and lively, while fish soufflés or terrines (unless there is a strong presence of dill) go best with complex wines.

For fried or grilled fish, a moderately good dry white will suffice, or a rosé if the fish is strong-tasting (sardines, anchovies).

Smoked fish is best enjoyed with dry whites of pronounced character, or even with sherry.

The great white Burgundies, the old Loire vintages (Vouvray) and the better class champagnes are still the best choice to accompany baked or steamed fish such as pike, fresh salmon or turbot, whether or not they are served with a rich sauce.

With any fish cooked in red wine (eel, trout or sole), serve the same wine or one slightly better. Bouillabaisse has to be served with unambitious rosés or dry whites, since the saffron will overwhelm any more complex or subtle vintage. Finally, caviar calls for a dry white of some distinction, such as a Burgundy or champagne.

Below left Ecrevisses à la nage *with Seyssel.*
Below *A seafood quiche with Listel Gris.*

Wine & Food 3

Poultry

At one time poultry was served before red meat, followed by game, and this called for a light red wine. Nowadays, however, poultry is itself the main dish of a meal and so can command a superior vintage of Bourgueil or Chinon in the case of white poultry (chicken) or a fuller-bodied red (Cahors, Madiran) if the flesh is dark (duck).

Local customs should always be respected: the area around Sauternes and Barsac, for example, is the home of roast chicken served with sweet, rich wines, while in the Champagne region, baked poultry is eaten with 'bubbly'.

Tannic red wines should accompany *confit d'oie* and *confit de canard* (Médoc, Saint-Emilion, Madiran); *coq au vin jaune* or *au Chambertin* of course call for the wine in which they are prepared.

White meats

Since roast white meats – veal, pork and lamb – have no very pronounced flavours, they prefer the company of delicate red wines; lamb and Médoc are a legendary combination, while if you prefer a Burgundy, choose a Côte de Beaune for the best results.

Veal sweetbreads and kidneys demand sophisticated culinary treatment and hence their table companions should also be wines of breeding and distinction: Médoc, Graves, Pomerol or first growths of Volnay, Pernand-Vergelesses from Burgundy.

Farinaceous dishes and vegetables

Vegetables do not as a rule complement wines to good effect. Asparagus, artichokes, spinach and sorrel possess a degree of acidity that never accords well with wines; fennel's aniseed flavour is too strong, but cabbage in the form of sauerkraut has found a firm friend in the wine of Alsace.

The mushroom is one vegetable that definitely goes with either reds or whites, and the truffle in particular represents the perfect complement to the better vintages of Pomerol, mature Jurançon, champagne, Côte Rôtie and others. Morels and *vin jaune* are yet another classical match, as are *cèpes* (boletus) and Saint-Emilion or Pomerol.

Finally, the farinaceous dishes (noodles, rice, pasta, etc.) are usually incapable of setting off a wine in spite of their relative neutrality, and go quite well with light red *ordinaire*.

Left Coq au vin jaune aux morilles *with a* vin jaune *from the Jura.*

Below Volaille au vinaigre *with Beaujolais-Villages.*

Red meats

Beef is a strong aromatic meat which of course loves the company of red wines. In its more modest form – beef stews – it goes well with Beaujolais and wines from the Mâcon region. For grilled beef, the better growths of Beaujolais, Burgundies or the minor *appellations* are perfect escorts, as is Saint-Emilion.

Roast beef calls for wines that are vigorous and forthcoming, such as good Burgundy AOC's and Rhône Valley wines. Beef dishes cooked in wine should of course be eaten together with a bottle of the same vintage but slightly superior in quality.

Game

Any game should be accompanied by wines that are warm and full-bodied to bring out the meat's own pronounced flavours. For feathered game, go for a classified growth of Graves or Médoc, a first growth of Côte d'Or, or one of the better years of Côte Chalonnaise.

All other game is perfectly enhanced by the great reds from the northern (Côte Rôtie) or southern (Châteauneuf-du-Pape) Rhône Valley. To follow this up when the cheese is served, choose a good Côte de Nuits or possibly a Saint-Emilion or Pomerol of distinction (Château Canon, Vieux-Château Certan).

Spicy dishes

Dishes which are heavily spiced, whether Indian, North African, South American, etc., pose real problems since a good bottle would certainly be wasted. Instead, choose a wine that is first and foremost 'gulpable' and thirst-quenching – a light fresh red or rosé, or even a white provided it is not over-acidic, otherwise it will taste harsh in the presence of certain spices and seasonings.

A Gewürztraminer may accompany a fairly subtle curry, while a full-bodied robust red (a Rioja, for instance) will stand up to a medium-strong chilli con carne.

Left Tarte aux cailles *with a Pinot Noir from Alsace.*

Wine & Food 4

Wine and Cheese

Although they combine perfectly, it is undeniable that cheese tends to benefit more from the accompaniment of wine than vice-versa.

Of course, there is cheese and cheese, and there are all too few really good makers. What is more, the same label often graces a variety of products that have little in common as regards taste and texture. There are all too many pasty concoctions that pass for the real thing, and once they start to run it is too late to eat them because of their excessively salty or ammonia-like flavour. A cheese of distinction, however, deserves a good vintage wine, and many local and regional wines and cheeses go naturally together: Munster with the wine of Alsace (Gewürztraminer), Epoisses and Burgundy (Côte d'Or), Banon and Côtes de Provence, Crottin de Cavignol and Sancerre, Morbier and Arbois Rouge, to name but a few.

As a rule, the choice of wine should be based on the cheese's actual raw materials and

Right Cheeses from north Burgundy (Montrachet, Langres, Gratte-Paille and Charolais mi-chèvre) with Côte de Beaune-Villages.

Left Roquefort, delicious with full-bodied red wines from the Rhône Valley.

method of manufacture. There are some guidelines:

All fresh cheeses: dry whites, rosés or light reds.

Goat's cheese: dry, fruity whites.

Soft blue cheeses: (e.g. Bleu d'Auvergne, des Causses, de Bressa, etc. made from cow's milk, or Roquefort from ewe's milk) wines with plenty of *sève*, robust, full-bodied wines from the Rhône Valley, or fortified wines. The traditional combination of Roquefort with Sauternes in south-western France originally derived from the British custom of eating Stilton with port.

Soft cheese in a wax crust (Brie, Camembert). The fruitiness of these cheeses often clashes with that of wines, but well-rounded, vigorous reds (local Côte d'Or *appellations*) are good accompaniments.

Soft cheeses with light crusts (Pont l'Evêque, Livarot). These should be enjoyed together with wines that are robust (Madiran, Bandol) and rich (Côte de Nuits growths).

Pressed hard cheeses (Gruyère, Emmentaler), hard cheeses from skimmed milk (Reblochon, St Nectaire, Edam, etc.). These cheeses go with a wide range of wines, although Cantal poses a problem because of its bitterness. Most hard cheeses go well with red wines from the Loire, Bordeaux, Burgundy or the Rhône; a Beaufort, for instance, will form an excellent complement to a mature Bordeaux, no matter how distinctive.

Wines and Desserts

Chocolate desserts, whether in the form of a mousse, a gâteau or hot sauce poured over fresh fruit, always rule out a wine accompaniment since the taste of chocolate fills the mouth, drowning the wine's aromas before they have a chance to develop. Lemon goes equally poorly with wine – its acidity kills any other flavour, as do most fruits (oranges, apricots, gooseberries, etc.).

Heavy, creamy desserts will cloy the mouth; the presence of alcohol in fruit salads or soufflés will overwhelm the flavour of a good vintage unless it is very discreet indeed. The same goes for too much sugar.

Among the desserts that can be enjoyed with wine are the following: Madeira cake or almond-based pastries, nuts, walnut gâteaux, light flaky pastries, plain pancakes, chestnut desserts, petits fours without cream, apple tarts, pear flans, etc. Such moderately sweet desserts should be eaten with medium-dry champagnes or a sweet wine from the Loire or south-western France. The *vins doux naturels* (Muscat, Rasteau, etc.) or sparkling wines made from aromatic grape varieties (Clairette de Die) may also be suitable.

Ices and sorbets are best enjoyed by themselves, but may be successfully followed by a drier white wine (Champagne Brut).

Finally, fresh fruit in red wine should never be accompanied by any wine at all, and certainly not by red.

Serving Wine 1

The right time to fetch the bottle

If you are fortunate enough to have your own cellar, the bottle should be brought up one or more hours before the meal depending on whether or not it is to be uncorked and/or decanted. A young wine should be carried and uncorked in the upright position, while an older vintage likely to throw off a deposit should be placed gently in a serving basket and poured from this near-horizontal position.

If you have no cellar and are therefore compelled to buy your wine from a retailer, you should make your purchase as late as possible on the day before consumption and leave it upright in a cool dark place overnight. Never allow a wine to stand for too long in a refrigerator, even if it is to be drunk chilled.

The right time to uncork

The reason why a wine should be uncorked in advance of a meal is to let the wine breathe and oxygenate, and to eliminate any foreign odours (sulphur dioxide, mercaptans, etc.). Since all air changes are minimal, oxidation is not a problem, except with particularly sensitive wines. The well-known Bordeaux oenologist Emile Peynaud even disregards this factor altogether, claiming that it makes little difference whether a bottle is opened three hours or three minutes before a meal, so that it might as well be done at the last minute.

Perhaps the best solution to the problem is simply to uncork the bottle, taste the wine and decide either to replace the cork (healthy young wines, very aged wines with subtle, volatile esters), leave the bottle open (to eliminate foreign odours), or decant it.

The right time to decant

Decanting enables the wine to throw off its deposit, an operation which necessarily brings the wine into contact with oxygen. Not all wines should be decanted; those that benefit most by such treatment are the wines of Bordeaux and occasionally certain red wines from the northern Rhône Valley, since their otherwise restrained aromas can be released more fully in this way. Whites, rosés and the more fragile reds, on the other hand, do not derive any benefit from decantation.

Some people, nevertheless, believe in decanting irrespective of bottle, and at Château Palmer, with its classified Médoc growths, they never serve a bottle, whatever the year, that has not been decanted well in advance.

Temperature

Generally speaking, wines that should be drunk chilled are usually too cold and those that must be consumed at room temperature (*chambré*) are too warm. In fact, the term *chambrer* has become somewhat redundant now that homes are centrally heated to as much as 24°C in winter, very much warmer than our grandparents' dining-rooms, which never went above 17 or 18°C.

Each type of wine of course needs an optimum tasting temperature, although this is always relative since a glass of wine at 18°C will taste different according to the season and outside conditions. Most white wines should be chilled, but this does not mean 'frozen', and anything much below 8°C is below the taste threshold. Always beware of labels requiring you to drink the wine 'well

Below Corkscrews should have wide coils free from sharp edges and be long enough to ensure good purchase on even the longest corks; l. to r.: wooden counterscrew, butterfly lever, screwpull, waiter's friend (above) and butler's friend (below).

Left Decanting a wine helps to release the more restrained aromas.

chilled' – the contents will probably have defects that will be concealed by a very low temperature. The temperature of the wine should also be reduced *gradually*. Place the bottle in an ice bucket half filled with water, then add ice cubes; once poured, the wine will quickly warm up by one or two degrees.

Sweet white wines Unless you specifically wish to accentuate the sweetness of the wine, it should be cooled to around 6°, bearing in mind what has already been said.

Champagnes and sparkling wines A good rule of thumb is 8° in the glass; one or two degrees more can suit sparkling wines that have matured for some years.

Dry white wines With these wines, the temperature will depend largely on the quality of the vintage. 'Little' dry whites (Entre-Deux-Mers, Gros Plant, etc.) should be consumed very cool (8°), while more complex whites, yet with a decidedly dry character (Graves, Alsace) are best enjoyed at 10–12°. The rich white wines that leave the merest hint of sweetness (the great Burgundies, white Châteauneuf-du-Pape, Condrieu, etc.) will not suffer from being drunk at 13–14° in the glass.

Vin jaune This is the only white that can be drunk relatively *chambré* (16°).

Rosés These are by their very nature young, fresh and fruity wines that should be served at cellar temperature, i.e. 9–10°.

Red wines Light reds drunk young or very young should also be enjoyed slightly chilled, since their fruitiness is damaged by too much warmth (Beaujolais, all Gamays, etc.).

Loire reds such as Bourgueil, Chinon and Saumur-Champigny are better structured and hence capable of withstanding one or two more degrees when drunk fairly young (13–14°). The great wines of the Rhône Valley and Burgundy give of their best at 15–16°, while the more tannic Bordeaux prefer top-of-the-range temperatures around 16–18°, the upper threshold (18°) being reserved for the older vintages.

Serving Wine 2

Right *Stages in the correct uncorking of a wine bottle.*

The right way to uncork

Start by cutting away the capsule about a quarter of an inch below the neck to prevent the wine coming into contact with metal.

The corkscrew should have wide coils that are free from any sharp edges and preferably long enough to withdraw corks of any size (screwpull, wine-waiter's knife, etc.). Never shake the bottle when opening – no good wine deserves rough treatment. Never 'pop' a champagne cork since a rapid release of gas will actually harm the quality of the contents.

Below *The suitability of the glass to the wine is of prime importance; l. to r.: ISO tasting glass, Burgundy, Bordeaux, Paris goblet (reds); tulip, goblet, Alsace (whites).*

A bottle that has been placed in a basket to allow the deposit to settle should always be opened in the same position. Just lift the bottle slightly, inserting a spare cork between the neck and the edge of the basket. This will slightly increase the slant of the bottle and so avoid the risk of losing any of the precious liquid.

Wine glasses

Wine should be poured gently into the glass – but not just any glass. Both the shape and the thickness are of prime importance. Generally speaking, a good wine glass is one that is colourless, uncut and with a stem and foot. At the Académie du Vin we use AFNOR (French standard) glasses which are suitable for whites, reds and sparkling wines, excellent for wine-tasting and ideal for everyday drinking at the dinner table. Of course there are others, such as the Bordeaux glass in the shape of a tulip, the bulbous Burgundy glass that is slightly narrower at the lip, the Alsace glass and the familiar champagne flute. A word of warning, however: never use the shallow *coupe* for sparkling wines; its lack of depth will not show the bubbles rising and its wide rim will let all the bouquet escape.

Whatever the shape of your wine glasses, the diameters of the foot and rim should be less than that of the body at its widest point, in order to hold in the wine's aromas. Glasses should be filled to half or three-quarters, never full. Finally, a clean white tablecloth is really the only acceptable background to set off the colour of any good vintage.

Below L. to r.: sherry, port, port/madeira, champagne flutes, cognac balloon and cognac recommended.

Fortified & Distilled Wines 1

These two styles of fortified wine are made in the same way as all fortified wine: alcohol is added to the must during fermentation, so that the fermenting process is stopped, leaving a lower degree of natural alcohol and an accordingly higher degree of natural sugar. The addition of alcohol can vary from 6° to 10° by volume. Only grapes possessing a minimum of 250 grams per litre of natural sugar (the equivalent of 14° alcohol) may undergo this operation, and they are thus specially selected varieties, grown in specific regions. The French word for this process is *mutage*, from *muet*, meaning 'dumb', since alcohol 'silences' the fermentation.

The difference between *vins de liqueur* and *vins doux naturels* in France is purely admin-istrative, the former being taxed as spirits and the latter as wines. They are all dissimilar in taste, because they are made in different regions from different grapes, but the methods of production are the same.

The best known French *vin de liqueur* is Pineau des Charentes, made from grapes picked in the Cognac region, with the addition of Cognac. It may be served either as an aperitif or a dessert wine – ice-cold – the alcoholic content varying from 16.5° to 22°. In Champagne a similar fortified wine, made from champagne grapes, is called Ratafia; and the allied Floc de Gascogne consists of grape juice and Armagnac. All three merit an AOC *appellation*.

The *vins doux naturels* are sweet wines pro-

Sweet Muscats are made in centres along the Mediterranean coast: at Lunel, Rivesaltes, Frontignan and also at Beaumes-de-Venise in the Vaucluse.

duced in the Roussillon, around Perpignan, in Languedoc and in the Rhône Valley. They are muted with neutral alcohol to a strength of some 96°. Wines made from the Muscat grape are vinified and matured in tanks in order to protect their aromatic qualities, while sweet reds are aged in casks or *bonbonnes* and deliberately oxidized to give them a slightly rancid flavour. Grenache is the most common grape variety used.

The finest of these wines are Banyuls and the Muscats. The former are always red, the latter always white. Banyuls is undoubtedly the finest VDN in France, grown in the Roussillon, almost on the Spanish frontier (also the home of Maury and Rivesaltes), from steeply terraced schistous vineyards.

The addition of alcohol may come early or late in the fermentation; the later the *mutage*, the drier the wine. To benefit from the *appellation* Banyuls Grand Cru, the must should ferment for at least five days before the addition of alcohol, and the wine must be aged in wood. A good Banyuls may rival a fine port.

The sweet Muscats (not to be confused with the Muscat d'Alsace, which is very aromatic but bone-dry) are found along the Mediterranean coast, at Lunel, Rivesaltes, Frontignan, and in the southern Côtes-du-Rhône at Beaumes-de-Venise. They have a wonderful golden colour, an explosive, richly aromatic bouquet, and a concentrated, sunny flavour. They must be served very cold, and they do not improve with age.

Ratafia is a fortified wine made in Champagne from champagne grapes.

Fortified & Distilled Wines 2

Fortified wines are produced, as we have seen, by adding alcohol to the must during fermentation. The best known wines in this category, far surpassing in international repute those made in France, are sherry, port and madeira.

Sherry

Sherry is different from other fortified wines in that it is fermented out to complete dryness, and the alcohol is added later. Since, in the usual fashion, the must is fortified during fermentation, leaving residual sugar in the wine, fortified wines are generally sweet. Sherry is dry, the sweetness in the richer blends arriving from the addition of wines specially selected for this purpose.

Sherry comes from vineyards to the south of Andalusia, between Cadiz and Seville, the best being grouped around the town of Jerez de la Frontera. The determinant factor of quality, however, is the nature of the soil, and the white, chalky *albariza* soil gives to sherry the finest breed and bouquet. On this soil, it is the Palomino grape that is universally planted, from which all types of the finer sherries are made. Several other grape varieties are planted for use in blending, especially the Pedro Ximénez; bunches of these grapes are dried in the sun for several days before fermentation to make a powerful, sweet wine to be used for the richer sherries.

After fermentation, the key to making sherry lies in selection and blending. A first selection will take place in December, follow-

ing the vintage in September. The lighter, finer wines will be set aside to make finos or amontillados, and will be fortified up to 15.5°; fuller wines, with less finesse, will be more heavily fortified to 17–18°, and will be destined for the oloroso family. The wine is still bone-dry. After fortification, the different wines are stocked in separate *criaderas* or wine-nurseries. The finos will develop a sort of milky skim (*flor*) on the surface of the wine (as is also found in the wines of Château-Chalon) in casks that have been left one-quarter empty. They will be bottled after one or two years, the result being a pale, clean, dry sherry. Amontillado is classically an aged fino, taking on colour and, curiously enough, alcohol through ageing in wood. The oloroso family may be aged and unsweetened, resulting in a complex, nutty wine, or be sweetened with PX (Pedro Ximénez) to be sold as a cream sherry. Throughout its life in cask, sherries are blended from butt to butt (the so-called solera system), which is also found in the making of madeira.

At Sanlucar de Barrameda, not far along the coast from Jerez, a sherry-style fino called manzanilla is made from the same grapes as sherry, but is said to get its very dry, tangy character from the salty sea breezes blowing in from the Atlantic.

Port

Port is probably the best known of the fortified wines. It comes from the Cima Corgo and Baixo Corgo regions of the Douro Valley

Right L. to r.: lighter, finer wines are used for the preparation of finos and amontillados; manzanilla is a sherry-style fino made exclusively at Sanlucar de Barrameda.

in north-east Portugal. Because of the schistous rock 'soil' and the steeply terraced vineyards, this is perhaps the most arduous wine-growing region in the world. There are many grape varieties, both red and white, but their character is of less importance than the soil, the climate and the human factor. The vintage takes place in mid-September, the red grapes having the maximum amount of colour extracted during the short period of fermentation, before the addition of alcohol – local *eau de vie* – to a minimum level of 16.5°. This will raise the 4–6° of natural alcohol to a total of 22.5–24.5°, incorporating a high level of residual sugar which gives port its sweetness. In the following spring the wine is brought down to the port lodges (as the above ground cellars are called), in Vila Nova de Gaia where it matures in preparation for its final blending.

There are two basic types of port: vintage port and wood port. The former is the product of a single year – and sometimes of a single domaine or *Quinta* – kept in cask until two years after the vintage, bottled and continuing to mature in bottle. Not all port shippers declare the same year as a vintage, some specialize in 'off'-vintages from their estates, and many offer a late-bottled vintage, bottled after longer in wood than the classic vintage. Wood port can be white, ruby or tawny. White port is generally fermented much drier than red port, but only the finest are very dry from several years in cask. Ruby is bottled after three to five years in wood, after which it

tends to lose its full colour and become progressively more tawny and less sweet with age. Port shippers do not use the solera system, but keep large reserves of older vintages and blend to match their house style. An old tawny will be a blend of several years, and if it carries a date – say 20 years old – the average age of the blend will not be less than 20 years. Ruby and white ports are less expensive than tawny port, as they are bottled earlier. A fine tawny is as good as, but different from, a mature vintage port. These styles are examined in the tasting on page 179.

Madeira

Madeira wine comes from the Portuguese island of the same name, and is almost as well known as port. It is, however, better known for its use in sauces and cakes, and not significantly appreciated as a fortified wine. The fame of madeira began when ships stopping off at Funchal on their way to the Americas for fresh water took on casks of the local wine as ballast. The lengthy sea voyage, during which the wine was kept at a high temperature, imparted a 'burnt' flavour that was much appreciated. Today, the same effect is achieved through the vinification process called *estafugem*.

Madeira grapes are grown on a volcanic soil infused with potash, and make four main styles of wine. Sercial, the palest and driest, is excellent as an aperitif. If it is aged in cask for many years it darkens in colour, develops an intense nuttiness, but never loses its acidity.

Left Oloroso sherries may be sweetened with the Pedro Ximénez grape to produce cream sherry.

Fortified & Distilled Wines 3

Distilled Wines

In France the right to distil wines or their by-products into brandies is being increasingly restricted to the major commercial distilleries. The great wine brandies – Cognac and Armagnac – enjoy AOC distinction, while others are entitled to display regulated *appellations*, for example the brandies of Burgundy, Champagne and other areas.

Distillation conditions are strictly enforced, with stills carrying out one run or more; they may be heated directly or by means of the water bath technique (*bain-marie*), with the *marc* being heated directly or indirectly by the steam which absorbs the alcohol vapour. The still's condenser must be cooled efficiently or some of the precious aroma is lost, and distillation is carried out slowly for the same reason. Hourly output and the specification of the raw material are also governed by official rules.

The distiller's art is to select the right apparatus for the distillation process itself, then to mature correctly in wooden casks; the timber, age and capacity of these casks all play as important a part as the ageing period itself.

Cognac

Distillation has been going on in the Charente region since the 18th century, and during that time the Ugni Blanc, known locally as 'Saint-Emilion', has taken over from the less reliable Folle Blanche which once went into the making of the finest Cognacs.

Vines planted in wide rows – two or three metres apart – and machine harvested produce a modest, sourish wine of 7–8° of alcohol which is never chaptalized or sulphured. Although the hectare yield is unlimited, the plants are pruned to give around 60,000 buds to the hectare. The area of production is divided into six different zones corresponding to six grades of Cognac, and in most instances these brandies are in fact a blend of the various grades.

Grande Champagne In the very heart of the region are some 13,000 hectares of crumbly limestone soil that yield the most delicate brandies with the most persistent aftertaste.

The **Petite Champagne** area is adjacent to that of the Grande Champagne, its limestone soil covering 16,000 hectares which produce fine brandies that mature more rapidly than those from the heart of the region.

Les Borderies This comprises 5000 hectares of silica-clay soil located to the north of the Grande Champagne which yield a Cognac notable for its roundness.

Les Fins Bois This huge area, some 40,000 hectares in all, encircles the preceding three. Its soil is silica-clay, and the Fins Bois Cognacs are well-balanced, elegant brandies which mature quickly.

Right *Checking the specific gravity of Cognac.*

Les Bons Bois Les Bons Bois in their turn enclose the preceding area, extending over 21,000 hectares of clay soil that yields a less balanced and less sophisticated brandy.

Les Bois Ordinaires These consist of 4000 hectares of Quaternary alluvial soil close to the Atlantic Ocean, yielding a more everyday type of brandy – said to taste of the salt sea.

The term *Fine champagne* does not indicate a region but denotes a blend of at least 50% of Grande Champagne with Petite Champagne.

Cognac is always obtained by double distillation: the first *chauffe* gives the *brouilli* which is collected at an alcohol content of around 30°. This is then re-distilled to give a final Cognac strength of 60–70°. It is placed in aged oak casks, during which operation some volume and alcohol content is lost. Estimates put the annual loss due to evaporation as high as 50,000 hectolitres, equivalent to seventeen million bottles!

The Cognac that is finally bottled will be blended from various different regions and different ages, while the alcohol content is reduced by watering. Caramel extract lends the brandy its characteristic hue and softness.

Cognac is never labelled by year, but its age can nevertheless be told by other distinctive markings. Three stars, for example, indicate that the contents are at least 2 years old, while VSOP, VO and Réserve denote 4 years. The designations Vieille Réserve, Extra and Napoléon are guarantees of over 5 years maturing in cask, while the average age of a blend is usually much greater.

Left *Stoking the stove under a Cognac still.*

Fortified & Distilled Wines 4

Historically, Armagnac is at least as old as Cognac, though only about one-tenth as much is produced. Additionally, its quality is less consistent and it is therefore more difficult to market. The region of *appellation* relates only partially to Armagnac itself, and this in turn can be divided into three zones, each with its own *appellation*. The Bas Armagnac covers more than 11,000 hectares of vines planted in a Tertiary topsoil of sand and pebbles, covering a silica-clay subsoil. This zone includes the Grand Bas Armagnac, close to Labastide d'Armagnac, where the very best Armagnac brandy is produced.

Le Bas Armagnac This Armagnac requires long maturing: at least 10 years but more often 40 (in casks). A delicate brandy, it is among the best in the world.

Le Tenarèze Over 8000 hectares of vineyards to the east of Bas Armagnac, covering limestone and clay soils, produce a brandy that is more flavoured and rustic than the Bas Armagnac, with a plum aroma.

Le Haut Armagnac This covers a vast area to the south and east of the two preceding zones, although only a mere 500 hectares are actually planted for the production of Armagnac, the rest being devoted to table wines. The soil is mostly limestone and as a region is undistinguished.

Grape varieties include the Folle Blanche (the best), and one of the most widespread is named after its inventor, Baco (22 A); others include the Colombard and the Ugni Blanc.

Distillation methods are by no means uniform, although lovers of true Armagnac

Right An Armagnac still; distillation methods vary from producer to producer.

prefer the brandy from the actual Armagnac stills. The brandy is not rectified, and has an alcohol strength of 50–55°.

The reduction in strength to 40–45° alcohol is done naturally, without watering, in casks made from local oak, each containing 400 litres. The brandy is never transferred from cask to cask, so each one is said to have 'its' Armagnac, and vice-versa, making for a unique marriage of oak and brandy.

The old original Armagnac stills are now hard to find, but each has its distinctive personality, and two different stills have been known to produce an identical brandy. The more modern stills are designed to produce brandies of around 60–65° alcohol. It is obvious that the lower the alcohol content, the more important the rôle played by other components, giving richness and character to the Armagnacs, which should be left in their casks for a very long time. After 40 years in the wood, however, the brandy 'dries out' and has to be bottled or transferred to smaller *bonbonnes*.

There is another method of distilling Armagnac similar to that used for Cognac (double distillation), but the finished product has less character and matures more quickly.

Unlike Cognac, the great Armagnacs are year-marked. Those that are not so good may bear three stars or the word Monopole, etc. to indicate they are over one year old; VO, VSOP and Réserve denote a brandy that is over 4 years of age, while XO, Napoléon, Vieille Réserve and Hors d'âge are older than 5 years.

Left Blending casks; the strength of Armagnac is reduced in the cask, but the brandy is never transferred from cask to cask.

Oak

A number of experiments have been carried out in Burgundy and the Bordeaux region to assess the importance of wood during the maturing of wine in casks. In Burgundy a *cuvée* of red Mercurey and one of Chassagne-Montrachet were systematically investigated in 1978, with tests done on a variety of different oaks: Limousin, Nièvre, Bourgogne, Tronçais, Vosges, etc., different sizes of pores and different tannin levels.

The way in which the staves are cut (split or sawn) is also important, and the timber may be seasoned naturally or artificially. The staves can then be bent with the use of steam or over a fire.

Wood is, of course, a permeable material and so permits the exchange of gases which alter the make-up of a wine's component parts; and wines that have matured in new oak casks will have different properties to those aged in old casks, or to wines that mature in enamelled metal vats.

During the above-mentioned tests, chemical and sensory tests were carried out at four-monthly intervals, with the following results:

There was a greater loss of alcohol from casks made from semi-split, steam-shaped Burgundy oak staves and from casks of Tronçais oak that had been sawn and split.

Volatile acidity was lower in used casks.

Malolactic fermentation took longer in worn casks.

Total acidity and dry extract was more or less the same in all types of container.

Wines kept in new woods were richest in colour and tannins; apart from tannin, the new wood also gave the wine polysaccharides (sugars).

Three tastings were held by 20 experts over the 16 months of maturing, the final tasting coming just before bottling. The overall decision was in favour of the new oak casks and against the old oak casks and metal vats. Yet that was not all. There were differences between the various new casks as well. Those with staves that had been shaped over steam were not as good for the wine as those with fire-formed staves. During the burning process the destruction of the lignin in the wood gives rise to a vanilla odour, while the sugars present in the hemicellulose molecules lend an aroma of caramel. Sawing of the staves, as opposed to splitting, did not seem to have any harmful effect on the wine.

In the case of red wines, the 'woody' character inherent in casks made from oak from the Tronçais, Nièvre and Bourgogne regions was superior in quality, while for white wines, the Burgundy oaks from around Mercurey and Cîteaux gave the best flavour. It was interesting to note that sawn oak from the Tronçais forests did more for the young wine than split oak from the same area.

These initial experiments will of course be complemented by further tastings once the samples have undergone several years of bottle-ageing. Clearly, more work needs to be done on the nature of the effect of oak.

Above *Forcing the hoops on to a new oak barrel, which will eventually modify the character of the wine stored in it.*

Wine & Health

It is quite untrue to say that wine is bad for the health; but obviously there is a distinction between use and abuse. Like any other food, wine becomes toxic if taken in excess, and too high a concentration of alcohol in the body cannot be eliminated without some damage being done, since in order to expel the excess alcohol whole body cells have to be burned up, and this means a waste of vitamins and proteins.

Levels of alcohol tolerance naturally vary from one person to another, and, more particularly, according to sex, owing to a weight difference. They also vary depending on the context in which the wine is consumed, i.e. whether it is drunk by itself, during a meal or with one food rather than another. Alcohol is more dangerous when the diet is lacking in meats, dairy foods and fish, while diets that are over-lean or excessively fat can reduce its elimination from the body by up to 20%.

Wine can benefit the health if taken slowly and in moderation. The French Academy of Medicine has fixed the daily intake at 1 gram of alcohol per kilogram of body weight, which means that a person weighing 155 pounds can quite safely drink one bottle of wine a day – in stages.

Wine as a foodstuff can provide up to one-quarter of our calorific needs; it is not rich in vitamins or mineral salts, but its alcohol is a source of calories that economize on lipids, glucids and amino-acids which are thus available for extra physical or mental effort. There is no better drink at table than wine – it is a source of water (85%) and many of its components actually aid digestion. The acids contained help the stomach muscles to flex and contract, assisting the natural stomach acids to digest starchy and albuminoid substances. The tannins present in wine stimulate the muscular fibres and promote the rate of metabolism; they also seem to be good carriers of vitamin C.

Wine is of course a depressant and as such has a calming, euphoric effect. Studies have shown that in old people's homes the atmosphere is considerably relaxed when a glass of wine is served with the meal.

The Wine Institute of San Francisco has even asserted that moderate wine drinkers live longer than teetotallers, and Dr Arthur L. Klasty believes this to be due in part to the beneficial effects of alcohol on the heart and circulation. Dr John P. Kane of the Cardiovascular Research Institute of the University

of California, San Francisco, claims that alcohol has beneficial effects on high density lipoprotein (HDL) levels in plasma, since high levels of HDL afford protection against hardening of the arteries.

Finally, it should be stressed that cirrhosis of the liver, caused by wine alone, is nowadays an extremely rare complaint. Indeed, like most other things taken in excess, wine can be harmful; but taken in reasonable quantity, it would seem to be more beneficial than otherwise.

Above Levels of wine tolerance vary from person to person, but it is generally agreed that wine drinking in moderation can actually benefit the health.

Tasting Cards

Tasting cards can take a number of different forms, of greater or lesser complexity. The card below is adapted from a form commonly used in France; its major advantage is that it compels the taster to make a precise examination of the various elements which will go into forming his final judgement of a given wine. A. Castell, 1967 (INAO).

Wine Type (White/Rosé/Red)			Appellation:
			Type:
Laboratory observations and conclusion			Date of Analysis
Specific Gravity Alcohol Residual Sugar Potential Alcohol Total SO$_2$ pH Free SO$_2$ colour index P/x Index of permanganate			Total Acidity Fixed Acidity Volatile Acidity (corrected for sulphuric acid)
Method of Vinification			
Visual Examination	**Surface of the liquid**		Brilliant – dull Clean – iridescent – oily
	Colour	**White Wine**	Pale with green or yellow tints – pale yellow – straw yellow – canary yellow – gold – amber
		Rosé Wine	Pale with violet or rose tints – grey – light rose – deep rose – partridge eye – onion skin
		Red Wine	Red with crimson or violet tints – cherry red – ruby – garnet red – red brown – tile red – mahogany – tawny
		Colour Hue	Frank – oxidized – cloudy
	Aspect		Crystalline – brilliant – limpid – hazy – cloudy – turgid – lead – grey/white – opaque, with or without deposit
	Legs/Tears		Quick or slow to form – non-existent – slight – heavy
Temperature of the Wine			**Any factor hindering the tasting**
Olfactory Examination	**First Impression**		Pleasant – ordinary – unpleasant
	Aroma	**Intensity**	Powerful – adequate – feeble – non-existent
		Quality	Very fine – racy – distinguished – fine – ordinary – common – not very pleasant – unpleasant
		Character	Primary – secondary – tertiary – floral – fruity – vegetal – spicy – animal – oxidized
		Length	Long – average – short
	Abnormal odours		CO$_2$ – SO$_2$ – H$_2$S – mercaptan – strongly oxidized – woody – lactic acid acescence – phenolic – corky flaw $\{$ temporary – permanent / slight – serious
	Details		
Any factor hindering or stopping the continuation of the tasting			

Gustatory	First Impression			
Examination	Flavours and sensations	Sweetness	Sugar	Heavy — very sweet — sweet — dry — brut
			Glycerine and alcohol	Soft — unctuous — velvety — smooth — rough — dried out
		Acidity	Excessive	Acid — green — tart — nervy — acidulous
			Balanced	Fresh — lively — supple — smooth
			Insufficient	Flat — flabby
		Body	Alcoholic strength	Light — sufficient — generous — heady — hot
			Flesh	Fat — round — full — thin — meagre
			Tannin	Rich — balanced — insufficient — astringent — bitter
		Aromas in the mouth	Intensity	Powerful — average — weak — long — short
			Quality	Very fine — elegant — pleasant — common — faded
			Nature	Floral — fruity — vegetable — spicy — wood — chemical — animal — other young — developed — complex
	Inherent or Abnormal Flavours	'Terroir'		Marked — noticeable — faint — non-existent
		Sickness		Grease — turned — aldehydes — sweet — sour — rancid — acetic acid — lactic acid
		Accident		Stagnant — mould — lees — woody — cork — metallic — H_2S — herbaceous — acrid
	Final Impression	Balance		Harmonious — bold — correct — unbalanced Xs acid, Xs sugar, Xs tannin, Xs alcohol
		After taste		Straightforward — unpleasant
		Resistance of taste and aroma		>8 sec 5–7 sec 4–5 sec <3 sec Very long long medium short
Conclusions	Conformity to appellation or type			
	Score out of 20			
	Summary of tasting (character of wine — future, readiness for drinking)			

Wine-tasting terms 1

(As formulated and defined by the Departmental Testing and Research Laboratory at Tours.)

In addition to long experience, keen sensibility and thorough knowledge, a wine taster must possess a specialized vocabulary so that he can express his exact feelings and conclusions.

We have therefore thought it worthwhile to include here a simple list of standard wine-tasting terms. These terms are used in the trade to define a wine's positive qualities and weaknesses, thus enabling the taster, whether amateur or professional, to describe it in some detail and with the greatest possible precision.

Sight

The wine's appearance

Bourbeux: miry; heavy cloudiness of a young wine that has not yet been racked.

Brillant: brilliant; great limpidity, associated with white wines.

Clair: see *limpide.*

Crémant: slight sparkle; sparkling wines in which the pressure is equal to 3.5 atmospheres. The 'Crémant de Loire' is a wine that can only be made in Touraine.

Cristallin: crystal-clear; perfect transparency and as bright as crystal.

Disque: disc; curved upper surface of the wine in the glass. The disc should usually be brilliant. When the wine has deteriorated, the disc presents a matt surface where various particles are to be seen.

Jambes: legs, also known as 'tears'; when the wine is swirled round the glass, it leaves a ringlet with an oily, colourless outline. This ringlet may be very noticeable or almost non-existent. The 'tears' which run down the inside of the glass from this ringlet and have an oily aspect are known as *jambes.* These 'legs' can be either thick or thin, form more or less quickly and vary in number. They are an indication of the richness of the wine in alcohol, sugar and glycerol.

Limpide: clear; perfect transparency with a complete absence of particles in suspension.

Louche: shady; cloudy of wine in which transparency and brilliance are slightly lacking.

Mousseux: fully sparkling, as with champagne; the bubbles rising to the surface are fine and persistent, with a pressure of from 4 to 5 atmospheres at its strongest. The bubbles leave a thin froth over the surface disc and then run away from the centre to the side of the glass where they form a ring round the inside known as the *cordon, collier* or *collerette.*

Perlant: beady, slightly gaseous; generally applies to young wines, wines that are kept on lees (Muscadet), sold straight from the barrel, or to those wines which are undergoing malolactic fermentation or a slight alcoholic fermentation.

Pétillant: slightly sparkling wine, made by the champagne method with a pressure of from 2 to 3 atmospheres. Carbonic gas is revealed by the fine but relatively few bubbles which rise to the surface to create a slight covering of froth, which quickly disappears. It is more noticeable on the palate because of its light tingling sensation.

Tranquille: still, non-sparkling; complete absence of bubbles.

Trouble: 'troubled', cloudy wine; wine lacking in clarity because of gel or particles in suspension.

The wine's colour

Robe: colour and clarity of the wine, taken together, as seen through its transparency. A wine is said to have a fine colour *(une belle robe)* when it is bright and clear.

Robe chatoyante: a glistening colour.

Red wines

Clairet: red wine that has a weak colour because of its short maceration period (Bordeaux region). Not to be confused with Claret.

Rouge grenat: garnet-red; colour that is taken on by certain wines as they age.

Rouge pelure d'oignon: onion-skin red; strong tawny-pink.

Rouge pourpré: crimson-red; dark red with a violet shade.

Rouge rubis: ruby-red; bright, firm colour of wines that are still young with good, steady acidity.

Rouge tuilé: tile-red; red with a shade of orange; colour taken on by wines as they age, similar to brick-red.

Rouge violacé: purplish-red; shade that is particular to certain wines lacking in acidity.

Rosé wines

Rose pelure d'oignon: onion-skin pink; dark, coppery-pink (rosé d'Arbois, Tavel, etc.).

Rose 'œil de perdrix': partridge-eye pink; clear, bright ruby-pink.

Rose saumoné ou ambré: salmon or amber-pink; pink with a yellow shade.

Rose vif: bright pink; a pink with great luminosity.

Gris rosé wines

Vins gris rosés: very pale rosé wines with a shade that lies between the white and rosé wines produced from direct pressing of red or grey grapes (Pineau d'Aunis).

White wines

Jaune ambré: amber-yellow; resembling the colour of yellow amber (fossil resin).

Jaune beige: beige-yellow; pale yellow with a shade of grey (dull colour).

Jaune citron: lemon-yellow; bright yellow like the colour of a lemon.

Jaune doré: golden-yellow; bright yellow similar to that of gold.

Jaune miel: honey-yellow; pale golden yellow with a slight tawny shade.

Jaune paille: straw-yellow; slightly pronounced yellow resembling the colour of straw.

Jaune plombé: lead-yellow; greyish yellow, noticeable in wine that has had tannin added.

Jaune vert: greenish-yellow; pale brilliant yellow with a green shade.

Vieil or: old gold; golden yellow with a sustained warm shade (found in old wines).

Smell

General terms of appreciation

Vins aromatiques: aromatic wines; wines with a very pronounced scent, such as wines from the Sauvignon grape.

Bouquet: the complex rich smell that develops during ageing (the wine is said to be *bouqueté*, having a bouquet).

Fumet: word used by some wine experts to describe the tertiary smells. (See *Odeurs tertiaires.*)

Nez: nose; the complex smell given off by the wine. A wine is said to have 'nose' when it is rich in scents.

Nez fleuri: flowery nose; a term used to describe a wine that has the scent of a flower.

Nez fruité: fruity nose; used to describe a wine that has a fruity smell. It is particularly used of young wine which still retains the smell of the grape from which it was made.

Nez subtil: subtle nose; used to describe a wine that has a fine, delicate smell.

Odeurs primaires: primary smells (sometimes referred to as 'natural' smells or original smells); describes those smells which come from the grape itself, found in young wines.

Odeurs secondaires: secondary smells (or fermentation smells); smells which appear during fermentation, caused by the yeasts.

Odeurs tertiaires: tertiary smells (or ageing smells); they develop as the wine ages in the bottle, guarding its secret of those subtle processes of oxidation and reduction. These are very complex scents, more abstract and richer than the afore-mentioned ones. They make up the real 'bouquet' of a wine (such as old Chinon or Bourgueil).

Perspective odorante: aromatic perspective (or convergence of smells); used to describe the complex smell of primary, secondary and tertiary scents given off by an outstanding wine, which in certain cases coexist and complement one another.

Smells by groups

Odeurs animales: animal smells; musk, ambergris, venison, game, fur, leather.

Odeurs balsamiques: balsamic smells; incense, vanilla, camphor.

Odeurs boisées: wood smells; cedar, liquorice, resin.

Odeurs empyreumatiques: smells of fiery origin; toast, grilled almonds, coffee, smoke, tobacco, tea, grilled herbs, hay.

Odeurs épicées: spicy smells; pepper, sandalwood, cloves, cinnamon.

Odeurs florales: floral scents; rose, violet, mignonette, jasmine, orange-blossom, iris, carnation, lime-tree, wallflower, primrose, verbena, hawthorn, acacia, syringa, honeysuckle, bluebell, peony, etc.

Odeurs fruitées: fruity smells; apple, raspberry, cherry, peach, quince, plum, blackcurrant, banana, hazelnut, lemon, strawberry, walnut, apricot, redcurrant, almond, etc.

There are, obviously, many other smells which do not fall into these groups. For example:

Odeur d'iode: iodine smell; can be found in those wines coming from maritime regions, or those made from grapes affected by 'noble rot', such as Vouvray or Montlouis. If this smell is too pronounced, it must be considered a defect.

Odeur de suie, de fumée: sooty, smoky smell; characteristic of certain wines.

Odeur de 'pierre à fusil': gun-flint smell; smell which recalls that obtained when two pieces of flint are rubbed together (characteristic of the white AOC wine of Jasnières).

Odeur de résine: resin smell; smell taken on by wine kept in conifer-wood barrels or found in certain Greek wines treated with pine resin.

Unpleasant smells

Odeurs dues à la vendange: smells which have their origin in the harvesting; earthy smell (presence of earth on the grapes), rambergue (presence of the *Aristolochia* plant at harvest-time), iodine smell (excess of 'noble rot'), foxy smell (characteristic of the native American vine).

Odeurs dues à une maladie: smells originating from an illness *ou à un mauvais traitement du vin:* or poor wine treatment; acescent smells (sour or stinging wine), stale or musty smells (formation of ethyl alcohol reminiscent of the smell of apples, wine that has been neglected and left open to the air), geranium smell (change in the ascorbic acid content), sulphuric hydrogen smell (SH_2, smell of rotten eggs, due to late sulphur spraying of the vine, or to sulphite treatment of the wine during fermentation).

Odeurs dues aux contenants: smells coming from containers; the smell of the cask, of dry wood, cement, plastic; stagnant, mouldy, corky smells.

Wine-tasting terms 2

Terms of taste and palate

Acerbe: sour; unpleasant, disagreeable, e.g. too much acidity.

Acre: bitter; wine with an excess of tannin, of volatile acidity – stinging, burning.

Agressif: aggressive; unpleasant, too much acidity (excess of alcohol).

Aimable: pleasant; agreeable and nicely balanced.

Alcalin: alkaline; wine rich in sodium chloride and potassium.

Altéré: wine that has deteriorated, having lost its normal characteristics as a result of illness or misuse of chemicals.

Amaigri: thin; wine whose natural colour and strength is exhausted (said of red wine, for example, that is too old).

Amer: bitter; bitterness coming from colouring matter or imparted by tannic acids – bitterness, disease coming from decomposition of glycerol (acroleïn).

Apre: disagreeable, rough, harsh, due to an excess of tannin or acidity.

Aqueux: watery; flat, diluted appearance, characteristics of a wine that has been 'watered down' or suffering from the disease known as *fleur* ('flower'), advanced stage of mould.

Austère: austere or harsh; hard wine with too much natural strength and unpleasant to drink (as with ordinary red table wine produced from certain hybrid vines).

Bien en bouche: a rich, well-balanced wine.

Bouchonné: corky; smell of cork mainly perceived by the nose.

Bref: short; leaving no pleasant or lingering aftertaste.

Brûlant: burning sensation given by an excess of alcohol in the wine; warm sensation.

Brut: very dry; applied to those sparkling wines with little sugar content (total absence of sugar gives Extra-Dry).

Capiteux: heady; high in alcohol, going to the head, intoxicating.

Charnu: fleshy; fills the mouth well, leaving a strong sensation on the taste-buds – full-bodied.

Charpenté: well constituted; rich constitution and high in alcohol.

Chaud: warm, rich in alcohol.

Corsé: full-bodied; wine with high alcoholic content and well-constituted; wine is said to have 'body' when it gives a sensation of fullness and rich consistency.

Coulant: pleasant, supple, not too high in alcohol, easy to drink.

Creux: hollow; lacking in body, unbalanced, excess acidity.

Cru: raw or coarse; used to describe a thin or young wine, under-developed, fairly acid, lacking in fullness.

Décharné: fleshless, thin of body; having lost its original qualities.

Délicat: delicate; fine, graceful, light wine.

Dépouillé: stripped; weakening of some of its substances as the wine ages (found in old red wines).

Déséquilibré: unbalanced; poor body, badly constituted and lacking in harmony, e.g. with a pronounced dominance of acidity.

Distingué: distinguished; fine quality wine with its own character.

Doucereux: sweetish; having an insipid, somewhat unpleasant sweetness.

Doux: sweet; having a certain richness in sugar which does not shock the palate.

Dur: hard; lacking in suppleness, rough to swallow due to an excess of volatile tartaric acid or tannin.

Edulcoré: artificially sweetened.

Elégant: elegant; distinguished and superb, as with wines from the great vineyards *(vins de cru)*.

Epais: thick; common, heavy wines without distinction.

Epanoui: well-developed; wines that wrap themselves round the palate.

Equilibré: well-balanced; well constituted in the right proportions (characteristic of all great wines).

Etoffé: full; well constituted, linked also with the rich colour of a wine.

Exubérant: exuberant; sparkling.

Fade: tasteless; weak, thin wine, lacking in character and taste.

Ferme: firm; lacks suppleness – rich in tannins and extracts.

Filant: ropy; forming viscous or gelatinous threads, suffering from *graisse* (grease or ropy) disease, or wine rich in dextran.

Fin: fine; describes wine of superb quality, well-balanced and harmonious (such as the *vins de cru* – the great wines).

Fini court: short-finish; short-lived taste.

Fondu: well-blended; well-matured, constituents in complete harmony.

Fort: strong; alcohol content predominant.

Frais: fresh; with a fair amount of acid, but not to excess; refreshing character; pleasant; thirst-quenching.

Franc: honest; natural, clean, sound wine without any faults.

Friand: delicious; wine with an agreeable taste, and pleasant to drink.

Fruité: fruity; still having the fresh, natural flavour of the grape.

Gazeux: gaseous; fizzy because of excess carbonic gas following refermentation in the bottle, or due to a disease.

Généreux: generous; noble, rich in alcohol, well constituted, full-bodied, rich in ester.

Gouleyant: easy to drink; light and pleasant.

Grain: excellent consistency; used to describe a first-class wine of superb quality, when it is said to have *du grain*.

Gras: rich in content; fleshy, full-bodied, sweet; rich in alcohol and glycerine (qualities associated with a truly great wine).

Grossier: vulgar; coarse, heavy wine, lacking in quality.

Harmonieux: harmonious; wine whose constituents are well balanced and in perfect harmony.

Jeune: young; new wine or wine that has kept its young character.

Joyeux: joyous; happy; a wine that cheers.

Léger: light; well-balanced wine, low in alcohol and extracts, but pleasant to drink (*vins rosés*, for example).

Liquoreux: liqueur-like; sweet wine, with rich sugar content and heady.

Long: long; wine whose taste lingers in the mouth with intense aromatic flavour. White wines have a more persistent flavour than reds. As a guide, the following time-scale gives some indication of the persistency of this 'aftertaste':
— *vin ordinaire:* ordinary wine; 1 to 3 sec.
— *vin de qualité:* good quality wine; 4 to 5 sec.
— *grand vin:* superb wine; 6 to 8 sec.
— *vin blanc sec:* dry white wine; 8 to 11 sec.
— *très grand vin:* superlative wine; 11 to 15 sec.
— *vin blanc liquoreux:* sweet white wine; 18 sec.
— *Grands Vouvray:* the great wines of Vouvray; 20 to 25 sec.
The term *caudalies* (caudals) is also used instead of seconds to describe the length of time.

Loyal: faithful; loyal; a natural wine that has been made following all the legal processes, without cheating, and having no hidden vices.

Mâche: chewy; full-bodied, filling the mouth well (when it is said to be 'chewy').

Mâché: chewed up; said of a wine where slight oxidation is present, a momentary deterioration after bottling.

Maigre: thin; lacking in alcohol and extracts, does not fill the mouth (opposite of *charnu*, full bodied). A large amount of volatile acidity makes a wine 'thin'.

Marchand: marketable; wine that has those characteristics required by all local commercial laws and regulations.

Mielleux: honey-like; wine in which the sugar content is predominant, throwing it out of balance with the other constituents.

Moelleux: mellow; full, well-rounded wine, with a certain amount of richness in sugar and glycerine, with little acidity. (Great dry white wine can be *moelleux*, e.g. Meursault.)

Mou: flabby, weak; lacking in body and freshness.

Muet: dumb; lacking in character and unattractive.

Mur: ripe, mellow; wine that has matured.

Nerveux: nervy; vigorous, with good body, a certain amount of acidity, and ageing well. These characteristics can stem from the soil from which the wine was produced.

Neutre: neutral; common and without any particular characteristics (a wine not capable of changing other

wines with which it is blended).

Normal: without fault.

Onctueux: unctuous; mellow wine with good viscosity, having a full-bodied feeling about it (rich in sugar and glycerine).

Pâteux: pasty; thick pasty consistency, rich in extracts, clinging to the palate.

Petit: little, in the sense of poor in alcohol and other constituents.

Piquant: sharp; tart, prickly, sensation on the tongue and palate, coming from carbonic gas (sparkling wines).

Plat: flat, lacking in body, alcohol and acidity.

Plein: full; well-balanced; wine with good body, rich in all its constituents, filling the mouth well.

Pommadé: falsified; thick, rich in sugar.

Puissant: powerful; rich, well-balanced wine.

Pulpeux: pulpy; thick in the mouth (having *mâche*, q.v.).

Qualité: quality; a good-quality wine is one that is above average, thanks to the grape and soil from which it was produced.

Raide: stiff; lacking in suppleness, acid.

Rance: rancid; defective wine (contact with air).

Râpeux: rough; raspy feeling on the tongue coming from the tannin in the wine.

Rassis: settled, well-balanced; wine that has finished ageing.

Riche: rich; high in alcohol and colour.

Rond: well-rounded and full; well-balanced, supple and mellow, generally full-bodied.

Savoureux: tasty; very pleasant on the palate.

Sec: dry; lacking in sugar. Applied to red wines, it means lacking in thickness (dry taste coming from deterioration of grapes at harvest-time).

Solide: solid; well constituted, keeping well.

Souple: supple; pleasant to drink, low tannin and acid content, soft on the palate.

Soyeux: silky texture; supple, recalls the feel of silk.

Tannique: tannic; wine having an excess of tannin.

Tendre: delicate; wine containing little acid, supple, light, slightly sweet.

Terne: dull; lacking vivacity and character; uninteresting.

Usé: worn-out; wine that is over-the-hill, too old, having lost its original qualities, keeping badly.

Velouté: velvety texture; supple, mellow, slipping easily over the tongue and palate, recalls the feel of velvet, soft in the mouth.

Vert: green in the sense of unripe; acid and young (excess of malic acid derived from picking of unripe grapes at harvest-time).

Vieux: old; characteristic adopted by the wine as it ages in the bottle. May be used in a pejorative sense when applied to a wine that is *usé* (q.v.).

Vif: lively; fresh, light wine, with average alcohol and acid content.

Vineux: having good vinosity; high alcohol content dominating other characteristics; warm to the taste.

Vintage Table

Vintage charts are a guide to the quality of the wine from a given region in a given year, but they can provide only the simplest indication of relative quality on the broadest possible scale. The Académie du Vin vintage chart is based on information from growers and *négociants* in the different wine districts, tempered by our own tastings.

All vintage charts should be reviewed once a year. Older vintages become of academic interest, particularly for white wines, and wines from younger vintages gain or lose quality. Some charts advise when a wine should be drunk, but they obviously cannot take into account who is drinking the wine, where it is drunk and how it has been stored. The French tend to enjoy their wines young; the British prefer them with more age; European wines in America or Australia may be drunk earlier than in, say, Belgium, to compensate for the sea voyage. Storage is the vital element for anything but the youngest wines, for it determines the eventual condition of the wine. No amount of fine service

		1920	'21	'23	'26	'28	'29	'33	'34	'37	'43	'45	'47	'48	'49	'52	
RED BORDEAUX	Médoc/Graves	18	15	12	16	19	19	13	16	13	14	20	18	15	19	16	
	Saint-Emilion/Pomerol	17	17	12	17	19	18	13	16	14	15	19	20	14	19	16	
WHITE BORDEAUX	Sauternes/Barsac	15	20	13	17	18	19	10	17	19	16	19	19	14	18	16	
RED BURGUNDY		15	16	17	15	17	19	17	18	18	16	19	18	14	20	18	

		1952	
RED BURGUNDY	Côte de Nuits	18	
	Côte de Beaune	17	
WHITE BURGUNDY		14	
BEAUJOLAIS		16	
RHONE	North, Côtes-du-Rhône	16	
	South, Côtes-du-Rhône	16	
LOIRE	Muscadet/Touraine/Anjou	14	
	Pouilly-Fumé/Sancerre	14	
ALSACE		13	
VINTAGE CHAMPAGNE		17	
GERMANY	Rhine		
	Mosel		
ITALY	Tuscany		
	Piedmont		
	Friuli/Veneto		
SPAIN	Rioja		
CALIFORNIA NORTH COAST	Red		
	White		

1952

or optimism can bring a wine back from the grave.

For the Académie du Vin vintage chart, we have used a 20-point scale, with the following ratings:

0–9 Bad, very poor, poor.
10–11 Acceptable.
12–13 Quite good.
14–15 Good.
16–18 Very good.
19–20 Exceptional.

We have chosen to start in 1952, in order to show a spread of 30 years. With the exception of the decade of the 1970s, we have omitted the generally accepted poor years, even though in some regions (1968 in Tuscany for example) the wines were very good. With improvements in viticulture and vinification as a result of continuing research and investment, there are fewer 'bad' vintages. Acts of God, like the 1956 frost in Saint-Emilion, will always be with us, but growers and winemakers can now make better use of what nature imposes.

'53	'55	'57	'59	'61	'62	'64	'66	'67	'69	'70	'71	'72	'73	'74	'75	'76	'77	'78	'79	'80	'81	'82
19	17	12	16	20	17	16	18	14	11	19	17	11	13	13	18	15	13	19	17	14	17	19
19	18	10	16	20	17	18	18	13	11	19	18	10	13	13	18	16	13	18	18	13	16	19
18	18	15	18	17	15	12	15	18	12	17	17	11	13	11	17	17	12	14	16	15	17	10
17	16	14	18	19	17	16	17	14	17	14	17	16	13	13	5	17	10	19	15	16	13	14
18	16	14	18	19	16	17	17	14	18	14	16	15	13	12	7	17	11	19	16	13	13	13
14	16	13	16	15	18	16	16	14	18	16	16	12	16	13	14	16	12	18	16	14	17	16
19	17	16	17	19	17	16	17	14	17	16	16	12	16	12	13	17	8	19	15	12	16	14
18	16	14	16	20	16	15	17	12	17	16	14	14	14	12	10	16	12	20	15	15	13	15
18	18	16	16	17	16	14	16	17	16	14	16	14	13	12	10	16	11	18	16	15	15	12
13	15	13	19	16	14	15	13	11	15	14	15	10	14	10	14	17	11	16	14	13	15	14
13	14	15	19	14	16	16	14	14	14	14	19	8	16	14	16	18	12	17	15	15	16	14
18	18	16	20	18	14	19	13	15	14	15	19	10	17	14	16	18	12	17	16	13	16	15
16	19		15	16	17	15	16	12	17	17	15		17		17	16		15	16	(14)	(17)	(14)
19	11		18	11		15	15	16	16	11	19	8	12	5	14	18	8	9	15	6	9	7
19	11		18	11		18	16	12	16	11	19	8	13	5	17	18	8	9	15	6	9	7
					('68) 16	12	16	16	16	20	8	8	14	16	8	16	20	16	16	16	12	18
					('65) 16	4	16	14	16	20	4	10	18	10	10	10	20	16	16	14	12	20
						12	12	14	14	16	16	16	14	12	10	14	14	16	12	16	16	16
		('68) 18		12	13	20	16	14	13	20	11	7	17	13	15	14	8	19	13	15	17	16
				18	14	19	16	16	17	20	18	14	16	20	18	18	16	19	18	18	17	15
				18	14	19	16	16	17	18	18	14	16	18	18	18	16	17	18	19	17	15
'53	'55	'57	'59	'61	'62	'64	'66	'67	'69	'70	'71	'72	'73	'74	'75	'76	'77	'78	'79	'80	'81	'82

Glossary of English and French Wine Terms

Alcool acquis   The actual alcoholic degree of a wine

Alcool en puissance   A wine's potential alcoholic strength

ampelography   The science of grape varieties

Anthocyane   A polyphenol that lends colour to young red wines

AOC   Appellation d'Origine Contrôlée. Better than VQPRD

Appellation   The name that guarantees a wine's origin and grape variety, but not necessarily its quality

Assemblage   The blending of wines of the same origin

Blanc de Blancs   White wine made from pressing white grapes

Blanc de Noir   A white wine made from pressing white grapes

Botryticine   An antibiotic produced from botrytis

Bourbes   Solid substances (waste matter) that are separated from the (white) must

Carbonic maceration   Maceration preceding the fermentation of light wines and wines made for quick consumption (*vins de primeur*)

Caudalie   Unit of measurement of aromatic persistence, equal to one second

Cépage   Variety of grape

Cépage teinturier   Ordinary variety that produces a red 'plonk', the chief characteristic of which is its colouring power

Chapeau   Cap of solids forming at the surface of the wine during fermentation

Chaptalization   Adding sugar to the grape-must to raise its alcohol content

Clone   A vine plant whose genetic make-up will be reproduced (cloned) over an entire vineyard

Coller (un vin)   Fining

Consume   Wine or brandy lost by evaporation (known as the 'angels' share')

Coupage   The blending of wines of different origins

Cuvée   In Champagne, 1. the first ten casks (205 litres) from pressing; 2. wine-blending

Débourbage   Separation of bourbes from grape must

Dégorgement   Removal of deposit formed during the second fermentation stage of sparkling wines

Ecoulage   Emptying a fermenting tank

Egrappoir/Erafloir   Machine that separates the grape berries from their stalks

Extract   Collective term for all the solids found in a wine

Flash pasteurization   Pasteurization at 70°C

Fleur du vin   Skin of yeasts or mycoderma that forms at the wine's surface

Fouloir   A machine for crushing grapes

Fouloir/érafloir   Machine that combines crushing with de-stalking

Franche de pied   A term used in reference to a non-grafted vine, i.e. native to the country in which it grows

Gravelle   Cream of tartar crystals in suspension in white wine bottles

Liqueur de dosage (or liqueur d'expédition)   Sugared liquid added to sparkling wines prior to corking

Liqueur de tirage   A liquor added to the wine to induce the *prise de mousse* (*méthode champenoise*)

Malolactic fermentation   Process in which the malic acid is turned into lactic acid under the action of malic ferments

Moût de gouette   Unfermented grape juice which runs off naturally

Moût de presse Unfermented grape juice from pressings

Mutage   Artificially halting the fermenting process

Oenolog   Anyone versed in the science of oenology

Oenologie   The science of wine; oenology

Oxydases   Oxidizing diastases which can cause a variety of grape diseases

Palissage   Method of training vines on wires and canes

Passerillé   Desiccated (grapes)

Pasteurization   Heating the wine to 70°C in order to kill off the biological components (e.g. ferments)

Phylloxera   Aphid which attacked and destroyed European vines from around 1865

Pigeage   Stamping down the 'cap' by hand (or foot)

Polyphenols   Tannins, anthocyanes and other bitter colourings

Porte-greffe   Vine stock, or root on to which the *greffon* or aerial branches are grafted

Pourriture noble   'Noble rot', a brown mould on the grape caused by *Botrytis cinerea* (fortified wines)

Première taille   The two casks of wine from the second pressing

Primary aroma   Aroma of the fruit

Prise de mousse   Corresponds to second in-bottle fermentation (*méthode champenoise*)

Rafle   Vine stalk or stem

Reducing agent   A substance that absorbs oxygen

Remontage   Immersion of the 'cap' by pumping up wine in the fermenting tank

Secondary aroma   Post-fermentation aroma

Seconde taille   The third cask, filled from the third pressing

Sélection clonale   Combination of characteristics

Sélection massale   Visual selection of the best vine plants

Soutirage   Tapping the wine from a vat or barrel

Sur lattes   Horizontal storage of wine bottles

Sur pointe   Vertical storage of bottles, neck down, in the *méthode champenoise*

Tannin   A bitter and astringent phenol compound

Tertiary aroma   Aroma after maturing

Thermolization   Partial pasteurization at 45°C

Tri, trie   Selective picking or harvesting of the grape (for fortified wines)

Ullage, ullaging   Replenishment of wine in bottles lost due to natural contraction, evaporation, etc.

VDQS   Vin de Qualité Supérieure. Not as good as VQPRD

Véraison   Moment when the berries start to take on colour

Vin de gouette   Wine drawn off from the fermenting tank

Vin de pays   Legal designation for *vins ordinaires* governed by certain rules

Vin de presse   Wine made by pressing the 'murk'

Vin de table   Legal term for *vin ordinaire*

Vin viné   A wine muted by the addition of alcohol, as an aperitif (cf. 'mutage')

Vin marchand   A wine that is reasonably saleable

Vinage   Addition of alcohol to a wine or grape-must

VQPRD   Vin de Qualité Produit dans des Régions Délimitées, i.e. a quality wine produced only in specific areas but complying with European quality regulations

Index

Page numbers in *italics* refer to captions to illustrations.
Abbreviation: Ch. = Château.

Bibliography/Acknowledgements

AMERINE, Maynard A. and SINGLETON, Vernon L.:
Wine: An Introduction, revised edition, University of California Press, Berkeley, 1978

ANDERSON, Burton:
Vino: The Wine and Winemakers of Italy, Little, Brown and Co., Boston, 1980; Hutchinson, London, 1980

BEZZANT, Norman and BURROUGHS, David:
The New Wine Companion, Heinemann, London, 1980

BLANCHET, Suzanne:
Les Vins du Val de Loire, ed. Jema S. A., Saumur, 1982

BROADBENT, Michael:
The Great Vintage Wine Book, Alfred A. Knopf in association with Christie's Wine Publications, New York, 1980;
Pocket Guide to Wine Tasting, Mitchell Beazley in association with Christie's Wine Publications, London, 1982

BRUNEL, Gaston:
Guide des Vignobles et Caves des Côtes du Rhône, ed. J. C. Lattès, Paris, 1980

DEBUIGNE, Gérard:
Dictionnaire Larousse des Vins, ed. Larousse, Paris, 1969

DION, Roger:
Histoire de la Vigne et du Vin en France des Origines au XIXe Siècle, ed. Paris, 1959

DOVAZ, Michel:
Les Grands Vins de France, ed. Julliard, Paris, 1979;
Encyclopédie des Crus Classés du Bordelais, ed. Julliard, Paris, 1981;
Encyclopédie des Vins de Champagne, ed. Julliard, to be published

DUYKER, Hubert:
Grands Vins de Bourgogne, ed. F. Nathan, Paris, 1980;
Bons Vins de Bordeaux, ed. F. Nathan, Paris, 1982

ENJALBERT, Henri:
Les Grands Vins de Saint-Emilion, Pomerol et Fronsac, ed. Bardi, Paris, 1983

FERET, Claude:
Bordeaux et ses Vins, ed. Féret et Fils, Bordeaux, 1982

FORBES, Patrick:
Champagne: The Wine, the Land and the People, Gollancz, London, 1972; Reynal, New York, 1968

HANSON, Anthony:
Burgundy, Faber, London, 1982 and Boston, 1983

JEFFS, Julian:
Sherry, 3rd edition, Faber, London, 1982 and Boston, 1982

JOHNSON, Hugh:
Pocket Encyclopaedia of Wine, Mitchell Beazley, London, 1977; Simon & Schuster, New York, 1977;
Wine, Nelson, Sunbury-on-Thames, 1973; Simon & Schuster, New York, 1975;
The World Atlas of Wine, revised edition, Mitchell Beazley, London, 1977; Simon & Schuster, New York, 1978

LEGLISE, Max:
Une Initiation à la degustation des grands vins, ed. Défense et Illustration des Vins d'Origine, Lausanne, 1976

LICHINE, Alexis:
(New) Encyclopaedia of Wines and Spirits, 4th edition, Alfred A. Knopf, New York, 1974; Cassell, London, 1979;
Guide to the Wines and Vineyards of France, Alfred A. Knopf, New York, 1979; Weidenfeld and Nicolson, London, 1979

LIVINGSTONE-LEARMONTH, John and MASTER, Melvyn:
The Wines of the Rhône, Faber, London, 1979 (revised edition 1983) and Boston, 1983

PENNING-ROWSELL, Edmund:
The Wines of Bordeaux, Penguin Books, London, 1979

PEPPERCORN, David:
Bordeaux, Faber, London and Winchester, Mass., 1982

PEYNAUD, Emile:
Le Goût du Vin, ed. Dunod, Paris, 1980

PIJASSOU, René:
Le Médoc, ed. Tallendier, Paris, 1978

READ, Jan:
The Wines of Spain and Portugal, Faber, London, 1972 (revised editions 1983); Monarch Books, New York, 1978

ROBERTSON, George:
Port, Faber, London, 1978 and Boston, 1983

ROBINSON, Jancis:
The Great Wine Book, A & C Black, London, 1979

SALE, Jacques:
Dictionnaire Larousse des Alcools, ed. Larousse, Paris, 1982

SARFATI, Claude:
La Dégustation des Vins, ed. Université du Vin, 1981

SCHOONMAKER, Frank:
Encyclopaedia of Wine, Hastings, New York, 1979; A & C Black, London, 1979

SUTCLIFFE, Serena:
The Wine Drinker's Handbook, David & Charles in association with Pan Books, Newton Abbot, 1982

VANDYKE-PRICE, Pamela:
The Taste of Wine, Macdonald, London, 1975; Random House, New York, 1975

VEDEL, A., CHARLES, G., CHARNAY, P., et TOURNEAU, J.:
Essai sur la Dégustation des Vins, ed. Société d'Edition et d'Information viti-vinicoles, Mâcon, 1972

WOUTAZ, Fernand:
Dictionnaire des Appellations, ed. LITEC, Paris, 1982

Photographs
Académie du Vin (Steven Spurrier), 15, 17, 19, 20, 23, 25, 41(bottom), 180–5, 187, 197, 198(left and right), 199(left and right)
Agence Photographique TOP, 1, 2, 38, 39, 48(right), 55, 60, 72
Comité national des vins de France (CNVF), 51(top and bottom), 58, 74(left), 75, 76, 80, 83
Food and Wine from France, 206, 207
Michael Freeman, 33, 41(top), 126(top), 133, 135
The High Commissioner for New Zealand, 137
Denis Hughes-Gilbey, 8–9, 11, 12, 16, 30(left and right), 31, 33, 34, 35, 36, 37, 40(top and bottom), 45, 46, 48(left), 49, 50, 52, 53(left and right), 54(top and bottom), 56, 57, 59, 61, 62(top and bottom), 64, 65, 69, 70, 71, 73(top and bottom), 74(right), 77, 81, 82, 88, 91(top and bottom), 92, 93, 94, 96, 97, 98, 99, 100, 101, 106, 188, 189, 190, 191(left and right), 192(top and bottom), 193, 194, 195, 204, 205, 208, 209
Chris Jansen Photography, 139
Lightbox Library, 63, 86, 89(top and bottom), 138
Geoffrey Roberts Associates, 29, 124, 126(bottom), 127, 134
Vinos de Espana, 118, 119, 120, 121

Wine Tasting Terms (pp. 212–15)
Laboratoire départementale et régionale d'analyses et de recherche de Tours;
Le centre technique expérimental de l'Institut technique du vin de Tours;
Le comité interprofessionel des vins de Touraine

Equilibrium diagram (p. 27)
E. Peynaud, *Le goût du vin*, Bordas, Paris, 2nd edition, 1983